The NGO Game

The NGO Game

Post-Conflict Peacebuilding in the Balkans and Beyond

Patrice C. McMahon

Cornell University Press
Ithaca and London

First published 2017 by Cornell University Press
Printed in the United States of America

Library of Congress Cataloging-in-Publication Data

Names: McMahon, Patrice C., author.
Title: The NGO game : post-conflict peacebuilding in the Balkans and
    beyond / Patrice C. McMahon.
Description: Ithaca : Cornell University Press, 2017. | Includes bibliographical
    references and index.
Identifiers: LCCN 2016047836 (print) | LCCN 2016049199 (ebook) |
    ISBN 9781501709234 (cloth : alk. paper) | ISBN 9781501709241
    (pbk. : alk. paper) | ISBN 9781501712722 (ret) | ISBN 9781501712739 (pdf)
Subjects: LCSH: Peace-building—Former Yugoslav republics. |
    Non-governmental organizations—Former Yugoslav republics. |
    Postwar reconstruction—Former Yugoslav republics.
Classification: LCC JZ5584.Y8 M35 2017 (print) | LCC JZ5584.Y8 (ebook) |
    DDC 327.1/7209497—dc23
LC record available at https://lccn.loc.gov/2016047836

To Hana and Julia

Peace is too important to be entrusted to states alone.
BOUTROS BOUTROS-GHALI, 1994

CONTENTS

Acknowledgments

The ideas for this book started in late 2000 when I visited Bosnia for the first time after the conflict ended. Generous funding from several sources allowed me to return to the Balkans on several occasions for extended periods of time. In 2000 and 2001, the National Research Council Young Investigator Program provided me with numerous opportunities and contacts throughout the region. In 2003 I returned with the Nebraska National Guard and I thank General Roger Lemke for this invitation. I also received a Policy Research Fellowship from the National Council for Eurasian and European Research (2003–2004), a research grant from the U.S. Department of State's Bureau of Intelligence and Research (2010–2011), and a Conference Grant (Building Coalitions to Build States) from the American Council for Learned Societies (2011). I am also grateful for the crucial funding I received from my university, including grants from the Department of Political Science, the Carl J. Schneider Research Grant, the University of Nebraska–Lincoln's Research Council, and the Harris Center for Judaic Studies. My interest in international politics is motivated by people and their lives. This requires that I leave my office to listen, observe, and witness. Without financial support from many sources, I simply could not imagine writing this book.

Throughout this project I have been fortunate to have had numerous supportive colleagues and friends to listen to me, read drafts of chapters, and provide feedback. Some of these colleagues are also good friends who have read chapters more than once and continued to give comments and criticism. David Forsythe is exactly the person I have in mind. Although he retired while I was writing this book, he has remained a mentor, coauthor, and good friend. Many others have helped as well, including: Mary Anderson, William DeMars, Dennis Dijikeul, Adam Fagan, Flora Ferati-Sachsenaier, John Furnari, Chip Gagnon, Jill Irvine, Jenny Miller, Ambassador Ronald Newman, Paula Pickering, Elton Skendaj, Jelena Subotic, Hans Peter Schmidt, Jack Snyder, and Jon Western. Conferences and workshops at Mount Holyoke College, the University of Delaware, the University of Westminster, and the International Studies Association, particularly the ISA Workshop on the Contribution of NGOs to International Relations Theory, all shaped this book in different ways. My colleagues and friends at the University of Nebraska–Lincoln, especially Jean Cahan, Courtney Hillebrecht, Chantal Kalisa, Alice Kang, Linda Major, Elizabeth Theiss-Morse, and Tyler White provided a tremendous amount of support and assistance on this manuscript. Thanks also to my graduate students, specifically Maria Benes, Kate Hunt, Ryan Lowry, Matt Morehouse, and Laura Roost.

In my trips to the Balkans I met many warm, inspiring, and helpful individuals. I have included an appendix of organizations and individuals I encountered and interviewed over the years. In particular I want to thank Fatime Aliu, Mujo Hadžić, Selma Hadžihalilović, Chris Hill, Saša Madacki, and Mirsad Tokača for their key insights and assistance. Merely listing organizations or including a quote from a particular individual, however, does not capture my gratitude or all that I have learned.

Roger Haydon has helped make this a much better book and one that I hope readers will enjoy reading. I thank him for his feedback and encouragement.

Many thanks to other caring friends who kept me grounded, including but hardly limited to Valerie Cuppens, Michelle Kaminsky, Rebecca McMahon, Kelly Smith, Sandi Zellmer, and Malia Zoghlin.

Finally, I would never have started or finished this book without my family's unwavering support, including my in-laws Carolyn and Tillman. I am grateful for their eternal optimism and perspective on life. As usual, my gratitude is greatest to Jeff, Hana, and Julia, who love me and keep me laughing. Thanks for allowing me to get some "good work done."

ABBREVIATIONS

CRS	Catholic Relief Services
CSCE	Conference on Security and Cooperation in Europe
DAC	Development Assistance Committee
EAR	European Agency for Reconstruction
ECLO	European Commission Liaison Office
ECOSOC	Economic and Social Council
EU	European Union
EULEX	European Union Rule of Law Mission (in Kosovo)
GHP	Global Humanitarian Platform
ICNL	International Center for Non-Profit Law
ICO	International Civilian Office
ICRC	International Committee of the Red Cross
ICVA	International Council of Voluntary Agencies
IGO	Intergovernmental or international organization
INGO	International nongovernmental organization
KFOR	Kosovo Protection Force

KWN	Kosovo Women's Network
KYN	Kosovo Youth Network
LNGO	Local nongovernmental organization
MBO	Member benefit organization
NGO	Nongovernmental organization
NSA	Nonstate actor
NPCG	NGO Peacebuilding Coordination Group
OECD	Organization for Economic Cooperation and Development
OSCE	Organization for Security and Cooperation in Europe
PBO	Public benefit organization
PISG	Provisional Institutions of Self-Government
PVO	Private voluntary organization
SRSG	Special Representative of the Secretary General
UNHCR	United Nations High Commissioner for Refugees
UNDP	United Nations Development Program
UNMIK	UN Mission in Kosovo
USAID	United States Agency for International Development

THE NGO GAME

INTRODUCTION

Booms and Busts in Peacebuilding

In most post-conflict countries, nongovernmental organizations (NGOs) are everywhere, but their presence is misunderstood and their impact exaggerated. I started visiting Bosnia-Herzegovina in 2000, almost five years after the horrific violence ended. At the time, I was captivated by the NGOs that existed in every city I visited. Returning to Bosnia many times and doing fieldwork in other post-conflict countries, such as Vietnam, Cambodia, and Kosovo, I noticed interesting but disturbing patterns in these very different countries. International actors and international NGOs (INGOs) descended on a country, local NGOs (LNGOs) popped up everywhere, and lots of money and energy went into creating and strengthening NGOs. In time, though, the frenzy of projects slowed, the internationals went home, and local groups disappeared from sight. Excitement and enthusiasm for peacebuilding turned to disappointment, if not cynicism, about these actors and their activities. After a few years, NGOs were no longer the ally and aide. They were part of the problem.

Scholars and policymakers tend to accept and even celebrate NGO in-volvement in post-conflict countries, but rarely do they examine *what* these ac-tors do or their impact on everyday life. This is the central concern of this book that focuses on the unintended and often negative outcomes associated with international peacebuilding. This book investigates *how* the surge of NGOs associated with international peacebuilding, what I call NGO booms, shapes post-conflict societies. In particular, this book investigates the development and behavior of local actors. Peace building in the Balkans, indeed, contributed to an explosion of NGOs both big and small, but this process and these organ-izations did not create strong domestic actors committed to liberal goals and building peace—as internationals had hoped and promised.

Instead, an NGO bust followed. INGOs did what they felt was best for stability and liberal democracy, and LNGOs, struggling to do something but also seeking to secure funds, followed their lead, competing with one an-other for international attention and foreign money. As interest faded and donor money went elsewhere, the NGOs disappeared, sometimes slowly but often overnight. For post-conflict countries, the decline of NGOs means the creation of a "disembedded civil society," or an environment where local groups look outside rather than inside their societies for support and direc-tion. It also nurtures disappointment with NGOs and disillusionment with liberal peacebuilding. This is why, in international peacebuilding, NGOs become part of the problem and not the solution.

There are many terms to describe what I alternately call *post-conflict peace-building*, *international peacebuilding*, or *liberal peacebuilding*, and others have gone to great lengths to discuss the differences between these terms and the many alternatives that exist.[1] There may be some distinctions, but I use a definition that is similar to the United Nations' definition, and my focus is on how Western governments and international organizations seek "to restore and build peace by promoting very specific political, economic, and social in-stitutions and practices" (Richmond and Franks 2009, 3–4). But unlike most who examine post-conflict peacebuilding, reconstruction, or state building, I am most interested in the role and behavior of nongovernmental organ-izations or NGOs in this process, a term that is also confusing and contested. Since others have dissected, disaggregated, and defined nongovernmental organizations "to nobody's great satisfaction" (Smillie 1995, 22), I will not. In-stead I adopt the UN's broad definition, seeing NGOs simply as all nonstate, nonprofit organizations that work for the public good.

Humanitarian NGOs have been involved in conflict zones for a long time, providing life-saving relief, care for the suffering, and shelter for the homeless. In some respects, there is nothing new about their involvement or their activities. Yet, the groups I encountered in Bosnia and other post-conflict settings were not traditional humanitarian NGOs, and their activities were not easy to summarize. Some were assisting refugees and providing relief to those in need, but other NGOs were working on education reform, memorial construction, or democracy promotion. In almost every city I visited, there were NGOs committed to women's empowerment. And whether they were international or local organizations, these groups implicitly claimed to be progressive actors, working alongside Western governments and international organizations to promote peace and liberal democratic change. As Roland Paris (2004) confirms, NGOs are now an important part of international peacebuilding, implicitly sharing in Western governments' and international organizations' liberal mission. The problem is that we do not know much about these actors or their unique role in post-conflict peacebuilding.

The NGO Reality

The NGOs I encountered in Bosnia and elsewhere surprised me in at least five ways that create the framework for this book. First, there was the sheer number and diversity of organizations both big and small. I never actually tripped over an NGO in Sarajevo, Bosnia's capital, but I often had that feeling that I might if I was not careful. This was especially the case in my first few visits to the country in 2000 and 2001. I found NGOs in the most unlikely places: isolated villages, refugee camps, and in newly built apartment buildings on the edge of town. They were also engaged in many more activities and sectors than the scholarship on NGOs suggested.[2] In my travels, I came across NGOs of all kinds that were committed to putting the country back together, empowering some segment of the population, or bringing attention to a neglected issue. They were not, to be sure, simply humanitarian NGOs, providing relief or basic assistance.

My second surprise concerning the NGO boom was how random and fundamentally unstable it was. In some cities, and for a particular period, there were lots of NGOs working in similar (though not necessarily cooperative) ways, while other issues, which were clearly urgent, were not addressed at all. The groups would appear and disappear suddenly, often without leaving a trace. With every visit back to the Balkans, there were fewer NGOs to visit and fewer people to interview, and the once plentiful civil society projects were hard to locate.

Third, despite what I had read, the NGOs in Bosnia were not just large international humanitarian groups providing short-term relief on the margins of political activities. The organizations were—or at least professed to be—local organizations involved in a dizzying array of political and social activities. Some were involved in very practical efforts: delivering food, helping with housing, or building war memorials. Others were working for abstract and ambitious goals like democracy, ethnic reconciliation, and transitional justice. Yet, most scholarship on NGOs, at least by international relations (IR) scholars and especially by those writing about post-conflict reconstruction, tends to focus only on international NGOs or local groups, separating them into neat categories that supposedly operate in different ways. If you believe what you read, NGOs engage in either service provision or in advocacy (Murdie 2014). In truth, post-conflict countries are not so tidy, nor are the activities of NGOs. For several years Bosnia was overwhelmed by foreign governments, international organizations, and INGOs, and all were intent on funding and creating all sorts of NGOs. Mostly in good faith, they were trying to "do something" and to make a difference. The NGOs I encountered often engaged in both service provision and advocacy, depending on the time period. The international–local distinction was also not clear cut. Since all of the NGOs received at least some of their funding from donors that came from outside the country, it was difficult to say whether they were international actors or domestic, local organizations. Agenda setting can be an imperceptible and even unintended process, and even the hint of foreign money can shift missions and inform strategies.

Fourth, it was apparent to me that many of the NGOs were not active simply to help the Bosnian people or to promote peace. NGOs are not businesses and do not make a profit, but their employees were often motivated by a mixture of misguided altruism and salaried self-interest. NGO scholars looking at development and the humanitarian industry make a similar point about the self-interested behavior of NGOs, but usually their remarks target INGOs (Anderson 1999; Cooley and Ron 2002). To be sure, not every NGO worker is misguided or self-interested, but it is clear that NGOs are created for many reasons by individuals with a range of motivations.

Finally, despite the NGO boom and the large number of activities and projects throughout the Balkans, it was often easier to observe their unintended and negative effects than it was to garner evidence that pointed to NGO achievements or success stories. How this messy group of actors, scattered haphazardly around the country, actually helped advance peace and democratic change remained a nagging question.

Despite these revelations, I was taken aback by what people said and seemed to believe about NGOs and their transformative power. International donors did not give an inordinate amount of money to either international or local NGOs, at least when compared to their investments in other sectors. The Bosnian government, struggling with its own economic woes, gave almost nothing to its nascent NGO sector. Yet, internationals and Bosnians alike often put naive faith in NGOs, giving them praise and attention as necessary or crucial partners in post-conflict peacebuilding. NGOs were even tasked with intractable social problems like ethnic reconciliation or gender inequality. Assumptions about NGOs were sometimes implicit, but they were generally optimistic; these increasingly popular nonstate actors provided crucial services and more importantly, they embodied and advanced certain values.

Fascination with NGOs seemed especially intense when Western governments lacked the will or the way to move forward on a particularly intransigent issue or with a deeply divided city. In other words, when all else fails, international actors reflexively turn to what is vaguely but ambitiously called civil society development and to NGOs. The reality on the ground, however, was quite different, and U.S. government officials like Secretary of State Colin Powell had no qualms about making clear their real function. As Powell put it in 2001, NGOs are "tremendously important" to the United States and its allies operating in war-torn countries, because they are a "force multiplier," extending the reach of the U.S. government and helping it achieve its goals.[3]

NGOs are the quick and easy solution in peacebuilding for good reason. First, they help fill in for the beleaguered state, providing significant relief and other services. At the same time, NGOs can give voice to people and certain issues, advocating for the population they claim to help. In policies and speeches, Western officials regularly referred to NGOs as "necessary" and "crucial partners," because they promote peace, democracy, and stability. At least early on, Bosnians shared their naïve optimism, embracing the NGO boom and seeing NGOs as independent, neutral actors that cared about their suffering and could somehow help them to develop necessary skills to change their country for the better.

Importantly, even when governments and international organizations did little, NGOs at least showed up and tried to do something. Most Bosnians realized that communism had stripped the population of both agency and accountability. Working for an international NGO—or better yet creating one of your own—put initiative and control back in their own hands. In a time of financial insecurity, externally funded NGOs provided Bosnians with a somewhat steady income and even some prestige. Despite their size and meager budgets, NGOs were assumed to be essential to connecting public and private actors and bridging international goals with local needs (DeMars and Dijkzeul 2015). In some places and in certain sectors, NGOs held both promise and power.

Unfortunately, much of this was a mirage, and as international peacebuilding unfolded in the Balkans, the facts about NGOs became crystal clear. With every visit back to the Balkans, I became more aware of the "difficult truths" surrounding civil society development and the work of NGOs. After flooding the streets of Sarajevo in the second half of the 1990s, international actors steadily returned to their home countries, and the NGO caravan moved to other, more urgent crises. Fortunately for the international NGOs, as interest and money in Bosnia started to dry up, events in neighboring Kosovo intensified, and international actors could scurry there. And after this crisis settled, they moved to Afghanistan where even more money awaited them to aid post-conflict reconstruction and development. However, for local NGOs dependency on foreign donors meant that once internationals started to leave, most of the Bosnian NGOs disappeared as well; others fought to stay afloat by changing their mission, and many local NGOs existed only on paper.

Bosnia's NGO boom only simulated a vibrant civil society, and the lists I had received containing dozens of NGOs in a city usually produced a handful of active organizations. Ironically, an NGO that might be well-known in Washington, DC, or London, a virtual darling of Western funders for its work on behalf of Bosnian women, might have a minimal presence among Bosnians. In fact, the NGO might even be dismissed by locals as a foreign-funded entity that lacked grassroots support and legitimacy. Even though a Bosnian NGO had a nice office with a few computers and staff who spoke perfect English, this did not translate into a successful indigenous organization with a constituency or a plan for development. By 2008, "paper NGOs" were common throughout Bosnia, and many acclaimed "agents of grassroots change" spent most of their time trying to finagle a way to keep their organization on the books, chasing after international donors and writing up complicated grant proposals with well-developed evaluation criteria. In post-conflict countries, creating an NGO requires a great deal more than just need. It demands a staff who writes well in English and has the know-how to construct winnable grant proposals. Sustaining an LNGO is even trickier and requires not only an abiding interest in and understanding of what international donors will support but also the shrewdness to figure out how Western money and good intentions can be used to advance local (rather than international) goals. NGO involvement in international peacebuilding yields many surprises, and its true character is hard to unearth and difficult to accept.

Over the years in Bosnia and in other post-conflict countries, I met many hardworking, well-intentioned people working for both INGOs and LN-GOs. Yet, their behavior rarely mirrored my vision of the noble humanitarian. Some of the NGO officials were generous and principled people who worked creatively and tirelessly to assist those traumatized by violence and instability. Others clearly were just grateful that they had a job. Certain personalities appeared to be more interested in their important position and the benefits it afforded them than in the causes or the people they claimed to help. I did not have to remind myself why so many foreigners ended up staying in the Balkans for so many years after the humanitarian crisis subsided. Sarajevo and Mostar, though run-down and recovering, are world-class cities, and the internationals living there were well-traveled professionals with an appetite for exotic locations.

The Bosnians working for NGOs were a far more diverse lot, and while only a few became relatively wealthy working in the NGO world, most readily acknowledged the advantages of working for an NGO—at least for a while. Bosnia's high unemployment and low salaries meant that any job with an international connection, even with a local NGO, was better than trying to find gainful employment in the local economy. And the networking opportunities and future job prospects provided incalculable advantages.

Yet, the NGO world is divided and hierarchical. Internationals and locals working in this sector inhabit the same geography, but they live in very separate worlds, and Bosnia's NGO culture reflected this reality. So-called local NGOs were sometimes staffed with foreigners who were inevitably paid better and given, as it appeared to the locals, unearned positions. How a recent college graduate from the United States with little knowledge of the country, no grasp of the native language, and scant relevant experience could be charged with directing an NGO that was operating in a complicated, post-conflict environment was maddening for Bosnians, many of whom were better educated or possessed years of experience. Locals held deep resentment for the hypocrisy of international peace builders and the dominant NGO culture with its endless fascination with "international experts" that parachuted into the country to rescue the downtrodden and backward Balkan people and develop its civil society.

As the anthropologist Séverine Autesserre (2014) explains in her book *Peaceland*, there is an obvious but inevitable disjuncture between the transnational community of expatriates who devote their lives to working in war zones and the locals. As well-intentioned as they are, the internationals inhabit their own space and political and economic reality. For example, international peace builders claimed to support women's rights and the empowerment of local organizations; yet, they had no qualms about decreeing how Bosnian women ought to act, and they regularly ignored the input of local women's groups. At best, the interactions in the NGO world were polite but awkward. At worst, the internationals were haughty and self-important, and Bosnians were hostile and defensive.

Like it or not, this is the NGO reality in many post-conflict settings. It contains an undeniably uplifting and moving quality of thoughtful professionals toiling away to promote change from the bottom up. A closer, more sustained look, however, exposes the darker sides of international peacebuilding and the self-interested organizations and professional humanitarians who engage in activities that are sometimes neither necessary nor particularly helpful—especially to those most in need. Liberal peacebuilding attracts large numbers of INGOs and it generates scores of LNGOs, but the presence of these actors and the flurry of their activities do not mean that crucial problems are addressed or that the population is helped. Although many believe otherwise, NGOs are not necessarily connecting, bridging, or giving voice to local groups and their interests. In fact, I submit that NGO booms in peacebuilding set the stage for NGO busts, as well as numerous unintended and detrimental consequences, especially for indigenous organizations and everyday life in post-conflict societies.

This book is different from most others on Bosnia and post-conflict peacebuilding in the 1990s, because it pays attention to organizations, processes, and groups that are often ignored or dismissed by Balkan experts and security studies scholars. Only a few books on Bosnia or the Balkans mention international promises to develop civil society, the work of NGOs, or what happens in everyday life.[4] Moreover, since many of the recent books on post-conflict reconstruction, nation-building or state building are written by security studies scholars, they too ignore the role of NGOs and local realities, focusing instead on the work of states and international peace builders. There are now many good critiques of liberal peacebuilding, but they usually do not provide in-depth field work, comparative research, or a focus on NGOs.[5] Human rights scholars and those writing about development and the problems of humanitarian work have, indeed, pointed out the shortcomings and unintended consequences associated with NGOs; unfortunately, their research has often been overlooked by IR scholars writing about conflict and post-conflict reconstruction.[6] In line with the more critical writings about liberal peacebuilding and with scholars interested in exposing the unintended and negative consequences associated with transnational involvement and foreign aid, *The NGO Game* provides an in-depth, comparative look at what actually happens in post-conflict societies, situating this phenomenon in a historical and interdisciplinary context.

The NGO Promise

Bosnia is well-known for the violence that shook Europe between 1992 and 1995. The stories of neighbors who became murderers, college students who dodged bullets, and doctors who treated concentration camp victims revealed some of the worst examples of violence to plague the continent since World War II. In total, perhaps as many as two hundred thousand people perished in the Yugoslav wars that started in Slovenia in 1991 and ended with the armed conflict in Macedonia in 2001. In Bosnia, the brutality and bloodshed damaged much of the country's infrastructure, but by 1999, and after just three years of intense international involvement, observers deemed the reconstruction efforts "remarkably successful" (Cousens and Cater 2001, 89–90). Yet, the scars of the conflict remained, particularly among the population and regardless of their ethnicity.

The conflict pushed almost half of the country out of their homes, it devastated the economy, and ethnic nationalism permeated public life.[7] In late

2000, I was talking to widows of the 1995 massacre in Srebrenica, many of whom had lost their husbands and sons at the hands of Bosnian Serbs. I asked: Who would identify their family members? Who would help bring closure to this horror?[8] At that point in time, NGOs were on the minds of these women. For them, nongovernmental organizations had money and energy, and their people-to-people orientation was a much-needed response for their miserable condition. Bosnian optimism and belief in the power of NGOs was no doubt fueled by the exuberant rhetoric of internationals in Bosnia who claimed that civil society development and NGOs were crucial to peacebuilding and ethnic reconciliation.

Whether by design or by default, NGOs were central to the international community's strategy for putting Bosnia back together and reconciling the Muslim, Serb, and Croat populations. International NGOs were involved in Bosnia during the conflict, but after the violence subsided their work evolved and their missions morphed. The shift from providing emergency relief to supporting reconstruction and strengthening civil society fueled an even larger explosion of national or local NGOs. The important point, however, is that local NGOs may have included some Bosnians (and over time this was increasingly the case), but this is not the same as saying that Bosnian organizations were indigenous actors. In fact, almost all of the NGOs in Bosnia were funded and sometimes created by external donors, with very specific ideas on how peace and democracy should unfold. In no time, the presence of these "local" NGOs was proof positive that Bosnian society was active, and that peace, democracy, and reconciliation were on track. Yet, as Michael Barnett and Peter Walker (2015, 32) explain, the wealthy and powerful "humanitarian club," or the organized and hierarchical network of powerful states, donors, international organizations, and NGOs that operates in post-conflict and developing countries, has certain goals in mind when it becomes involved in a country. This means that NGOs do many good things, but they are also there to carry out the will and agenda of Western governments and large international aid organizations. The presence of NGOs may be a gift, but these groups come with strings attached.

Money from several international donors allowed the widows of Srebrenica that I had interviewed to form their own NGO with the purpose of raising awareness of their plight and to fund the identification of their families' bodies. In time, the Widows of Srebrenica Association became involved in a range of civil society activities; among them was helping refugees and their families. Westerners visiting Bosnia regularly met with the Widows of Srebrenica Association and heard their heart-wrenching first-hand accounts of pain and sorrow. Although this NGO represented more the exception than the rule, Bosnian NGOs more generally benefited from their story and experiences. Consequently, Bosnian NGOs were looked to and relied on because they addressed local concerns and engaged in activities that helped Bosnians rebuild and take their country back. Indeed, the promise of NGOs was well entrenched, even among those who had experienced so much tragedy but desperately wanted peace and reconciliation.

The mythological importance of NGOs did not end with their assumed ability to provide emergency relief or certain services. By some unknown process, NGOs were heralded as the legitimate and rightful voice of "the people." By connecting different groups and advancing the goals of the Bosnian people—as if they were a unified group with agreed-upon objectives—NGOs were regarded as essential to laying the foundation for political and social goals, including democracy, reconciliation, and even peace. Again, all of this was more aspirational and imagined rather than real. NGOs were like the proverbial noodle on the cupboard door; they are thrown at problems in the hope that something will stick. Even though these ideas were neither examined closely nor proved in any way, the logic was nonetheless clear: since Bosnia had so many challenges and dilemmas, more NGOs meant more assistance, more collaborators, and by extension, more partners in advancing liberal peace.

On many levels, the United Nations and Western government documents supported the vague but ambitious NGO agenda. Such ideas and policies remind us that a primary lesson from the conflicts in the 1990s was the urgent need for international actors to identify local structures and support domestic capacity to strengthen civil society and sustain long-term peace. For better and for worse, NGOs were the primary beneficiary of this rhetorical exercise. Although their actions were intuitive and even defensible, too often international peace builders took short cuts; they were heavy on words and short on deeds. Instead of carefully identifying local actors and grassroots initiatives in what should have been a comprehensive, given-and-take process to cultivate trust and relationships with domestic actors committed to liberal peacebuilding, civil society development and NGO support were carried out haphazardly and halfheartedly.

A few scholars writing about the Balkans acknowledge the ubiquity of NGOs as well as some of the shortcomings associated with Western efforts to build civil society (Belloni 2008b; Fagan 2012), but no book examines the medium- to long-term effects of NGOs or interrogates how the NGO boom shaped everyday life in different post-conflict countries. In part this is due to the challenges of getting reliable information on NGOs, especially in conflict-ridden countries. One study on Bosnia, for example, indicated that by 1999 over 170 international and 360 local NGOs were involved in what it described as "civil society development" in Bosnia (ICVA 2000). Another source claimed that between 1992 and 2001, at least eight thousand NGOs were registered as "humanitarian organizations," working on some twenty thousand projects throughout the country (Sejfija 2006, 125).[9] These widely divergent estimates not only reflect inconsistent terminology, but they point to the need for a more systematic investigation into the activities and effects of these plentiful organizations.

The NGO Game

In 2008, I was talking to the director of a Sarajevo-based NGO, asking him what had happened to all the NGOs that once filled the city.[10] Frankly, I missed the buzz of activities and all the excitement that went with these projects. My Bosnian interlocutor smirked and replied by telling me a story about a conference he had recently attended for NGO leaders from post-conflict and transitional countries. He confided how the group, containing an eclectic assortment of people from the Balkans, Africa, and other "troubled lands" that the West wanted to save, sat together swapping experiences and best practices. He explained that everyone there knew and even joked about the NGO game and what it entailed. There are many variations, but the game always includes Westerners showing up in a conflict-ridden or transitional country with lots of money to spend and tons of good intentions. Astonishingly, though, many of the internationals have little knowledge of the country or the reason for its problems. Without ever defining it in this exact way, others I have interviewed in Bosnia, Kosovo, and elsewhere described shockingly similar circumstances or portions of this complicated scenario.

There is no doubt that Westerners want to promote peace, democracy, and development in conflict-ridden countries. Yet, well-intentioned humanitarians have other more immediate tasks that usually take priority. First, they need to justify their presence and the urgent need for financial or in-kind support. They also need to convince their governments, their boards, or their donors that their organization or some specific project will have a positive impact on peace and change. In some amount of time, they will need to provide tangible, if elusive evidence to this effect. The country and people in question are undeniably important, but because of the structural environment and the game that everyone is forced to play, locals, their needs, and their goals are often secondary. A recent comprehensive report of humanitarian assistance by the international NGO Oxfam found evidence of the NGO game and this specific truth. Although Western governments and international organizations provide a substantial amount of money to post-conflict and transitional countries, less than 2 percent of this aid actually goes to national or local actors, and even less humanitarian aid makes its way to local NGOs (Gingrich and Cohen 2015, 14). At least at the beginning, the game gives internationals money to throw at civil society projects and local organizations. But foreign aid does not come without a price.

Although the Western "partners" were always different (some were governments while others were international organizations or private foundations), and the domestic conditions of the troubled countries varied even more so, the processes essentially contain the same kinds of organizations and operate according to similar rules of thumb. And the game is, in fact, simple to play because of the structure of international aid, the interests of the actors involved, and the ideas that permeate conflict-ridden and transitioning countries. To satisfy the Westerners, but more importantly to get them to open their wallets, locals needed to listen intensely to what was said about the goals of a particular government, INGO, or private foundation. Using this crucial information, they then needed to attend meetings, create projects, and organize activities that fit their funders' vision and mission. In the end, the dynamics, assumptions, and behavior were essentially the same.

The well-intentioned Westerners did their thing: they created lots of "local" partners, they invested in capacity building, and they funded scores of important projects—all in the name of peace, democracy, and stability. All the while, the locals did what was necessary and rational: they showed up to meetings, organized activities, and feigned interest in the newest pet theories of donors. My interviewee summarized the NGO game with a key phrase: we (the NGO leaders) waste the Westerners' money, and they waste our time. He was not being cynical or judgmental; he was merely describing a complex and important phenomenon that created lots of diverse, if overlooked dynamics and behaviors. It also fueled a NGO boom.

There are many problems with the NGO game. Although numerous organizations and countless activities are funded, these interactions rarely create a strong network of sustained domestic organizations and alliances. And because of the temporary nature of these transnational relationships, the unequal power dynamics between internationals and locals, and the actual amount of money that is ultimately transferred to locals, the results are "projectification," "NGOization," and disembedded societies. In other words, despite international rhetoric and the buzz of activities and projects, the NGO promise is rarely fulfilled, the short-term benefits do not endure, and strong, indigenous social organizations seldom emerge. For a short-time, the dysfunctional relationship between internationals and locals benefits everyone who plays, but the situation cannot last, nor should it. Inevitably, international interest wanes and foreign funds disappear. The Western players become impatient, and local partners grow tired of pretending that these actions make an important difference in their lives or in their countries.

Frustration and futility aside, NGO booms and busts were a common feature in many post-conflict and transitioning countries throughout the 1990s, and such dynamics, though they have different players and objectives, continue in some form today in these same countries. Games are usually played for fun, but the policies and practices in post-conflict countries are a serious, billion-dollar business with high stakes. Although these promises and behavior may not inflict immediate harm on anyone, NGO booms have damaging consequences. The game and the machinations that go along with it end up making locals dissatisfied and disillusioned. Without real power, NGOs accomplish little, and struggles with donors bleed into other areas and into peacebuilding more generally. The realities of what happens in the NGO world make it even harder to deal with the hypocrisy and self-righteousness of internationals who have all the answers and fail to listen but leave little behind.

In theory, international peacebuilding in the 1990s was different from similar international rebuilding efforts of the past, in part because external actors focused their attention on conflict-ridden societies and local groups, aiming to restructure state–society relations and transform attitudes. A plethora of new organizations and top-down and bottom-up strategies, alongside

other changes in international politics, meant that liberal peacebuilding produced two different but related effects: lots of money for international and
local NGOs, and a slew of policies, institutions, and practices focused on supporting and sustaining local NGOs and civil society. In certain sectors, or at
least for a while, the sudden and dramatic increase in the number of NGOs
may be positive as many of these organizations engage in timely humanitarian work. NGO work can also genuinely inspire individuals to participate
in society because they feel like they can genuinely make a difference. However, a numerical expansion of organizations should not be misunderstood
or exaggerated. In fact, the dramatic growth of NGOs in a society may mean
just the opposite, and a closer look at the situation in the Balkans reveals that
the number of NGOs in a country is neither symptomatic of nor synonymous
with the existence of local partners committed to peace or other liberal goals.
Moreover, with so many actors on the scene that are neither elected nor accountable to those they claim to serve, surprising and unwanted consequences
inevitably follow.

If words mean anything, international peace builders genuinely wanted
Bosnians to own the process of rebuilding and reengineering their society.
Yet, the structure of international assistance and the environment associated
with the funding of peace-building initiatives, civil society development, and
NGOs created perverse incentives that inadvertently discouraged capacity
building and empowerment. Historical relationships, cultural bias, and certain
ideologies confounded these structural problems, making it even harder for
peace-building initiatives to construct strong, embedded local organizations.

Institutional theories and insights are common in political science, but they
often focus either on material, structural factors, highlighting incentives and
constraints, or they emphasize the role of history, identities, and ideas. Research
on "new institutionalism," however, often concludes that there are many benefits to integrating different institutional approaches to explain outcomes (Hall
and Taylor 1996; Thelen 1999). Given the complexity of peacebuilding in the
Balkans, this book tries to bring together the insights of different institutionalist approaches, drawing attention to the structures and material factors that
shaped outcomes while emphasizing how actors' identities, perceptions, and
beliefs inevitably shaped and misshaped perceptions and behavior. In other
words, the international community's inability to create self-sustaining local
NGOs in the Balkans is a function of the dynamic created by powerful
Western governments, international organizations, and financially dependent

NGOs. But the NGO bust is also a product of actors' goals, their historical practices, and fundamentally different understandings of how political and social change should take place.

In the short-term, international peacebuilding produces a welcome influx of international actors, but the behavior of donors and INGOs and the NGO game, with its top-down processes and conflicting agendas, has unintended and negative consequences. NGO leaders in post-conflict and transitioning countries may accept the inevitability of these processes and even joke about the game, but over time these policies and practices become an annoying ritual that no one likes but everyone is still pressured to follow.

What's at Stake?

A lot. NGO booms, busts, and the NGO game tell us a great deal about international peacebuilding in the late 1990s and early 2000s, the activities of some NGOs, and how recipients of top-down international policies often feel. Although others have pointed out some of these same dynamics in different kinds of post-conflict environments, and in different regions, the concepts developed here of booms, busts, and the game itself capture important dynamics and reasons why international peacebuilding often fails and why, despite the initial growth of NGOs, their numbers and reputation decline quickly. International peacebuilding in the Balkans is unique in many respects, but this is just one of many peace-building exercises orchestrated by the international community in the post–Cold War era.

There are also many cases of peacebuilding that were not led by international actors (for example, Rwanda and Sri Lanka) or where violence did not stop completely (Afghanistan), but NGOs have still been prominent, if not pervasive in peacebuilding. Thus, the arguments made here are inductively generated by several years of observations in the Balkans. But I suggest that location is less important than the structure and dynamics of peacebuilding itself, naive beliefs about NGOs, and the behavior of the actors involved. Indeed, scholars writing about post-conflict reconstruction and peacebuilding in Asia and Africa describe many of the same outcomes and problems.[11] In addition to naming these dynamics (booms, busts, and games) as phenomena associated with transnational involvement and international aid to post-conflict countries, this book explains international and domestic actors' behavior given the incentives, constraints, and ideas associated with international peacebuilding.

More than two decades of peacebuilding in more than a dozen countries, alongside U.S.-led misadventures in Iraq and Afghanistan have left little money and no stomach for extensive international involvement in conflict-ridden countries. Even those who favored military intervention in Libya in 2011 stopped short of pretending that there was any support for internationally led peacebuilding (Western and Goldstein 2011; Hitchens 2011). The question is: What will replace extensive and intentional international efforts to rebuild conflict-ridden countries? And what role will NGOs play in future international peacebuilding?

Liberal peacebuilding may indeed be under attack in 2016, but this does not mean that the international community will necessarily ignore internal conflicts, failing states, or problems of the past. And it certainly does not spell the end of NGOs in peacebuilding. In fact, because of the problems with comprehensive, top-down liberal peacebuilding in the 1990s, even more money and attention may end up going to NGOs and other nonstate actors, if we are not careful. Today, as in the late 1990s, when international actors lack the will or a plan to move forward in a troubled country, they often turn trustingly, but naively, to NGOs or other organizations that they hope will advance their agendas quickly and inexpensively. It is clear why Western governments may not want to work with authoritarian or weak regimes, but this does not necessarily mean that NGOs will be more effective or their involvement problem-free.

Disbursing aid directly to locals and investing in domestic groups sounds both noble and intuitive, but increasingly, more critical scholarship is documenting what actually happens with this aid: much of the money meant for locals goes to those outside the country or to a few privileged groups within a targeted country. And most of it does not even make it to these countries.[12] Yet, in conflict-ridden countries where authoritarian leaders rule or where state institutions are weak, that there are often few alternatives to NGOs. Understandably, everyone wants peacebuilding to be easy and cheap. This is why, disappointments and difficulties aside, NGOs have managed to retain some cachet as effective and even legitimate partners in building peace and constructing post-conflict society.

When I started travelling to the Balkans in the early 2000s, little was written specifically on NGOs in post-conflict countries.[13] Although many IR scholars ignored their growing presence, others assumed that since NGOs were there and engaged in lots of activities, this was proof enough that they were increasingly important agents of liberal peacebuilding. More recent IR scholarship has given some attention to NGOs, and it has been critical of them, often demonizing NGOs for a lack of transparency and account-ability. The following summarizes some of literature, situating this book in wider IR debates. While it is certainly true that NGOs are not elected by anyone, and no framework exists to hold them accountable, instead of criti-cizing all NGO involvement in conflict-ridden and transitioning countries, I instead maintain that their role in peacebuilding is both exaggerated and misunderstood.

Like others, this book is interested in exposing "the NGO turn" for what it often is to some international actors—more of a game and diversion than an actual strategy for engaging domestic actors, building local capacity, and promoting long-term peace. I also contend that although NGOs will likely continue to be popular and even pervasive in post-conflict and transitioning countries, the golden age of NGOs in international peacebuilding is coming to an end as academics and policymakers unearth the problems and unin-tended consequences of NGO involvement. In fact, in the last few years there have been many calls for major changes in how the international commu-nity deals with war-torn, transitioning, and failing states and how humani-tarian assistance should be provided. The stakes are high indeed, but it is time to put an end to assumptions and embellishments about NGOs and instead scrutinize their activities and effects in post-conflict environments.

From Marginal Actors to Magic Bullets

The NGO reality I observed in Bosnia was hard to make sense of, especially by reading IR literature, particularly books that focused on post-conflict op-erations, nation building, or state building (Dobbins et al. 2003; Doyle and Sambanis 2006; Jarstad and Sisk 2008). The fact is security specialists dismiss and discount NGOs and nonstate actors. Even when IR scholars acknowledge the growth of nonstate actors or their reach into new areas, international NGOs are generally viewed, as Fred Halliday (2001, 21) puts it, as "interna-tional tiddlywinks"; they are a distraction, akin to a child's parlor game but "with no great importance" to issues of peace and security. In the last two decades, a number of IR scholars have revisited this flawed assumption, and there is now great interest in the work of NGOs in international politics, and even in issues of war and peace.[14] However, as a field of study, IR still has a way to go to catch up with the tremendous growth, diversification, and presence of NGOs and other nonstate actors in international politics. As well, IR scholars have a long way to go to catch up with their peers in sociology, anthropology, and even comparative politics, who have all interrogated NGOs more thoroughly. The following suggests three basic ways to organize IR research on NGOs. These categories may generalize and condense a lot of literature, but they provide a somewhat chronological overview for how this field has viewed these nonstate actors.

Historically, IR as a subfield has been dominated by NGO critics, or those who overlook or devalue NGOs and other nonstate actors in international politics. Since others have explained the roots and core features of this subfield and the dominance of realist assumptions in great detail, I merely point out that IR scholars have long concentrated almost exclusively on states and, specifically, the behavior of great powers (Waltz 1979). Even in the 1980s, as the global balance of power shifted, international organizations became more involved in international politics, and the number of NGOs exploded, scholars regularly, if not eagerly, dismissed nonstate actors, maintaining that they mattered little in a world of states.

Realists old and new, both classical and structural, maintained that despite the obvious growth of intergovernmental and nongovernmental organizations, international politics was dominated by nation-states, their militaries, and national self-interest. John Mearsheimer (1994, 7) makes the realist argument clearly: if international institutions matter at all, it is only because they reflect the interests and calculation of the most powerful states, not because they are separate from them. Books and articles on post-conflict reconstruction, state building, and peacebuilding are written largely by security studies scholars who implicitly or explicitly embrace such a perspective. Not surprisingly, NGOs are overlooked in discussions of military operations, and if they are considered, it is "perhaps as an afterthought" but little more (Aall 2005, 365).

Liberalism, neoliberal institutionalism, and approaches of this ilk all emphasize the importance and sometimes even the autonomy of intergovernmental organizations and international regimes, because they are able to encourage states to cooperate and, under certain conditions, even change states' interests and behavior.[15] Despite an acknowledgement of the importance and even independence of intergovernmental organizations, liberal scholars are often equally as inattentive to nongovernmental organizations, treating them no better than their realist contemporaries. For example, in the 2005 edition of *After Hegemony: Cooperation and Discord in the International Political Economy*, Robert Keohane (2005, xvii) admits that his neoliberal institutionalist theory of cooperation circa 1984 is not valid in the twenty-first century. This is because it fails to consider how NGOs, transnational, and transgovernmental networks affect states' behavior. William DeMars and Dennis Dijkzeul (2015, 9), in their recent book *The NGO Challenge to IR Theory* even assert that "liberal theory has actively discouraged NGO scholarship for decades." To be sure, NGO critics represent a diverse lot, and I do not attempt to represent them comprehensively here. Nonetheless, their common failing is their neglect, if not total disregard of NGOs as meaningful actors in international politics.

Most of the research on NGOs in IR literature has come from NGO enthusiasts, and whether they focus on economic development, the environment, or human rights, these scholars tend to take almost the opposite perspective as the skeptics, viewing nonstate actors and NGOs as positive and even transformative actors in international politics. With roots in the transnational revolution of the 1970s, enthusiasts draw attention to the ways that nonstate actors influence outcomes. Whether it is multinational corporations (MNCs), private foundations, or NGOs, these nonstate actors can make a difference by impinging on states' power, shaping global agendas, and altering domestic politics.[16] Implicitly, NGOs are viewed as progressive actors that are a positive force for liberal, democratic change. Transnationalism lost some of its luster in the 1980s, in part because scholars suggested that the growth of transnational actors came at the expense of states, and this was clearly was not the case. Nonetheless, research on NGOs continued unabated, and with greater sophistication and wider application.

The associational revolution of the late 1980s, combined with the Cold War's end, shifted academic thinking and lines of inquiry, pushing scholars from various disciplines to reexamine the role of NGOs, networks, and nonstate actors. IR scholars were certainly part of this emerging research program, but most of the enthusiasts looked at human rights, foreign aid, the environment, and development, focusing on various parts of the world that had been overlooked (see for example Fisher 1998; Hilhorst 2003; Goonatilake 2006; Jalali 2013). The problem with some of this early literature is that it fails to provide more than anecdotal evidence for the praise heaped on NGOs. Moreover, enthusiasts tended to look at NGOs as either international or domestic actors, disregarding the transnational characteristics of these organizations and ignoring how transnational influences often shape domestic politics and the development of local NGOs. As Peter Willets (2010, 1) explains, this is because it is a gigantic task to consider all the NGOs involved in some way with international issues; thus, he concentrates only on the NGOs that work internationally.

Such a division is understandable, because it is easier conceptually to do this, and there is far more information on INGOs. But in post-conflict peacebuilding, as in many contexts, it is almost impossible to separate international and local actors. International actors and even INGOs are deceptively powerful, indirectly shaping agendas and the strategies of local actors. By trying to study the behavior and effects of international and local NGOs separately, scholars are inherently discounting their important transnational power. Also left behind in the fold is the fact that NGOs regularly operate as international, transnational, and domestic actors—simultaneously.

Not all enthusiasts pretend that it is possible to separate international from local NGOs. As Margaret Keck and Kathryn Sikkink's (1998) seminal book on transnational advocacy networks (TANs) observes, these networks of public and private actors include international and domestic NGOs as well as international organizations, states, and other civil society actors. But before this groundbreaking work, IR scholarship barely recognized the unique character of NGOs as domestic, international, and transnational actors that sometimes work with states and international organizations in overlapping and complementary ways.

In the years since, scholars in anthropology, comparative politics, humanitarian studies, and development have used insights about transnational politics to consider NGOs as actors working on various levels simultaneously. For example, Julie Fisher (1998) and Dorothea Hilhorst (2003) both aim to tease out the complex relationships among international, domestic, and grassroots NGOs operating in the field of development. However, the chief shortcoming of NGOs enthusiasts is that they are often so enamored with the growth and potential of NGOs that they portray them in an exclusively positive light. NGOs are thus viewed as enabling, progressive actors that can resolve complex international issues, advance progressive agendas, and represent the will of so-called global civil society. Up until recently, scholars operating in this group have paid too little attention to NGOs' negative and unintended consequences as they scramble for money, attention, and influence to keep their organizations afloat (Cooley and Ron 2002). It is also unfortunately the case that even recent research that focuses on the negative and unintended effects of foreign aid does not pay attention to post-conflict peacebuilding (Coyne 2013).

This book acknowledges the incredibly important insights identified by NGO enthusiasts, namely that NGOs are increasing in number as well as in political and economic clout. It also agrees that NGOs can, especially in certain sectors, be crucial transnational agents in peacebuilding. Yet, an important point of this book is that numbers alone tell us little about who the NGOs are, what they do, or how they actually shape post-conflict societies. To understand and assess the complex and unintended outcomes we must look to other disciplines and to the work of comparativists who have looked closely at when transnational advocacy networks are successful, how foreign aid impacts certain segments of societies, and the unintended effects of transnational social movements (Risse, Ropp, and Sikkink 1999; Tarrow 2005; Hertel 2006; Jalali 2013). We also need to look closely at what happens on the ground and to the everyday lives of people affected by NGO booms.

To some extent, NGO skeptics are the most recent to engage in sustained research on when and how NGOs (and well as other transnational actors) shape outcomes in international politics. Importantly, many writing from this perspective have come from inside the NGO community, providing crucial evidence of the policies and everyday practices of NGOs in different contexts and issue areas (Anderson 1999). As Oliver Richmond (2003, 2) explains, scholars writing from this more critical perspective eschew the traditional utopianism about NGOs and adopt "a more skeptical position of both the opportunities and constraints" NGOs face. In some cases, extensive field exposure has provided these scholars with sobering insights into NGO activities but also highlighted the paradoxes, challenges, and unintended consequences of their well-intentioned work. For example, Mary Anderson's (1999) groundbreaking book, *Do No Harm*, explains how NGOs can undermine peace efforts and encourage discord among the local population. At the same time, this practitioner recognizes the crucial role of NGOs as the primary arm of relief and development and their potential to support and transform peace. To be clear, the "consequentialist turn" is not inherently dismissive or even necessarily critical of NGOs. As Michael Barnett and Jack

Snyder (2008, 144) put it, scholars using this orientation want to "to see whether, which, and how the actions" of aid providers and others save lives and improve societies, with the goal of developing a more strategic orientation for future work. And by revealing certain negative or unintended dynamics, researchers seek to improve aid's effectiveness and, by implication, the work of NGOs.

Given their empirical bent, NGO skeptics often spend a lot of time identifying the many obstacles to studying NGOs and their effects systematically. Admittedly, part of the reason IR scholars like to focus on states is because of parsimony and the need to simplify complex environments. It is also because of the nature of NGOs and the bewildering array of activities and programs they undertake, and these also vary by country and sector. Unfortunately, NGOs are hard to count and monitor and thus it is difficult to theorize about their effects. Complicated funding relationships and overlapping projects further mean that it is almost impossible to know the impact of any single NGO.[17] In peacebuilding environments, the challenge of discerning the unique effects of NGO activities is even greater, because international policies and practices always include a wide assortment of governments and international organizations and a broad array of international NGOs as well as other public and private actors. Involving such a concoction of actors may make peacebuilding more legitimate than earlier forms of international intervention, but it also means that it is impossible to say with much precision what NGOs alone actually accomplish.

There is no getting around it; NGOs are hard to study, especially in post-conflict environments, and questions related to causality and impact are almost impossible to answer with much accuracy. Yet, the presence of NGOs all over the world and in so many sectors reminds us that despite these challenges, they cannot be ignored or dismissed. In post-conflict peacebuilding, NGOs have arrived and even thrived, and much is expected of them. On the other hand, a NGO boom that started in the 1990s should not be interpreted as the dawning of a new era full of actors that are transformative, more democratic, or more representative. Since the effects of NGOs are indirect, cumulative, and even unintentional, institutional theories and frameworks are helpful in exposing surprising and counterintuitive outcomes (Ohanyan 2009; Henderson 2003; Cooley and Ron 2002).

Peacebuilding and NGO effectiveness are topics that are equally important to policymakers and NGO practitioners as well as academics. Policymakers and NGO practitioners have expertise and first-hand experiences in conflict-ridden environments, but they have little time and money for long-term evaluations. Incorporating lessons learned or best practices, while laudable, are often a luxury because countries facing crises need assistance and action, and this often means engaging various actors. Academics are interested in evaluating NGOs and their strategies, creating and testing propositions to understand causes and outcomes, but often this is done without fieldwork or in-country experience. This book aims to speak to all who care about NGOs and peacebuilding to clarify their relationships and better understand their activities.

The Plan

This introduction described the questions that motivate this book, including: *Why* were NGOs involved in peacebuilding in the Balkans and other countries in the 1990s? Chapter 1 answers this question by providing a historical backdrop to the NGO boom, explaining *why* and *how* NGOs became involved in liberal peacebuilding. Others have offered different explanations for the growth of NGOs in international politics. This chapter does not necessarily disagree with these other accounts, but it highlights how understandings of violent conflict and security changed the strategies that governmental actors used, the actors that were implicated, and thus ideas on *how* and *who* should respond to post–Cold War threats.

Given the growth of internal conflicts in the 1990s, new norms, and different expectations associated with who and how peacebuilding should take place, chapter 2 provides evidence of what can only be called the NGO revolution, documenting the growth of NGOs and measuring their power. This chapter not only describes *how* NGOs have changed as they have grown in number, but it explains what is new about their behavior in the post–Cold War period and how their involvement in post-conflict countries differs from the past. This chapter also exposes the disjuncture between the discourse Western actors use when they talk about peacebuilding and international assistance and the realities on the ground.

My interest in this project began with my experiences and observations in the Balkans, starting in the early 2000s. Chapters 3 and 4 look at these dynamics closely in Bosnia and Kosovo, respectively, incorporating interviews that started in 2000 and ended in 2011. In both Bosnia and Kosovo, there was a discernable NGO boom followed by a bust as international assistance declined. NGOs grew competitive with each other, and people became disillusioned with international promises to build civil society and invest in local actors. In both countries, many NGOs were disembedded from local structures, proving unwilling or unable to advance international goals.

Rational and historical institutionalism allows me to contextualize the interactions and effects of liberal peacebuilding as a set of policies and practices in light of certain domestic institutions and local conditions. This comparative, historical framework helps tease out relationships that might otherwise be overlooked. There are many advantages to this approach, which attempts to trace the links between international peacebuilding and the development of local NGOs and other activities in society (George and Bennett 2005, 7–9). Importantly, it helps isolate the effects of the NGO boom, which is difficult because of the large number of public and private actors that are always involved in peacebuilding. To be clear, I am not focused on demonstrating the effect of NGOs on peacebuilding per se or evaluating specific NGOs. Instead, I discuss *what* happens *after* NGOs arrive and multiply, and *how* this group of actors shapes peacebuilding and post-conflict societies.

Post-conflict countries are not easy to access, and doing research on social and political changes requires more than a cursory knowledge of a country. I chose two countries from the Balkans that I know well and which have a lot in common. These new states were once part of Yugoslavia's multiethnic federation and they both attracted substantial international involvement. Both were also safe enough for me to conduct fieldwork and interviews and, especially in Bosnia, to study these processes and dynamics over time, asking locals at different points about the international community's policies and NGO effects.[18] To some extent, this was an opportunistic process, and the book is primarily about the effects of international peacebuilding in the Balkans. However, as I discuss briefly in my conclusion, NGO booms and busts and some versions of the NGO game exist in other contexts, and thus these concepts and processes are not necessarily limited to these countries, this region, or to internationally led peacebuilding.

The conclusion summarizes the book's main contributions and provides a sampling of boom and bust dynamics in countries as diverse as Afghanistan, East Timor, and Sri Lanka. I end by discussing the future of peacebuilding and NGOs more generally. Given the conflicts and crises we face today, alongside the glaring problems of the current system of international aid and post-conflict reconstruction, it is clear that future policies will require more knowledge of everyday realities as well as a greater appreciation for genuine partnerships. This book, thus, wholeheartedly supports Boutros Boutros-Ghali's observation that peace is too important to be entrusted to states alone. At the same time, it warns that building peace is far too difficult and complex to be left to mere assumptions and wishful thinking about NGOs or any actors involved in this messy and difficult process.

Chapter 1

UNCERTAIN TIMES

Robert Kaplan's writings (1993; 1994) in the early 1990s reveal a great deal about the concerns presented by the Cold War's end. They also help explain why NGOs became so prevalent in post-conflict peacebuilding in the Balkans. Ostensibly a travel memoir, Kaplan's *Balkan Ghosts* (1993) has an important message to tell: southern Europe is "a powder keg for 21st-century cultural and religious warfare between Islamic groups and Christianity, and identity conflicts such as these will spread from Athens all the way to Muscovy."[1] His follow-up article in the *Atlantic* (1994) and book by the same title, *The Coming Anarchy* (2002), provided an even more alarming picture of how ethnic conflict, environmental degradation, and transnational crime would change our understandings of security and conflict. These ideas, deemed stunning by then President Clinton, claimed that resource scarcity and urban poverty would exacerbate ethnic tensions and become bloody, violent battles. The menacing future would not just be rife with violence but borders would be weakened and the nation-state system destroyed.[2]

Clearly, neither ethnic conflict nor environmental degradation was a new issue, but Kaplan's writings (1993; 1994) exploited post–Cold War uncertainties. Kaplan and others may have exaggerated emerging threats, misrepresenting history in the process, but fears of global instability wrought by diverse and indeterminate factors demanded attention and a response. Earlier well-known scholars like Richard Ullman (1983) and Jessica Tuchman Mathews (1989) had called for the broadening of security studies to include economics, the natural environment, and other nonmilitary factors, but the debate over "redefining security" remained largely an academic one until the Soviet Union collapsed. It was not until the early 1990s, when violent internal conflicts suddenly but decisively turned states and theories on their heads, that policymakers and academics scrambled for new strategies *and* different partners.

It was in this context of transition and perceived chaos that Western states and international organizations looked expectantly to NGOs, submitting that these "representatives of civil society" were effective, efficient, and even legitimate actors in international relations and post-conflict peacebuilding.[3] A more sober analysis of these developments is that leaders of states and international organizations wanted to do something, but they did not want to do a lot. Unwilling to invest the time and money needed to respond carefully and comprehensively to emerging crises, international actors turned desperately and naively to nonstate actors. For many reasons NGOs were an attractive solution to post–Cold War threats. Not only did Western governmental actors see them as flexible organizations that could respond quickly to situations, but many also believed that NGOs were efficient and could save governments both money and time. In truth, the motivations for engaging NGOs in post-conflict peacebuilding were never fleshed out, nor were the plans to solicit and engage these organizations. Nonetheless, it was easy to assume that NGOs belonged in peacebuilding in some seamless way and to exaggerate their ability to counter nebulous threats while bridging international and local actors. Clarifying the historical context in which NGOs were implicated is different from answering the question: *What* prompted the NGO turn in the early 1990s? After decades of neglect, how did these once marginalized actors suddenly become engaged in post-conflict reconstruction and peacebuilding—issues so central to security and sovereignty?

NGOs had good timing. In the last decade of the twentieth century, not only did government leaders start to fear new threats, but they decided to address these complicated concerns differently. Given important changes in international politics, states and international actors started to look beyond peacekeeping and conflict management and commit themselves to restructuring and reengineering countries in ways that were both ambitious and wide-ranging. In other words, as Cold War threats disappeared, the liberal peace-building agenda emerged, generating different expectations for *how* and *who* would respond to the post–Cold War disorder.

Interpretive analysis based on policy statements, governmental reports, and secondary sources highlights the changing post–Cold War norms and how the reframing of states' understandings and interests opened spaces for the growth of NGOs (Stephenson and Zanotti 2012, 4). Broadly speaking, interpretive methods seek to understand the intentions of social behavior from the language that actors use (Abdelal et al. 2009, 6). Sometimes language is used instrumentally and for other purposes, but I contend that the language of government officials and academics in the first half of the 1990s sheds light on *how* governments perceived and sought to counter emerging threats. In the end, ambitious but fundamentally deceptive statements about NGOs informed policies and behavior, ultimately giving rise to NGO booms, busts, and the NGO game in international peacebuilding.

Other explanations exist for the growth of NGOs in international relations that are grounded in the Cold War's demise and the rise of neoliberal economic policies or certain structures and ideas. I do not reject these explanations entirely, but I maintain that to understand the role and importance of NGOs in post-conflict environments, three key factors need to be highlighted: the rise of violent internal conflicts, how state leaders started to think about responding to these events, and to whom governments and international actors looked for help in addressing complex humanitarian emergencies and dealing with conflict-prone states. Uncertain times mandate innovative strategies; they also call for new actors.

New Wars

Journalists are often the first to report on changes that are happening on the ground, but in the early 1990s they were hardly alone in drawing attention to the dramatic shift from interstate conflicts and conventional warfare to intrastate violence and complex humanitarian emergencies.[4] After decades of nuclear standoff between the United States and its allies and the Soviet Union and its bloc of socialist countries, intrastate violence was not only more likely, it was frightening and destabilizing. Initially, international relations scholars maintained that the causes and dynamics of internal conflicts were not that different from what animated interstate wars of the past. Concepts like the balance of power and the security dilemma, which were used by security studies scholars to explain interstate war, were thus still useful for explaining and predicting intrastate ethnic violence.[5] The rapid and disruptive expansion of these conflicts, however, pushed scholars to rethink and revise earlier concepts and theories. No unified theory emerged to explain intrastate wars, but a cluster of variables, including ethnic composition, domestic institutions, and elite politics, were all tenuously linked to post–Cold War violence.[6]

Actual causes aside, so-called new wars were cast as qualitatively different from the large-scale, interstate wars of the past (Kaldor 1999). In a nutshell, post–Cold War conflicts were deemed unusually brutal, criminal, and predatory. As the title of John Mueller's (2000) article "The Banality of Ethnic War" proposes, contemporary ethnic wars were about thugs and criminality rather than ethnicity or ideology. According to this interpretation, post–Cold War violence was driven by profit and greed and was characterized by gratuitous violence, while interstate wars of the past were depicted as ideologically driven, enjoyed broad support, and practiced controlled and disciplined violence (Kalyvas 2001, 101–2). According to Mary Kaldor (1999), who coined the term *new wars*, this new form of organized violence was not caused by the Cold War's end, by colonial boundaries, or by ethnic differences. New wars were instead the result of a revolution in the social relations of warfare and the erosion of the autonomy of states. The point is that something bigger, more complex, and far nastier was generating horrific new wars, and they required a different, innovative response.

Using the Bosnian conflict as her only example of new identity-driven wars, Kaldor explains how globalization transformed both how and where wars would be waged in the twenty-first century—in living rooms and by neighbors, not on battlefields between states and soldiers. In this emerging system, interstate wars would be replaced by low-level violence within states with transnational ties and accompanied by massive human rights violations. Kaldor's (2007) subsequent book, *Human Security*, develops these ideas further, linking new wars to failed states, peacebuilding, and economic development and discussing the changes in sovereignty and the rights of individuals. For her, the revolution in warfare and the erosion of states' sovereignty shifted the focus of security away from states and *national* security to individuals and *human* security.

This reframing of threats and security advances the position that the key to preventing new wars and resolving human security dilemmas rests with civil society, which is supposedly led by nongovernmental organizations and other so-called representatives of the global community. Just who these actors would be and how they would represent "the people" is never explained or explored in much detail. But in this unfolding, uncertain world, NGOs would become crucial international actors. NGOs would not work alone but would be part of a multiactor response to internal conflicts, giving voice to marginalized interests and vulnerable groups and to concerns of "the people." At least this is the narrative that some were peddling: international stability and peace in the twenty-first century are linked to factors and forces coming from within countries and thus depended on NGOs and other so-called "representatives of global civil society."

Many authors tried to characterize and account for the restructuring of states, international security, and the post–Cold War world. Samuel Huntington's (1996) clash of civilizations thesis perhaps provides the most pessimistic, if cogent, picture for how these forces came together, squarely pinning the causes of future violence on issues of identity and culture. Huntington ominously predicts that fault line wars would not only mean ruthless violence against civilians, but these civilizational conflicts would bring about the end of multiethnic states. The post–Cold War world was characterized in various ways, but there was some agreement on the central message delivered: in the era of new wars and human security, nation-states beware!

Although terms like *ethnic conflict, complex humanitarian emergencies*, and *new wars* were increasingly used to characterize messy internal conflicts, not everyone bought into the notion that these conflicts were profoundly different from wars of the past. Careful research on the history of warfare, in fact, casts serious doubt on the idea that this violence was either new or unusually brutal to civilians.[7] Stathias Kalyvas (2001, 101–2), for example, does not deny the sudden rise of internal conflicts in the early 1990s, but he does take issue with the claim that they were somehow qualitatively different or somehow "more criminalized, de-politicized, and privatized" than previous wars. At best, the characterization of new wars was incomplete if not ahistorical. At worst, the term and ideas surrounding them fundamentally misrepresented reality. Claims about new wars were tenuous and largely unsubstantiated, but this was nonetheless how the post–Cold War world was being depicted by some policymakers and academics. Yet, as some suggest, international responses to emerging intrastate conflicts were less influenced by the threats themselves and their severity than they were an outgrowth of ill-prepared actors and inappropriate policies (Crawford and Lipschutz 1998).

The Need to Act

The Coming Anarchy argument (Kaplan 1994) may have been exaggerated and based on incomplete information, but emerging threats and the expanding number of failing states were difficult challenges that required a global response (Helman and Ratner 1992, 3). Statements and policies early in the decade clearly endorsed perceptions that the post–Cold War world was not only dangerous for civilians but threatening to states and world order. According to Michael Doyle and Nicholas Sambanis (2006, 1), the United Nations grasped the fragility of the moment, adopting a "strikingly interventionist tone" starting in 1990, because of the threats and the "perceived need for a coherent international response." From 1990 to 1993 alone the United Nations' Department for Peacekeeping Operations (PKO) took on fourteen new operations—even though it had not taken on a single operation in the ten years prior. With no obvious actor or overriding strategy equipped to respond to the growth of internal conflicts, the United Nations needed to take the initiative and respond to the problems as well as the opportunities presented by the Cold War's end.

The *Agenda for Peace* (Boutros-Ghali 1992) lays out the rationale for fundamental changes in the UN's structure and the institutions and strategies it needs to both prevent and respond to emerging international threats. This and subsequent UN documents describe the changing nature of war in the post–Cold War era and assess what this implies for international action (Diehl and Druckman 2010). The United Nations' post–Cold War message was strong and focused on the threats to the world system: "This is a time of global transition" that is marked by "uniquely contradictory trends," where cooperation between Western states and international organizations is evolving while "primitive, brutal rivalries threaten world order."[8] Paradoxically, and despite the Soviet Union's peaceful demise, a menacing international environment was unfurling. On the one hand, long-standing ideological barriers had collapsed, making cooperation and peace more likely, especially among Western states. On the other hand, fierce new assertions of nationalism and ethnic identity were reemerging, threatening the stability that took decades to foster.

New wars were not just horrific and bloody for those living within these countries, but they "fundamentally impact the cohesion of States." The nation-state system was directly "threatened by brutal ethnic, religious, social, cultural or linguistic strife."[9] Moreover, because these wars did not tend to involve powerful states, the United Nations, or other international organizations, the actors involved lacked the military might needed to incorporate new resources and strategies to push things back on track. Consequently, the *Supplement to an Agenda for Peace* (Boutros-Ghali 1995) elaborates on the new and varied sources of internal conflicts while it reaffirms the need for comprehensive, multileveled responses. As events in the former Soviet Union in particular demonstrated, for many, "Today's conflicts are *within* States rather than between States."[10] For the United Nations, the single most important international concern was not militarily powerful states; it was weak and failing states, because these states engaged in human rights abuses and provoked humanitarian disasters, threatening the security of all states in the system (Fukuyama 2004, 93–94).

During this same period, U.S. leaders also acknowledged the surprising and unfortunate turn of events that accompanied the Cold War's end. As President Clinton's 1993 inaugural address stated, "Today, a generation raised in the shadows of the cold war assumes new responsibilities in a world warmed by the sunshine of freedom but threatened still by ancient hatreds and new plagues."[11] The choice of terms like *ancient hatreds* and *plagues* suggests that the Clinton administration believed that internal conflicts, while unleashed by communism's demise, had deep roots that made them both unmanageable and unwinnable for the United States alone. A year later, in his State of the Union address (1994), President Clinton elaborated on the dangers of rampant arms proliferation, regional conflicts, ethnic and nationalist tensions in new democracies, severe environmental degradation, and fanatics who seek to cripple the world's cities with terror.[12] For the United States, and after decades of responding to the nuclear threat coming from the Soviet Union, new threats were suddenly everywhere, emerging from far-flung sources. All of this meant that even the most powerful country in the world lacked the tools to respond.

Unlike the United Nations' inclination to respond vigorously and proactively to new threats, the United States initially signaled that it was unwilling to get involved in the messy internal affairs of states, seeing them as beyond the interest or the reach of U.S. military power. As the then-U.S. secretary of state Warren Christopher reminded, "The death of [Yugoslav] President Tito and the end of communist domination of the former Yugoslavia raised the lid on the cauldron of ancient ethnic hatreds."[13] Such age-old hatreds prevented the United States—or any other international actor—from swooping in and quickly solving these domestic problems. At least some U.S. leaders appreciated that despite the unique, unipolar moment where the United States enjoyed unparalleled military power and a tremendous international prestige, the global hegemon needed to restrain itself and use its power judiciously and sparingly. At the same time, even if new wars and failed states were not direct threats to the homeland, they still impacted allies and undermined world order. More problematically, there was no easy or quick solution.

In 1994, the U.S. Department of Defense and the Central Intelligence Agency (CIA) jointly published the first post–Cold War examination of threats to the United States, outlining its strategies for the future of American security policy.[14] *Redefining Security* makes plain the threats of the post–Cold War era and the challenges facing the United States, because they are diffuse, multifaceted, and dynamic. Importantly, these complex, internal problems could easily pull the United States in many unproductive directions: "National security concerns now include a daunting array of challenges that continue to grow in diversity in our unstable and unpredictable world. . . . Burgeoning ethnic and religious rivalries that cross traditional boundaries endanger both new and long-standing peace agreements, drawing the United States into an expanding role in peacekeeping and humanitarian missions."[15]

The September 11, 2001 terrorist attacks changed American security policy in obvious ways, but in terms of perceived threats these events only intensified fears that the wars of the twenty-first century would be different, unpredictable, and centrally related to the problem of weak and failing states.

As an independent task force studying American capabilities in the post–9/11 world stated in the report, "In the Wake of War: Improving U.S. Post-conflict Capabilities" (2005, 6), although poverty does not make poor people into terrorists or murderers, weak institutions and corruption can turn vulnerable and failing states into homes for terrorist networks and drug cartels. For the United States, the terrorist attacks on American soil perpetuated the view that post–Cold War violence was random and directed toward civilians and emerged from multifaceted causes. Moreover, states and military might were no longer the primary security concerns for the world's hegemon.

The European response to emerging internal conflicts became more obvious and decisive, given the violence and instability in neighboring Yugoslavia and the Soviet Union. Understandably, European countries were more focused on the threat of aggressive nationalism and ethnic conflict. Individually and in regional gatherings, European leaders agonized over how the internal affairs of countries in the East might affect stability and prosperity in Western Europe. Regional organizations like the Conference on Security and Cooperation in Europe (CSCE) openly warned of the specific and imminent threat of ethnic and civil conflict, not only states' integrity but also to European security. According to the CSCE's 1992 *Challenges of Change*: "This is a time of promise but also a time of instability and insecurity. Economic decline, social tension, aggressive nationalism, intolerance, xenophobia and ethnic conflicts threaten stability in the CSCE area. Gross violations of CSCE commitments in the field of human rights and fundamental freedoms, including those related to national minorities, pose a special threat to the peaceful development of society, in particular in new Democracies."[16] In response to the real and potential violence erupting within states in Central and Eastern Europe, in 1995 the CSCE morphed into the Organization for Security and Cooperation in Europe (OSCE) with the intention of focusing on early warnings of conflict and conflict prevention within fragile states. These same threats redefined and reinvigorated other regional European organizations, including NATO, the Council of Europe, and the European Union.[17] By the middle of the 1990s, a clear consensus had developed: internal conflicts, rather than interstate wars, were the primary threats to states and security, and something needed to be done.

Action of some sort was clearly needed, but in actuality the 1990s turned out to be far less war-prone and bloody than predicted. It was also the case

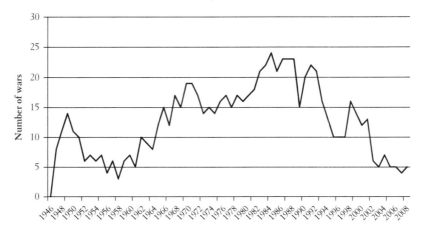

Figure 1.1. Number of wars, 1946–2008. Source: Adapted from the Human Security Research Group. "Number of Wars." *Human Security Research Project.* 2009. http://www.hsrgroup.org /docs/Publications/HSR20092010/Figures/20092010Report_Fig10_2_NumberOfWars.pdf.

that while the overall number of wars jumped dramatically in the early 1990s, these conflicts should be considered in a broader, historical context which is far more complicated. As figure 1 shows, the number of wars, in fact, started to increase in the 1960s, and they decreased quite a lot by the middle of the 1990s.

The trends associated with intrastate conflict were, however, quite worrisome, and in the 1990s there were many more conflicts within states than between them, with the former increasing sharply in the early 1990s, as figure 2 demonstrates. Yet, the images of bloodshed in places like Bosnia and Rwanda did not tell the complete story, because intrastate conflicts rose dramatically in the 1970s and declined steadily in the second half of the 1990s.

In building the case for states to respond quickly and vigorously to these new wars, scholars and policymakers often implied that post–Cold War violence was more awful and inhumane than in earlier conflicts, disproportionately harming civilians. These claims also turned out to be exaggerated and poorly supported. Supposedly, some 90 percent of the fatalities in the new wars of the 1990s were civilians (versus less than 50 percent for wars in the 1960s). When examined closely, however, researchers maintained that determining civilian casualties is so difficult that it is simply impossible to compare wars in this way (Barakat 2005a, 22; Roberts 2010, 115–66). Deaths from

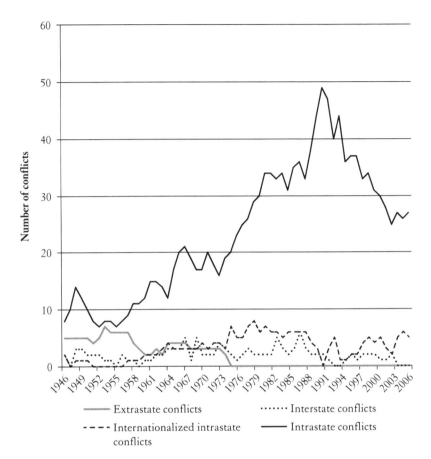

Figure 1.2. Types of conflict, 1946–2006. Source: Adapted from the Human Security Rearch Group. "State Based Armed Conflicts by Type, 1946–2006." *Human Rights Security Report Project*. 2007. http://www.hsrgroup.org/docs/Publications/HSB2007/Figures/2007HSBrief _fig3_1-StateBasedArmedConflictsByType.jpg.

intrastate conflicts in the 1990s were no doubt high, but post–Cold War violence was not nearly as fatal as wars of the past, as figure 3 demonstrates. In terms of battle deaths, for example, the conflicts of the 1990s did not hold a candle to the slaughter that happened during World War II.

The United Nations' *Human Security Report* (2012) confirms that although some forms of violence increased in the first few years after the Cold War ended, state-based armed conflicts and average battle deaths declined

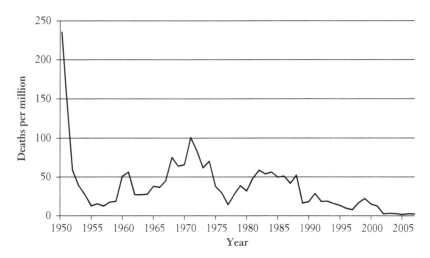

Figure 1.3. Number of battle deaths, 1950–2005. Source: Adapted from the Human Security Research Group. "Battle Deaths per Year per Million of World Population, 1950–1970." *Human Security Research Project.* 2010. http://www.hsrgroup.org/docs/Publications /HSR20092010/Figures/20092010Report_Fig6_6_BattleDeathsYearMillionPopulation.pdf.

in the last decade of the twentieth century and continued to shrink in the twenty-first century.[18] These facts notwithstanding, the chaotic post–Cold War era was regularly portrayed as uniquely and particularly threatening to individuals, states, and world order (Fukuyama 2004, 96). Unfortunately, policymakers are often more burdened by perceptions than facts, and mounting fears required new strategies to respond to intrastate violence and failing states.

From Management to Transformation

Given the perceived assault on states and the international system, it is somewhat surprising that governmental actors turned to nonstate actors and NGOs in particular for help. But not only had ideas changed about the threats facing states and the causes of future conflict, but so too did expectations for how international actors ought to respond to the coming anarchy and its grave consequences. During the Cold War, international actors and particularly Western states engaged in what was appropriately called conflict management. Conflict management is outcome-oriented and focuses on ending interstate wars, primarily through coercion and diplomatic, state-led initiatives. In the early 1990s, because of changing understandings of war and security, there was a deliberate shift from managing violent conflicts to transforming them. Conflict transformation is process-oriented and focuses on the underlying conditions and actors involved in intrastate violence through a variety of institutional and societal mechanisms. In other words, the end of superpower rivalry, combined with the uncertainty of new wars and their presumed nastiness, resulted in new ideas about what states should expect and how they should behave. Conflict transformation is aimed at restructuring and rebuilding conflict-prone environments rather than merely containing their effects.

As we know, this was not the first time that international actors became extensively involved in trying to rebuild war-torn countries, but liberal peacebuilding at the Cold War's end aspired and pretended to be different. As Oliver Richmond and Jason Franks (2009, 6) put it, liberal peacebuilding was "both wildly ambitious and comprehensive in what it sought to achieve," focusing on the roots of violence, seeking to reengineer states and societies, and reaching out to various actors at different levels. Liberal peacebuilding not only had grand goals, but it sought to implement them differently, supposedly relying on innovative bottom-up methods that involved creating democratic institutions and restructuring a country's society. Yet, creating new institutions and transforming a country is no simple feat, and it also involves dilemmas and contradictions that cannot be addressed easily or quickly (Jarstad and Sisk 2008).

Following World War II, there were many chances for members of the international community to become involved in countries' internal disputes, but only rarely was there any sort of collective, sustained international response. The most successful examples of post-conflict reconstruction, or what some call nation building, were those that were led by the United States immediately after World War II (Dobbins et al. 2003; Dobbins 2012). The American occupations of Germany and Japan were quite different from what transpired in the 1990s; in particular, the former were postconquest interventions that relied largely on America's military might. They were unilateral in nature and premised on pursuing reconstruction through the spread of American-style institutions (Suri 2011). Liberal peacebuilding was similar in important respects, but it was not based largely on American military power or unilateralist policies. In theory and in practice, liberal peacebuilding aimed for a certain consensus among many actors who adopted overlapping and reinforcing strategies at different levels to restructure states and their societies.

In comparing American nation-building efforts after World War II from Germany to Iraq, the Rand Corporation, for example, makes it clear that U.S. investments in postwar reconstruction, measured in terms of troops on the ground, financial assistance, scope of activities, and time spent in country, were not replicated in any of its post–Cold War missions (Dobbins, et al., 2003, 149–66). In more recent examples of liberal peacebuilding, U.S. involvement was crucial, but its level of involvement was quite different, if not modest; so too was American behavior. Unlike the post–WWII period, in the 1990s the United States responded reluctantly, encouraging the involvement of allies, and subcontracting responsibilities and activities to nonstate actors. This does not necessarily mean that the United States did not direct or even dominate many aspects of international peacebuilding in the 1990s and 2000s, but its hegemonic position was not permanent in every sphere of activity. As James Dobbins (2012, 43) explains, in post–Cold War operations, and particularly in the Balkans, the superpower operated as part of a broader, multilateral coalition. In fact, in many of the post–Cold War undertakings, it was the United Nations and not the United States that organized and led peace-building efforts.[19] Thus, in spite of its unique position as the unrivaled superpower, the United States defied both history and expectations by not seeking to exploit its power and dominate others, even when it came to rebuilding post-conflict countries—at least before its misadventures in Afghanistan and Iraq.

During the Cold War, when the international community intervened in the domestic affairs of another country, it did so in the form of UN peacekeeping. The activities of the United Nations were, by intention and design, temporary and limited, manifesting minimal interference in domestic affairs and the management of conflict. When UN peacekeeping started in 1948, activities were mostly defensive in nature and included observation, supervision, and interposition. This meant that UN troops were sent to a country to act as a neutral monitor with circumspect tasks to observe and to keep the peace. Peacekeeping troops could use force but only in self-defense, and they avoided invasive political or social processes. In other words, peacekeeping did not include engagement in nation building, and before 1990 there were only a few attempts by the United Nations or any other international organization to engage in multilateral, comprehensive post-conflict reconstruction aimed at changing countries' internal structures and transforming conflict-prone environments.

These strategies and assumptions changed as new wars spiraled and thinking shifted from managing violence to transforming countries and the underlying conditions that led to violence in the first place. For Ted Robert Gurr (2002, 50), evidence of "new post–Cold War norms" were reflected in the level, intensity, and variety of the activities undertaken by the United Nations, Western governments, and other international organizations throughout the 1990s. For better and for worse, this destabilizing period pushed the United Nations to find its new calling, which it alternatively called conflict prevention, conflict transformation, and peacebuilding. However, these new roles were not the United Nations' alone and many Western governments and other international organizations as well as international NGOs followed the United Nations' lead, creating a cottage industry of organizations committed to transforming and rebuilding conflict-prone countries.

Focusing on the underlying conditions that gave rise to violence and the concept of peacebuilding was not completely new. In fact, the practice of peacebuilding dates back to the 1960s, peace studies literature, and to scholars like Johan Galtung. But peacebuilding on the scale proposed in the 1990s had never been attempted. At the Cold War's end, the term was revived by the United Nations as top-down and bottom-up mechanisms were created to restructure countries' political, economic, and social institutions. These conflict-transforming instruments and strategies are laid out clearly in the *Agenda for Peace*, which called for nothing short of a "radical transformation of societies from structures of coercion and violence to an embedded culture of peace" (Keating and Knight 2004, xxiv). In the years since, United Nations' multifaceted, multilayered peace operations have reflected this transformation, emphasizing healing and reconciliation as well as civil society development.

Like preventive diplomacy, post-conflict peacebuilding embraces a variety of activities and instruments that are undertaken on the far side of conflict to reassemble the foundations of peace and provide the tools for building on those foundations (Report of the Panel on Peace Operations, 2000). For the United Nations, peace-building activities include but are not limited to: reintegrating former combatants into civilian society; strengthening the rule of law; improving respect for human rights through the monitoring, education and investigation of past and existing abuses; providing technical assistance for democratic development and promoting conflict resolution and reconciliation techniques. As former secretary-general Boutros Boutros-Ghali clarified, peacebuilding in the 1990s implied the "creation of a new environment," not merely the cessation of hostilities facilitated by traditional peacekeeping (Diehl 2008, 8).

The United Nations' post–Cold War agenda certainly kept it busy. In the 1990s, it created more missions requiring more forces and much larger budgets. As figure 4 demonstrates clearly, after agreeing to only twenty-one peacekeeping missions in forty years, the United Nations took a radical turn at the Cold War's end, sending out forty-three new missions in about fifteen years (between 1990 and 2006), requiring many more UN troops.

Of the wars that ended between 1988 and 2007, the United Nations played a major role in peace efforts in at least half of these countries, helping with stabilization, reconstruction, and political and economic development.

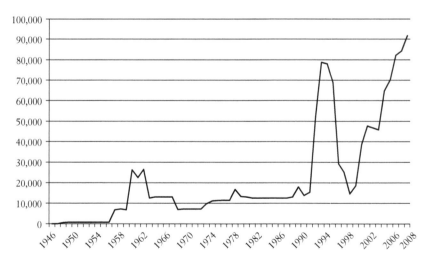

Figure 1.4. UN peacekeeping force size, 1947–2008. Source: This chart represents UN Peacekeeping force levels by year. The figures show the highest month for each year, rounded to the nearest hundred. Figures include troops, military observers, and police. Adapted from data compiled by Global Policy Forum, *Peacekeeping Tables and Charts: Size of UN Peacekeeping Operations*, https://www.globalpolicy.org/images/pdfs/images/pdfs /Size_of_UN_PK_force_by_year_-_2011_.pdf.

The United Nations also led comprehensive peace-building missions in Kosovo, Cambodia, and East Timor. But in these peace operations, the United Nations never worked alone; instead, as the *Agenda for Peace* report (Boutros-Ghali 1992) proposed, UN troops worked alongside a blend of international actors that were engaged in activities aimed at creating structures to consolidate peace and advance a sense of confidence and well-being among people. By adopting these strategies and tactics, it acknowledged that post-conflict peacebuilding in the 1990s was different from its top-down activities of the past. As the Panel on UN Peace Operations put it, peacebuilding is "a complex and multifaceted process, and it is clear that to prevent conflicts in the future, the UN must work with other actors and focus on the root causes of violence and, thus, the environment that promotes it."[20]

The UN's commitment to conflict transformation as well as prevention resulted in an immediate increase in the number and composition of its operations, significantly affecting it peacekeeping budget (see figure 5). Moreover, on average, UN missions during the 1990s were both more numerous and lasted longer than peacekeeping missions in any other previous decade or in the first decade of the 2000s (see figure 6).

The United Nations' peace-building agenda certainly challenged the organization in obvious ways, but it also presented it with opportunities to resolve long-standing conflicts and to cultivate what it referred to as "a culture of peace movement" based on dialogue and negotiation with individuals and groups as well as nation-states (Alger 2007, 534). In a world increasingly marked by civil wars and the collapse of states, the United Nations recognized that it needed a range of positive inducements to encourage actors to follow its lead and focus on the root causes of violent conflict.

UN leaders appreciated the difficulties of their ambitious plans as well as the challenges of cultivating a movement of peace based on dialogue and negotiation. The 2000 Brahimi Report that evaluated post–Cold War UN peace and security activities, for example, explained that for such a movement to happen, a doctrinal shift in how the United Nations approached peacekeeping was necessary. This new approach needed to emphasize "a team approach" because of the interest in upholding the rule of law, respecting human rights, and helping communities achieve national reconciliation.[21] The UN report also acknowledged the importance of creativity and flexibility in responding to future operations, particularly with domestic institutions and local actors. Commenting on the Brahimi Report, Kofi Annan, the then

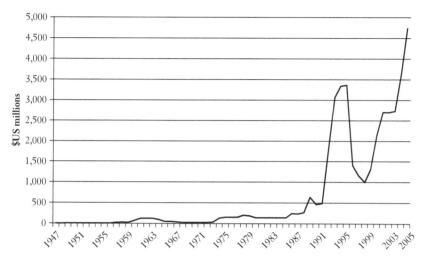

Figure 1.5. UN peacekeeping operations expenditures, 1947–2005. Source: All sums are rounded in $US millions. Since 1996, the United Nations' peacekeeping budget is measured on a July to June basis instead of by calendar year. Global Policy Forum has calculated the calendar year figures since 1996 by adding the prior and the current years' figures and dividing by two. From 2000 onward, peacekeeping data represent approved budgets rather than actual expenditures. Adapted from data compiled by Global Policy Forum, http://www.globalpolicy .org/tables-and-charts-ql/un-finance-tcql/the-un-peacekeeping-operations-budget.html.

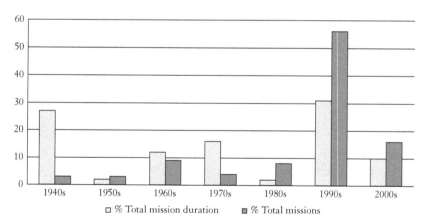

□ % Total mission duration   ■ % Total missions

Figure 1.6. Comparing UN missions. Sources: Adapted from data compiled by Global Policy Forum, https://www.globalpolicy.org/security-council/peacekeeping/peacekeeping-data.html.

secretary-general, confirmed that peacekeeping operations and conflict management were no longer sufficient and should not be used as a substitute for transforming environments and focusing on the root causes of violent conflict.[22]

In the age of liberal peacebuilding then, UN operations were not just more numerous, their involvement was broader and bolder, because of the international organization's interest in involving more sectors and establishing new patterns of interaction with other international agencies, regional organizations, and governments. Working with donors and other stakeholders, the United Nations established a post-conflict needs assessment (PCNA) for conceptualizing, negotiating, and financing post-conflict recovery strategies in cooperative and comprehensive ways.[23] By 2005 the UN Peacebuilding Commission was established, recognizing that "development, peace and security and human rights are interlinked and mutually reinforcing."[24] Moreover, it acknowledged the importance of thinking creatively about how the United Nations works with other organizations to stop violence while laying the foundation for democratic governance and sustainable development.

Mirroring the UN's activities, other international organizations and Western governments adopted similar rhetoric and policies, establishing their own capacities to transform internal conflicts and promote peace. In 1997, for example, the World Bank created a post-conflict unit, because although it was established after World War II to help with reconstruction and economic development, post–Cold War peacebuilding was different and posed new challenges. In fact, liberal peacebuilding defied "the exact boundaries of traditional forms of assistance"; it was not just sustainable development, but it was also not a strictly humanitarian response (Tschirgi 2004, 6). The nature, scale, and professionalization of these conflicts were also different and meant that the activities supported by the World Bank could not be stand-alone projects; the activities needed to be "part of a comprehensive and interrelated package of interventions designed to facilitate the transition from conflict to peace" (World Bank 1998).

By the beginning of the twenty-first century, the World Bank was involved in post-conflict reconstruction in more than thirty-eight countries, working in consultation with donor governments, civil society actors, NGOs, other UN agencies, and the private sector in different and overlapping ways to promote peace. A 2006 report explained exactly how the World Bank's interest in post-conflict peacebuilding had changed its overarching strategy, from an "outcome-oriented approach associated with conflict management to a relationship-oriented approach based on conflict resolution and transformation" (World Bank 2006, 5–7). Like the United Nations, the World Bank's peace-building agenda combined a focus on short-term management with the cultivation of relationships with public and private partners at the international and domestic levels. The World Bank also aimed to be more inclusive, using a team-based approach to working with domestic actors for long-term change.

Similarly, the Organization for Economic Cooperation and Development (OECD) developed its own mechanisms in the 1990s to support the emerging liberal peace-building agenda, emphasizing the importance of economic development to conflict transformation and long-term peace. Its Development Assistance Committee (DAC) even created a Task Force on Conflict, Peace and Development Co-operation "to help orient the actions of donors working in rapidly changing situations of conflict and potential conflict" (OECD 1998). The OECD's Task Force however did not just coordinate the involvement of donors, but it created new strategies, underscoring the need to build on existing practices and actors for more effective peacebuilding. First published in 1997, the OECD–DAC *Guidelines on Conflict, Peace and Development Cooperation* reflects the international community's fundamental shift in thinking about the relationship between conflict and development and the need for "conflict-sensitive strategies" that are multidimensional and multileveled ("Peace and Conflict-Sensitive Approaches to Development" 2000). Like other organizations of the time, the OECD maintained that successful peacebuilding required coordinated and coherent policies that addressed the root causes of conflicts as well as their consequences.

The United States responded somewhat differently to emerging post–Cold War conflicts, hesitating to act, because it feared that it would spread itself too thin or become unnecessarily entangled in the internal affairs of other countries. The Clinton administration instead promoted what it called "active multilateralism," embracing and supporting the involvement of allies and new private actors to address global instability. A more straightforward interpretation of the U.S. government's behavior is that the United States wanted to limit its resources and involvement to counter direct threats to American security. Recall that Bill Clinton campaigned on the promise that he would focus on the country's economy, even though he accused the Bush administration of doing too little in the Balkans. Later President Clinton's position shifted, maintaining at least for a while that the conflict in the Balkans was Europe's problem, and European countries and regional organizations should take the lead (Forsythe and McMahon 2016). In the end, but only after three years, the United States led the international intervention in Bosnia, but its involvement was half-hearted.

Domestic public opinion ensured that the U.S. government adopted cost-effective strategies that avoided putting American people in harm's way or exhausting the country's treasury. But regardless of its motivations, American behavior in the early 1990s reflected a liberal internationalist mindset that assumed that Western countries and international organizations needed to cooperate and even coordinate their efforts in post-conflict countries to create specific political, economic, and social institutions in war-torn countries. Even in Afghanistan after 2001, there was some appreciation of the benefits of liberal peacebuilding, which allowed the United States to assume a leadership position in certain areas without having to be responsible for all aspects of reconstruction and development (Ignatieff 2003; Fukuyama 2004).

The military interventions in Afghanistan and Iraq in 2001 and 2003, respectively, were indeed different; initiated by the United States and motivated largely by American geostrategic goals, U.S. behavior changed markedly under George W. Bush's administration. Although the United States had the military muscle to intervene and to act unilaterally, when it came to post-conflict reconstruction and peacebuilding, the United States still wanted the help of others, relying on the United Nations as well as a "consortium of industrialized countries and public and private organizations" to maintain the semblance of liberal goals and democratic means in both Afghanistan and Iraq (Fukuyama 2004, 26). Others clearly see America's "empire building" actions differently, but still contend that U.S. behavior in the 2000s was not that much different from what transpired in the 1990s in places like Bosnia or Cambodia. As Michael Ignatieff puts it, "Washington may have been in the lead (in Afghanistan), but London, Paris, Berlin and Tokyo all followed reluctantly in what can only be called a shared Western mission and a commitment to stability, democratic reform and market economics" (2003, 17).

Naturally, American behavior toward conflict-ridden countries and peacebuilding depended on the country and the context; nonetheless, its projects and plans were increasingly carried out by international organizations and a growing army of nongovernmental organizations. In this way, the agents of peacebuilding were not only in agreement on the new emerging threats, but they generally agreed on the strategies and institutions that were necessary to transform countries as well as the various organizations that needed to be involved. Yet, unlike previous international interventions, liberal peacebuilding emphasized the importance, if not the urgency, of both top-down and bottom-up strategies to transform (rather than just contain) conflict-prone environments into peaceful, democratic countries.

It is easy to exaggerate the effects of the 2001 terrorist attacks on the United States, but the impact on U.S. policies toward post-conflict peacebuilding was both immediate and meaningful. Overnight, President Bush went from deriding nation building and promising to end U.S. involvement in the Balkans and other multilateral peace-building activities, which he saw as a costly and unnecessary distraction, to embracing what his administration pointedly called post-conflict stabilization and reconstruction in failing states. The motivations for American intervention in Afghanistan and Iraq were unmistakably different from the interventions in the Balkans or U.S. involvement in other conflict-ridden countries during the 1990s. Yet, the instruments and the strategies the United States employed and the institutions it promoted did not change markedly. Establishing an Office of Conflict Management and Mitigation in 2002, USAID explicitly recognized that the multiple, converging causes of violence and conflict required multidisciplinary solutions that no single institution or unit could address alone.[25]

After the terrorist attacks, the U.S. government declared that one of its central objectives was identifying fragile states and ensuring that they did not become a home for terrorists or extremist groups. While fighting terrorism became an overriding goal, it only reinforced perceptions about post–Cold War threats: they would come from diffuse and nontraditional sources, and ensuring peace in the twenty-first century required innovative strategies that went beyond military might and focused on creating the conditions for democracy and stability.

Into the Void

Post–Cold War threats and new wars demanded different strategies and creative responses. Uncertain times also meant reaching out to and incorporating new actors. According to Tim Murithi (2009, 7), liberal peacebuilding is qualitatively different from other kinds of international intervention, because the policies and practices explicitly recognize that this is a *process* that engages actors at different levels and is carried out by a range of organizations and initiatives. Thus, unlike American nation building in Germany and Japan following World War II or post-conflict stabilization in Iraq after 2003, liberal peace-building exercises aspire to include various actors with different resources, attributes, and orientations. Liberal peacebuilding is also touted as a long-term undertaking where no single organization, institution, or UN agency operates alone; policies and processes instead seek out private and public actors and encourage them to work together in overlapping and reinforcing ways. It is this final shift in understandings and norms that explains the prevalence of NGOs in post-conflict environments in the 1990s. NGOs are actors that operate on different levels, theoretically connecting public and private organizations and making peacebuilding easier and more legitimate, to say nothing of lowering costs.

Transforming new wars, indeed, created spaces for different actors, especially those with the knowledge and on-the-ground experience that governments lacked and did not want to develop. In 1992, the UN Security Council passed Resolution 688 that demanded protection for humanitarian NGOs working in Iraq, while Resolution 808, which came just a year later, established an ad hoc international tribunal to prosecute those charged with committing crimes against humanity in the Balkans. These and other UN actions in the early 1990s laid the foundation for what Oliver Richmond (2003, 5) calls "an emerging human security ethos," which provided a central and legitimate place for NGOs in peacebuilding and global governance. Years later, a meeting led by the UN NGO Working Group on Women and International Peace and Security took the recognition of NGOs even further, pushing the UN Security Council to pass Resolution 1325 on Women, Peace and Security.

UN Resolution 1325 explicitly acknowledges the role of women's groups and NGOs in peace processes while the passage of this resolution itself demonstrated the growing clout that both international and local women's groups already had in shaping the UN's peace-building agenda. Even before the passage of Resolution 1325, the Security Council had informally allowed representatives of women's NGOs from Sri Lanka, Guatemala, Somalia, and Tanzania to submit information and recommendations to the Security Council. The Security Council then took this information to the field, ensuring that future UN missions took gender into account and included "thorough con-sultations with local and international women's groups" (Hill 2002, 27). The UN Security Council does not formally acknowledge any official role for NGOs in post-conflict peacebuilding, but in the twenty-first century it expects NGOs and other nonstate actors to shape and implement policies in conflict zones and complex humanitarian emergencies. The *Supplement to an Agenda for Peace* (Boutros-Ghali 1995) explains why this is: NGOs play essential roles that go far beyond fundraising and the delivery of services, working in areas that include research and information outreach, policy formulation, and advocacy.[26]

This is why throughout the 1990s, NGOs were increasingly sought out by UN agencies, because of their perceived comparative advantage in operational matters, their proximity to their members or clients, and their flexibility. Others emphasized different advantages to their presence and participation in post-conflict environments, namely that NGOs connected with people on the ground, providing them with "the capacity to inform and mobilize opinion" (Richmond 2003, 5). As the UN Assembly explained in 1998, NGOs play "a very significant and helpful role by establishing bridges between the United Nations and civil society at large."[27] The former UN secretary-general Boutros Boutros-Ghali confirmed the unique, bridging role of NGOs, observing that "NGOs are a basic form of popular participation and representation, and peace in the largest sense cannot be accomplished by the United Nations system or governments alone" (Weiss and Gordenker 1996, 8). Other statements and policies demonstrated that the United Nations was rethinking not only *how* it operated in post-conflict countries but also *whom* it worked with, emphasizing the role and importance of different actors to increasing the United Nations' effectiveness and legitimacy and also to minimizing its costs.

Liberal peacebuilding is premised on and promoted as a multilateral and multileveled international response to conflict—even if it is not always im-plemented as such. However, Sir Brian Urquhart, undersecretary-general of the United Nations for more than a decade, maintains that liberal peace-building is different from what happened in the past: "In the twentieth century war was pronounced, belatedly, to be too important to be left to the generals; in the 21st century, prosperity and security have turned out to be much too complex to be left to the politicians, and the old distinctions between national and international, private and public, have become increasingly blurred" (Urquhart 2004). This complexity and blurring of issues and actors in liberal peacebuilding is addressed in the 2000 Brahimi Report that calls for more openness to different strategies and even a shift in how the United Nations conceives of and utilizes civilian actors, because "effective peace-building requires active engagement with the local parties, and that engagement should be multidimensional in nature."[28]

Importantly, it was not only the changing, ill-defined boundaries between international wars and internal conflicts that forced the hand of the United Nations and other governmental actors toward engaging and encouraging more nonstate actors and specifically NGOs to engage in peacebuilding. It was also the sheer complexity of post-Cold War wars as well as rising costs which were drawing down the UN's budget and undermining its focus. On this latter point, the Brahimi Report is clear: "Peacekeeping is a 50-year-old enterprise that has evolved rapidly in the past decade from a traditional, primarily military model of observing ceasefires and force separations after inter-State wars to incorporate a complex model of many elements, military and civilian, working together to build peace in the dangerous aftermath of civil wars."[29]

Other UN documents echo the ideas of Johan Galtung and others who remind us that because peacebuilding is a complicated multilevel process, there are "tasks for everybody;" thus, there are many ways that NGOs and other private actors can make a difference.[30] Several meetings in the early 2000s focused on the need for the UN Peacebuilding Commission and the UN Development Program (UNDP) to grow into organizations that were able to leverage their strengths through partnerships with international and local NGOs. Indeed "cooperation," "partnership," and "collaboration" with NGOs and other civil society actors were the catchphrases of the day.

When the UN Peacebuilding Commission was established in 2005, it explicitly recognized the value and contributions of civil society and nongovernmental organizations, even though it failed to distinguish the important differences between these entities. Simply put, the problems of the world were too large for public actors alone, and since the Cold War's end the United Nations worked hard to reach out to incorporate NGOs into its activities, bringing to bear the energy of civil society, the resources and technology of the private sector as well as the knowledge and expertise of foundations and universities. In fact, there are both short-term, practical reasons and long-term, process-driven motivations for cooperating with NGOs to cultivate a culture and movement of peace from the bottom up. In its words and its deeds, the United Nations increasingly referred to these benefits and to NGOs as unique transnational actors that are able to deliver assistance and services while connecting people and actors in post-conflict environments. With more idealism and rhetoric than thoughtful discussions about what this would mean for policies, practices, and funding, UN documents consistently recognize NGOs for their unique abilities and neutral character.

Although technically part of the UN structure, the World Bank is an autonomous organization and a key player in post-conflict peacebuilding. In the 1990s, it too started to pay attention to the importance of soliciting new actors and particularly the input of NGOs, making them partners in the Bank's post–Cold War mission. From 1970 to 1985, for example, development aid disbursed by the World Bank through international NGOs increased tenfold, and by the decade's end about 15 percent of World Bank aid was channeled through international NGOs.[31] The World Bank's interest in NGOs only increased throughout the 1990s, and by 1997 it was focused centrally on post-conflict peacebuilding, endorsing new policies to guide its activities. Its post-conflict unit explicitly acknowledged the need for new players, especially those from the private sector, and recognized that NGOs had become central to the Bank's new approach of economic peacebuilding.

A 1998 World Bank report confirmed that for its programs to be effective in post-conflict countries, it had to "develop strong and constructive relationships with civil society and the private sector" (World Bank 1998, vi). Ever since, the World Bank has underscored the significance of their new partners, establishing meaningful collaborative relations with intergovernmental organizations, states, NGOs, and local actors. In these partnerships, civil society plays a crucial role in restoring public confidence in peace and connecting different populations and cultures. This is why, ever since, the World Bank has continued to open up a space for new actors, essentially mainstreaming cooperation with civil society organizations throughout its policies. As with other UN agencies, civil society organizations and NGOs were deemed crucial to delivering services to the poor, but they were equally important for holding governments and global institutions accountable to their citizens. Of utmost importance to the World Bank was developing strong and constructive relationships with both civil society and the private sector (Flores and Nooruddin 2009).

Recent peace agreements also recognize the normative shifts in postwar peacebuilding, stating the importance of international and local NGO assistance in reconstruction and the transformation of conflict. As one study of peace agreements in the post–Cold War period observes, making peace last requires reaching out to new actors and specifically to "civil society actors" to lay the foundation for long-term peace (Alger 2007, 544). This is because new wars are caused by numerous internal factors and demand both top-down and bottom-up strategies to transform these conflicts and focus on their causes. According to another study, of the 389 peace agreements made after the Cold War's end, which addressed 48 intrastate conflicts, 139 mention a role for NGOs or civil society; and 41 of the agreements make specific provisions for what NGOs and civil society organizations can do to help, such as providing humanitarian relief, monitoring human rights, legitimating public participation, protecting and promoting democracy, or pursuing transitional governance (Bell and O'Rourke 2007). Like the international actors involved in liberal peacebuilding, peace agreements in the twenty-first century are also more likely to underscore the importance of democratic means and ends as well as the different ways that peace must be promoted.

The international community is far from a homogenous group that has identical interests and priorities. However, to a great extent, liberal peacebuilding in the 1990s was viewed by governments, international organizations, and even international NGOs through a similar lens: as a unique international undertaking that emerged because of diverse drivers of violence that necessitated multifaceted and multileveled responses. The nature of post–Cold War conflicts and the strategies international actors converged upon emphasized the transformation of states and societies using bottom-up as well as top-down approaches. Yet, despite consistent references to civil society and NGOs as partners and allies, writings rarely explain or define *who* these actors are or *how* these partnerships will be pursued. What is clear is that one-time marginalized actors were not only recognized, but they were embraced as important agents of international peacebuilding.

The Roots of the Growth

Since NGOs have been overlooked in research on post-conflict reconstruction and peacebuilding, security studies scholars have rarely inquired into the growth of NGOs. There are, however, different explanations for the NGO revolution in international politics, each of which offers important insights in how NGOs became so popular and prevalent in peacebuilding. The most common explanation observes that the growth of NGOs in the second half of the 1980s was due to an increase in funding by governments. Indeed, between 1990 and 2006 there was more than a three-fold increase in humanitarian assistance, and much of this was channeled through international NGOs and to local NGOs (de Jonge Oudraat and Haufler 2008). Increased funding for humanitarian assistance certainly explains *how* NGOs were able to grow in number, but this only describes what happened. It does not clarify *why* governmental actors gave more money and support to NGOs, especially in post-conflict environments.

Some observe that the explosion of NGOs coincided with communism's decline and the triumph of laissez-faire economics. Thus, in important ways the Cold War's end provided a permissive environment for Western governments to engage NGOs. The end of Soviet one-party rule in Europe, combined with fiscal crises in the West and revolutionary changes in global communications, indeed, provided NGOs with an unparalleled opportunity to step in, fill in for retreating states, and become engaged in different sectors. Interestingly, both the economist William Easterly (2006) and the journalist Naomi Klein (2007) point to neoliberal economic ideas and calls to scale back the state to explain the explosion of NGOs in the 1990s. Neoliberal thinking (liberalization, privatization, and a decrease in public spending based on a market-driven model) did push governments to downsize in many areas, while NGOs were cast as natural mobilizers of financial, material, and human resources. Nurtured by Western disillusionment with large-scale international aid efforts in the 1970s, governments eagerly looked to nonstate actors, subcontracting out responsibilities to cut costs and promote efficiency. According to this explanation, economic calculations and states' preferences, but also certain ideas stimulated the NGO turn in international relations (Uvin 1995, 163–64).

A final explanation offered rests on the assumed, if not mythological, power of NGOs as actors in their own right. This explanation is somewhat similar to the argument that is made by NGO enthusiasts. In this view, since governments cannot manage international problems alone, and because of the presumed capabilities of NGOs, such as their on-the-ground experiences, flexibility, and nimbleness, NGOs help states address complex problems

(Edwards, Hulme, and Wallace 1999). Thus, it is the qualities and character of NGOs that pulled them into the vortex of liberal peacebuilding, and they became involved whether states wanted them to or not. Seen from this perspective, NGOs are powerful indeed, because they hold a distinct representative mandate and do what is ethically correct on behalf of the people they claim to represent (DeMars 2005). This might be true in some respects, but we cannot forget the complexity of NGOs; they are engaged in many areas, operate in confounding ways, and cannot be controlled. In the words of William DeMars (2005, 3), NGOs are "wild cards" that cannot be counted on nor discounted because they behave in unexpected ways. This is both the promise and problem with NGOs in peacebuilding: we do not know who these organizations are working with or their effectiveness in promoting change. Nonetheless, a great deal is assumed and expected of them.

The explanations for the growth of NGOs in international politics tend to be grounded in material factors or they focus on specific events, but there is no single explanation for why NGOs and other private actors became more prevalent and powerful in international politics starting in the late 1980s, much less in post-conflict peacebuilding. I maintain that the involvement of NGOs in post-conflict environments stems from a perfect storm of structural, political, and ideational changes. New threats and the rise of internal conflicts were certainly important. At the same time, governments were determined to act differently, seeking to address the conditions that gave rise to violence in the first place. To transform rather than just manage these conflicts, states and international organizations as well as nonstate actors were called to duty.

Some dismiss states' intentions when it comes to involving NGOs in post-conflict countries, claiming that state interest in NGOs was "more of a marriage of convenience than a passionate romance" (Aggestam 2003, 19). This may be true, but once policies change, behavior, practices, and expectations shift accordingly. NGOs were once regarded as easy and convenient answers to complex problems, but increasingly they are referred to as crucial partners and even preferred bedfellows, engaging willingly with states and international organizations to promote liberal peacebuilding.

Kaplan (1993) may have intentionally painted a dramatic and one-dimensional picture of the Balkans and other fragile states to attract and sustain an audience. Yet, as the 1990s unfolded, his tales of ethnic hatreds abolishing states and upsetting world order were starting to look alarmingly prophetic. The Yugoslav wars began in Slovenia in 1991, but since the republic contained few Serbs, the violence was brief, and the Yugoslav army withdrew quickly. The next target was the republic of Croatia, where about 10 percent of the population was Serbian. After a few years, but with much bloodshed, the focus shifted again to the more ethnically mixed republic of Bosnia–Herzegovina where the Yugoslav government's goals were clear and its resolve unwavering. Unfortunately, by the middle of the decade, Balkan ghosts were haunting the region, if not the world, with reports of ethnic cleansing, concentration camps, and mass rapes.

The drama in Yugoslavia was just one of many new, post–Cold War conflicts that were threatening states and upending theories. The Soviet Union was also in the process of disintegrating, roughly half of Somalia's population was at risk of starvation, and in 1994, almost a million people were slaughtered within a month in the east African country of Rwanda. Perhaps Kaplan had not overstated anarchy's coming at all, as many parts of the world were ablaze with violence and instability. With the prophesized chaos already upon the international community and with no ready-made solutions or obvious actors able to respond, NGOs became an attractive and low-risk solution to mounting crises. There were other obvious advantages to working with these nonstate actors; they allowed governments to do something without actually spending a lot of money or getting directly involved. The real beauty of NGOs, however, lies in the deceptive rhetoric that was used to justify their involvement, promising fundamental shifts in how Western states interacted with war-torn and conflict-prone states and their populations.

A World Bank report is revealing in its simplicity if not insincerity, observing that the presence of a large number of NGOs offers unique opportunities to transform institutions and change attitudes in post-conflict environments. NGOs, according to the report, boost public confidence in peace and act as a bridge between different populations, groups, and cultures (World Bank 1998, 49). In other words, NGOs not only deliver humanitarian assistance but they change institutions and empower individuals. Tellingly, the report provides little explanation of *who* these powerful NGOs are and scant details on exactly *how* they will deliver aid, transform attitudes, and bridge groups and cultures. As is always the case, the devil is in the details.

In uncertain times, much is unknown but even more is feared. At the Cold War's end, a great deal was assumed of and promised by NGOs regarding their activities and impact. Beyond new expectations and wishful thinking, what changed with NGO involvement in liberal peacebuilding? Answers to this question and an explanation of *what* NGOs actually do—and do not do—in post-conflict peacebuilding are found in the next chapter.

Chapter 2

Of Power and Promises

Mostar is in the southern part of Bosnia, close enough to the Adriatic Sea and brimming with so much history and rich architecture that it is a regular stop on any tour of the Balkans. Sitting on the Neretva River, Mostar is most famous for its *Stari Most* (the Old Bridge) that was built by the Ottomans in the sixteenth century. Before the war, the bridge and Old Town area wove together Ottoman, Mediterranean, and European architectural features, creating what UNESCO calls "an outstanding example of a multicultural urban settlement that exists harmoniously with its natural surroundings."[1] The war changed Mostar's tranquil environment and much more.

Mostar has always been a cosmopolitan city, boasting an ethnically diverse and culturally proud population. When it was part of Yugoslavia, almost an equal number of Croats, Muslims, and Serbs lived side by side and married outside their ethnic group. About a quarter of the population identified as Yugoslav. Although the east bank was predominantly Muslim and the west bank mostly Croat, minorities lived without concern or censure in majority-dominated areas. Once Bosnia declared its independence from the

Yugoslav federation in 1992, the city's multiethnic charms became its curse. Mostar is now infamous for being one of the most heavily bombed cities during the war and one of the most divided since its end.[2] Not only has this city experienced violent clashes since the peace agreement was signed, but its institutions are dysfunctional and inhabitants estranged.

During the siege of Mostar in the spring of 1992, Croats and Muslims initially worked together to push out the Yugoslav army (JNA) which was dominated by Serbs. Once the JNA was driven out, Croats turned on Bosnian Muslims and "a war within a war" ensued. The fighting in Mostar killed thousands and, with equal intensity, demolished mosques, churches, and monasteries. Eventually, the violence brought down the Old Bridge. The Croat army claimed that the bridge was targeted because of its strategic importance, but most believe that it was attacked because of its symbolic value. The engineering marvel of its time, it was built in harmony with nature, and the bridge and surrounding area showcased the city's unique diversity and its multiethnic, religious pluralism. By killing memory in this way, Mostar's shared cultural heritage and history of peaceful coexistence were deliberately attacked.

By 2000, remnants of the Old Bridge were barely noticeable, but its memory and what it represented were giving life to a budding NGO community funded by Western donors. Interviewing NGOs involved in reconstruction and peacebuilding, I fortunately crossed paths with a Croatian woman, a Christian, who was working for what she called "a local NGO," even though the organization was funded entirely through donations from international donors.[3] At the time, the organization provided healthcare and information on housing to internally displaced people living around Mostar. I learned quickly, though, that the Croat, Muslim, and Serb employees had other, more ambitious goals in mind. In addition to its stated activities, this NGO doled out messages of peace and reconciliation.

The Croatian woman was not a doctor or a nurse, and to explain how she ended up working for this NGO, she revealed that her husband was Muslim and that the war had been hard on them in many ways. Fortunately, her children had escaped Bosnia and were living safely in the United Kingdom. She smiled widely as she talked about her children, their comfortable lives abroad, and their futures. Mostar's rich history and natural beauty were impressive, but I could not imagine why anyone would choose to stay in this beleaguered city, particularly when their children were safely ensconced in a Western country. After I inquired about the history of her organization and its activities, I asked directly why she chose to remain in Mostar. Her answer surprised me. She acknowledged that she could easily retire or join her kids abroad, but she was convinced that this nongovernmental organization and its work had an important, if not urgent, mission.

Too many Croats, Serbs, and Muslims had tried to destroy Mostar's history and its tolerance, she reflected, but they could not succeed. And they would not if people like her continued their work and if NGOs were successful in Bosnia. At least at this point in time she, like many in Bosnia, believed in the promise of NGOs. International NGOs had indeed arrived in droves, helping the locals create their own organizations, and these groups provided Bosnians with an opportunity to "do their part" to help the country rebuild, advancing peace one person at a time. This woman's hope was that, with so many people and organizations representing Bosnia's peaceful past, NGOs would help the city return to what it once was: a safe, multiethnic, and cosmopolitan center of Bosnian life. By remaining in Mostar, with her Muslim husband and working for an NGO that served Croats, Muslims, and Serbs equally, this activist had, in her words, "found her place in the sun, and she would not be going anywhere."

Unfortunately, such faith and optimism did not last long. In Mostar, as throughout Bosnia, promises turned problematic as internationals implemented their peacebuilding mission, ignoring locals and forgetting partnerships. Despite the ambitious goals of the Dayton Peace Accords, signed in 1995, international interest faded quickly, and money for so-called civil society development was neither forthcoming nor particularly appropriate. Civil society leaders in Mostar, like elsewhere in Bosnia, realized that if they wanted money from foreign donors, they could not do what locals requested or what they themselves wanted. Instead, local organizations had to follow the lead of international organizations which had very specific ideas for how the country's development should unfold. In Mostar, in particular, internationals spent surprisingly little time getting to know groups or cultivating relationships. As Adam Moore (2013) writes, international practices in Mostar were unfortunately characterized by rapid turnovers in international staff, many of whom spent less time in the city than they did in places like Sarajevo or Brčko. Even if internationals did not speak the language and parachuted in and out, Bosnian NGOs were still wise to heed their sage advice because, after all, most of them had "done this all before" and they knew better. Bosnians came to realize that if they did not listen to those doling out the money, NGOs would disappear—regardless of need or effectiveness.

Appreciating the power of NGOs in terms of local stakeholders and perceptions cannot be measured easily, but it does not mean that local understandings of NGOs and their impact on everyday life are irrelevant, especially to the success of international peacebuilding.[4] In fact, local's perceptions are essential to understanding both why and how international efforts fall short. Nonetheless, most research on post-conflict peacebuilding minimizes the role of NGOs or ignores ordinary peoples' views of international activities and practices, assuming that these processes are the work of states and international organizations and thus international strategies and resources matter most.[5] The reconstruction of buildings and the creation of new institutions are certainly paid for by governments and international organizations, but the implementation of international assistance, the cultivation of relationships, and the one-on-one interactions are increasingly the domain of NGOs. And since the success in peacebuilding depends on ordinary people, their experiences and perceptions of the behavior and practices of omnipresent NGOs are important indeed.

While not without problems, there are ways to measure the expanding role of NGOs in post-conflict environments.[6] Numbers, economic resources, and new relationships provide some evidence of their influence in international politics, but this is only the start. Only by looking at what was said and promised of NGOs, as well as what happens on the ground can we understand the disillusionment and disempowerment associated with liberal peacebuilding in post-conflict societies. Measuring NGO power is admittedly not easy, but the following analysis provides clear evidence of their growing numbers and larger budgets in the 1990s. I then analyze the inspiring rhetoric of governments and international organizations and what was stated about NGOs and their importance. With their numbers, money, and access, it is clear that NGOs had significant sway in Bosnia's rebuilding. Yet, there is little evidence that the NGO boom had much to do with empowering locals or advancing peace.

What the Numbers Say

Joseph Nye is best known for his research on the different dimensions of state power, but he has also commented on the growing importance of NGOs in international politics, asserting that these actors are more powerful than ever and are "increasingly able to get governments' attention and to set their agendas."[7] It is hard to prove or disprove such a statement, because measuring power in international relations is notoriously difficult. However, research on international associations does provide ample proof that these particular international actors, with their increasing numbers, larger budgets, and powerful friends, might indeed, be able to get governments' attention and inform agendas.[8] Missed, however, in this analysis is the obvious fact that NGOs are not all the same, and while international NGOs, based largely in Western countries, may be growing in number, increasing in economic clout, and shaping policies and agendas, this says precious little about national or local NGOs. The United Nations, for example, has created a range of mechanisms and institutions to solicit NGO input, incorporating them into their decision-making process and policies. More often than not, however, these mechanisms engage and incorporate international NGOs based in the West, not national or local NGOs in post-conflict or developing countries, an important but often overlooked difference.

In the mid-1990s, IR scholars started to acknowledge the explosion of NGOs, even comparing the so-called associational revolution to the rise of the nation-state in the nineteenth century and other such transformative events. Unfortunately, few provided accurate numbers regarding the incipient NGO boom or even a sense of its scope and domain (Edwards and Hulme 1996, 2). Many questions associated with the NGO boom remain to this day: How many NGOs exist in the world? What do they do? Are they genuinely transformative actors? It is hard to answer these questions with a lot of precision, but the Union of International Associations (UIA), which claims to have the most detailed and reliable information on registered international NGOs (INGOs), confirms that there has been steady growth in INGOs around the world for quite some time.[9] Comparisons of INGO growth with the expansion of intergovernmental organizations (IGOs) during the same period make the NGO boom even more obvious and important.

As figure 2.1 shows, from 1900 until before World War II, between twenty-five and one hundred INGOs were established every year. After World War II, INGOs grew significantly, with a noticeable spike occurring in the second half of the 1980s and peaking in 1986 with more than one thousand new INGOs founded in one year.

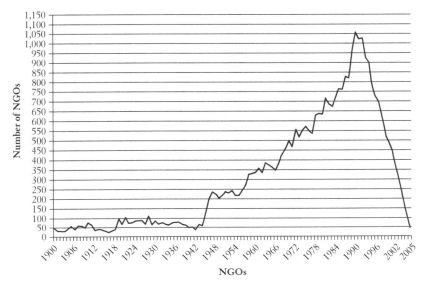

Figure 2.1. NGOs founded by year, 1990–2006. *Source:* Adapted from data available in *Yearbook of International Organizations, Vol. 5* (Munich: K.G. Saur Verlag, 2007), 241–49.

The explosion of INGOs after 1950, as figure 2.2 shows, is quite different from the steady but gradual growth of intergovernmental organizations (IGOs) during this same period.

As these figures make plain, the NGO boom is real, and by 2013 there were almost sixty thousand registered INGOs but only about eight thousand IGOs. With this said, the associational revolution may be coming to an end for INGOs. The total number of international NGOs continues to increase, but the pace of growth has slowed noticeably in the twenty-first century as figure 2.3, that looks at newly registered NGOs, shows. Thus, although hundreds of new INGOs were established every year throughout the 1990s, in the 2000s the number dropped to about fifty new INGOs founded every year.

Given the American tradition of strong civil society associations and the U.S. government's support of these organizations since the 1930s, it is not that surprising that it is home to some of the largest and most well-known international NGOs. Unfortunately, we do not even know how many U.S.-based NGOs are engaged in international work. Part of the problem in producing an exact number is that even within the United States there is no

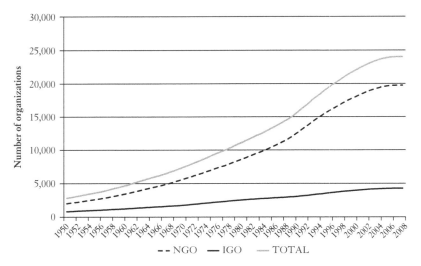

Figure 2.2. Growth in international organizations 1950–2007. *Source:* Adapted from
data available in *Yearbook of International Organizations, Vol. 5*
(Munich: K.G. Saur Verlag, 2007), 241–49.

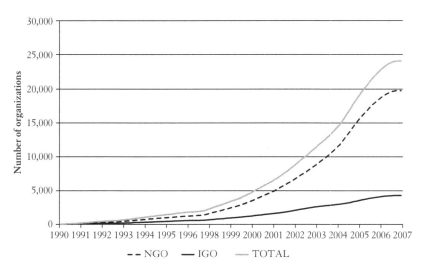

Figure 2.3. Growth in international organizations 1990–2007. *Source:* Adapted from
data available in *Yearbook of International Organizations, Vol. 5*
(Munich: K.G. Saur Verlag, 2007), 241–49.

consensus on the term that should be used to describe these actors. American academics usually use the word *NGO* to describe the eclectic group of private nonstate actors that engages in international work. The U.S. government prefers *private voluntary organizations* (PVOs), while practitioners who often work in both domestic and international realms often opt to call them *nonprofit organizations*. There is naturally some overlap in these terms and more attention is being paid to nonstate actors working internationally, but definitional challenges still make it hard to calculate the growth or impact of NGOs on post-conflict peacebuilding.

Although there are different estimates of the number of U.S.-based private actors working abroad, their growth appears to mirror the global INGO boom documented by the UIA. Rachel McCleary (2009), for example, looks at PVOs in American foreign policy, observing a steady rise between 1939 and 2005. American PVOs working on relief and development grew steadily after World War II and exploded in the second half of the 1980s, just as the global associational revolution was taking place. According to Charity Navigator, by 2011 at least five hundred American PVOs were working internationally in one of four areas: development, peace and security, humanitarian relief, and on single-country projects. The National Center for Charitable Statistics, which claims to have assembled "the most comprehensive information on the U.S. international nonprofit sector," claims that the American global footprint in this sector is actually much larger, and thousands of U.S. nonprofit groups are involved in a variety of international work (Reid and Kerlin, 2006). The National Center is a clearinghouse for the nonprofit sector, recording not only the work of registered NGOs but also the activities of organizations providing direct services and training and those promoting exchanges, research, and education. In 2013, it estimated that more than seven thousand U.S.-based private actors were working internationally, making up more than a quarter of the world's NGO community. In other words, the NGO world is not an American contrivance, but it is disproportionately influenced by this country and its interests.

Some of the U.S.-based NGOs are large and well-known, but most are actually quite small and specialized. But neither size nor celebrity determines an NGO's importance or its ability to shape outcomes. According to the Urban Institute, "the widespread contributions of small, grassroots international organizations are often overlooked in favor of highly visible efforts by global mega-organizations in the field of development and relief"

(Reid and Kerlin 2006, 3). This is unfortunate, because while the efforts of small U.S.-based NGOs often go unnoticed, their numbers and efforts reflect the civic depth of this sector, providing "a window into social capital building on an international scale where person-to-person interactions build goodwill and meet need" (Reid and Kerlin 2006, 3). As William DeMars and Dennis Dijkzeul (2015) put in their book *The NGO Challenge to IR Theory,* measuring and conceptualizing NGO power in international relations is indeed difficult, but it is clear that their policies and practices are crucial to both international and domestic politics. NGOs are complex and multifaceted actors that perform many functions while engaging in distinct practices, bridging actors and issues, and embodying, reflecting, and also transforming relationships.

There is no consensus on the exact number of the INGOs that exist in the world, but all the research, using slightly different terms points in the same general direction: toward an increase in the number of nonstate actors after World War II, with a significant rise starting in the second half of the 1980s. However, the recent explosion of NGOs is historic for other, more important reasons. For one, previous discussions of NGOs almost always focused on the activities of international groups that were based in North America or Western Europe but were working in the developing world or the global south. In the twenty-first century this is simply not the case. Most international NGOs are still based in the global north, but in the last two decades NGOs of various sizes have mushroomed in almost every corner of the world. In fact, in the 1990s the highest NGO growth rates were in Central and Eastern Europe and Central Asia, but during this same period, every country examined—with the exception of Iraq and Somalia—experienced an absolute growth in the number of independent nongovernmental organizations (Anheier, Glasius, and Kaldor 2005). The NGO boom *within* countries and the growth of local NGOs is thus a significant turn of events.

Organizational structures, relationships, and money flows are also more complex and contain new kinds of private actors. In other words, the growth of NGOs that started in the late 1980s is not only a global phenomenon but it has different characteristics, with organizations that are international, transnational, and local. This is precisely why NGO numbers are even more difficult to calculate. To capture the growth of these private actors and their new relationships, researchers at the London School of Economics started to do research on what they call *global civil society*, which includes the vast array of international, transnational, and local NGOs (as well as associations, networks, and values) located between the family, the state, and the market, and which operate beyond the confines of national societies, polities, and economies (Anheier, Glasius, and Kaldor 2005, 2). Without solving the methodological problems associated with studying these very different actors, this research confirms what everyone suspected and perhaps even hoped for: all around the globe, nonstate, private, voluntary civil society actors were multiplying. Another report, quoting figures from the United Nations Development Program (UNDP) confirmed that by 2005 between thirty-seven thousand and fifty thousand NGOs were actively involved in international politics in the areas of international development, human rights, and security and peace politics (Fischer 2006).

These numbers are impressive, but they tell only part of the NGO story, and relying on numbers alone can be misleading at best. Focusing on numbers can divert attention away from what the NGOs are actually doing—or not doing. Narrowing on numbers alone also ignores the appropriateness of NGO activities as well as the impact that they have on individuals and broader outcomes. As Kenneth Anderson and David Rieff (2005, 26) remind us, a lot of assumptions are made by researchers studying global civil society, particularly about international NGOs, transnational actors, and even new social movements, specifically regarding the representativeness and legitimacy of these actors. In post-conflict countries, looking at the number of registered NGOs basically reveals how many groups received money from external donors and an organization's stated mission, but little more. As important as the registration of NGOs might be to establishing the cast of characters involved in reconstruction and peacebuilding and getting a handle on the number of actors involved, NGO lists and databases provide little meaningful information about their activities or influence.

In 2011, for example, when I visited Kosovo's Department for Registration and Liaison with NGOs within the Ministry of Public Administration, the director proudly reported that Kosovo had more than six thousand registered NGOs.[10] Yet, reports, interviews, and fieldwork confirmed that there were perhaps one hundred NGOs active during the past year, and my Kosovar interlocutors assured me that maybe a couple dozen NGOs were able to influence policies or support ongoing projects. I was also told that some of the most interesting and effective NGOs in Kosovo were grassroots initiatives that did not receive money from abroad and thus had no need to register with a government office. Frustratingly, in many countries the registration of NGOs fails to distinguish international organizations from national or local ones. But even if organizations have no internationals on staff, so-called local NGOs in post-conflict countries still rely heavily, if not exclusively, on external donors to keep their organizations afloat and their projects going. The blurred boundary between what is international and what constitutes the local foreshadows one of the most serious problems with NGOs in peace-building: NGO booms that are followed by busts, NGOs' disappearance, and the disillusionment that sets in.

Money for Something

States are alternately credited or criticized for the growth of NGOs and their expanding budgets, but rarely is the relationship explored in much depth. In fact, while NGOs have more money, a whole host of public and private actors, in addition to states, are now involved in creating and funding NGOs. Michael Barnett and Peter Walker (2015) refer to this elite group of public and private actors involved in complex humanitarian emergencies as the humanitarian club. It is this same cartel of Western governments, international organizations, private foundations, and international NGOs that funds and fashions the NGO game, providing assistance and supporting NGOs at various levels. The problem with it is, despite their professed interest in creating local partners, these organizations still control the resources and the agenda, embracing only changes and actors that reinforce their central position and interests (Barnett and Walker 2015, 131).

The OECD tracks official international assistance, and although NGOs and private funding are increasingly included in the international aid framework, the OECD acknowledges its shortcomings in tracking funds that go *through* NGOs and *to* NGOs.[11] That is to say, the OECD knows that governments are channeling a larger percentage of official assistance money through international NGOs, and this is easier to track, but it does not know how much aid money actually makes its way to local NGOs or to those organizations organized and working *within* countries. Between 1970 and 1985, for example, OECD assistance going through international NGOs rose by 40 percent (Edwards and Hulme 1996, 2). By the late 1990s, OECD countries, on average, were disbursing between 25 and 50 percent of their emergency assistance through international NGOs (Goodhand 2006, 89). By the beginning of the twenty-first century, the European Commission's Humanitarian Aid Office was sending more than 60 percent of its humanitarian assistance to international NGOs to use and disburse as they saw fit. This meant that by 2011 more than $19 billion, or about 20 percent of official bilateral aid, was going through INGOs, an increase of about $2 billion over the 2008 to 2011 period (OECD 2013).

On the surface, all of this demonstrates governments' growing interest in giving more economic power to NGOs; in truth, it tells us little about who the NGOs are or what the funding is for. The OECD understands well that channeling money *through* international (or donor-country) NGOs is different from providing money directly *to* national (or developing-country) NGOs or to groups within targeted countries.[12] This is a crucial but overlooked distinction in the aggrandizing discussions about NGOs and all the money that increasingly flows to these assumed representatives of global civil society. Unfortunately, the transfer of funds to national NGOs or groups within countries is almost impossible to measure since there is no separate OECD category that tracks all the different kinds of funding that may end up going to domestic groups. Thus, aid for humanitarian assistance, democracy promotion, or women's rights could end up going directly to fund local NGOs, but since this aid is not earmarked for local NGOs specifically, the OECD cannot say exactly how much official international assistance makes its way to local NGOs working within countries.

A reasonable proxy is OECD assistance to government and civil society, which has been recorded since the 1970s. OECD data confirms that as rhetoric and interest in civil society increased, so did official development assistance for government and civil society.[13] However, OECD assistance to these sectors did not increase significantly in the 1990s; only in the 2000s were significant investments in government and civil society made when funding went from less than $2 billion (in 1999) to more than $16 billion by 2008 (See figure 2.4).

Tracing NGO funding is complex and confusing, but what is not, as the OECD realizes, is the conclusion that most official development assistance does not end up going to national or local organizations within targeted countries. A recent OECD study shows, for example, that in 2011, donors

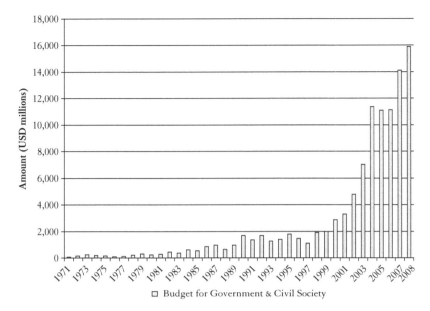

Figure 2.4. OCED official development assistance for government & civil society, 1971–2008.
Source: This graph shows the amount of official development assistance (ODA) committed
by OECD countries; the countries included are Australia, Austria, Belgium, Canada,
Denmark, Finland, France, Germany, Greece, Ireland, Italy, Japan, Korea, Luxembourg,
the Netherlands, New Zealand, Norway, Portugal, Spain, Sweden, Switzerland,
United Kingdom, and the European Union. Adapted from data from the *Organization for
Economic Co-operation and Development: Query Wizard for International Development*
Statistics. http://stats.oecd.org/qwids/.

provided more money for NGOs based within donors' own countries than
to international NGOs or local NGOs. In fact, funding for NGOs within
donors' own countries was ten times more than the funding that went to
NGOs based in developing countries or local NGOs. Figure 2.5 shows clearly
where development aid actually goes, despite promises and calls for partnerships with local groups and individuals. In post-conflict, transitioning, and
developing countries, Western governments are still giving far more money
to "their own" than to international NGOs or to organizations based inside
other Western countries.

Governments are usually credited or blamed for the rise of NGOs, but
these nonstate actors have more than governments to thank for their growing numbers and swelling budgets, adding another wrinkle to the compli-

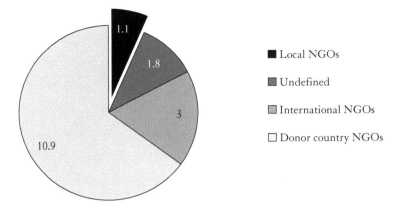

Figure 2.5. Where the money goes: Development aid to different types of NGOs, 2011 in $US billions. Source: Adapted from "Aid for CSO" DAC CRS 2013, 8. http://www .oecd.org/dac/peer-reviews/Aid%20for%20CSOs%20Final%20for%20WEB.pdf.

cated international funding structure. After World War II, there were only a few international funding mechanisms that provided assistance, and Western governments doled out most of the funding to create and sustain NGOs. In the last few decades, but particularly in the 1990s, the international aid system changed dramatically as the number of private foundations, corporations, and other private financing mechanisms expanded. Following governments' lead, private investment funds and philanthropic giving increased in the 1990s, and during the ten-year period from 1994 to 2004, private financing for international development increased dramatically (see figure 2.6). With almost one thousand international financing mechanisms in 2004 and a significant number of private mechanisms providing money for global public policy goals, the current assistance architecture is best described by the OECD as "spontaneous disorder" (OECD 2008, 14). Because of the large number of private actors, which are difficult to monitor and evaluate, the current "non-system of international assistance" is characterized by mission creep, duplication, and inefficiency (OECD 2008, 15).

The increase in private funds for international assistance is due, in part, to the tremendous growth and wealth of private philanthropies, which exploded in the last two decades. In 1990, for example, the United States was home to about thirty-two thousand private foundations. Less than a decade later, the number more than doubled, jumping to more than seventy-five thousand

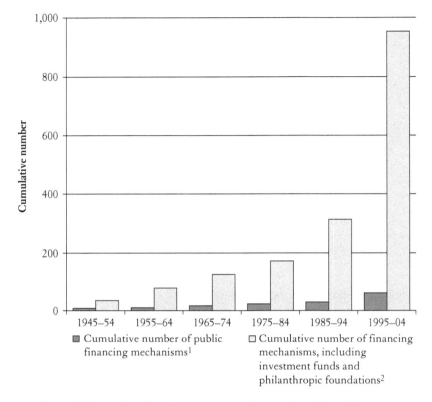

Figure 2.6. International financing mechanisms. Source: Adapted from "Financing
Development 2008: Whose Ownership?" OECD, 2008.

foundations in the United States alone (Center for Global Prosperity 2008, 20).
More actors involved in international assistance and post-conflict peacebuilding
might, indeed, help more people and lend legitimacy to certain causes, but
it also adds to the complexity and incoherence of the peacebuilding process.
For good and for ill, in the twenty-first century there are many distinct pots of
public and private money available for post-conflict and transitioning countries, many of which are also channeling money through and to NGOs.

More data is becoming available on private financing actors, but it is even
harder to calculate how these new actors and relationships influence the development and behavior of NGOs. With private foundations "multiplying
like wildfire" and international NGO budgets rising significantly, we do

know for sure that certain INGOs and private foundations are now giving out more international aid than many public actors (OECD 2008). This means that international NGOs like World Vision and Save the Children, and also private foundations like the Bill and Melinda Gates Foundation and Soros foundations are significant global donors, giving out more international aid than Western governments. For example, the 2006 budget for World Vision International was more than what Italy gave in foreign aid but about the same as Denmark's generous budget (OECD 2008). Similarly, although the Bill and Melinda Gates Foundation gave less international aid than World Vision International in 2006, its giving amounted to more than the aid given by five European countries (Ireland, Finland, Austria, Greece, and Portugal).

Regardless of where NGOs get their money, they clearly have substantial economic power. As figure 2.7 shows, a comparison of the budgets of registered NGOs with intergovernmental organizations (IGOs) demonstrates the significant economic resources that are available to NGOs. In general, NGOs tend to have larger budgets than IGOs, and by the second half of the 1990s, eight of the largest NGO families received almost half of all global

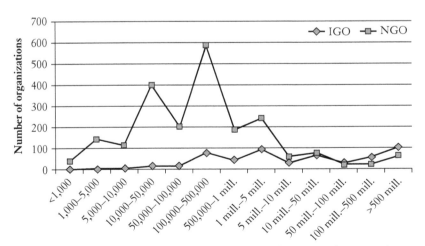

Budget amount (in Euros based on September 2002 exchange rates)

Figure 2.7 Budgets of IOs versus NGOs. *Source*: Adapted from data available in *Yearbook of International Organizations, Vol. 5* (Munich: K.G. Saur Verlag, 2007).

humanitarian assistance funding with combined budgets of more than $8 billion (Gordenker and Weiss 1996, 91). By the end of the decade, the wealthiest four hundred NGOs together spent as much as $10 billion on humanitarian issues and peace alone, reaching at least 250 million people worldwide (Abiew and Keating 1999, 94–95). In 2010, the largest NGO, World Vision, with a staff of forty-six thousand and a budget of almost $2.6 billion, was not only a major player in peacebuilding but it had more economic resources for international aid than most Western governments (OECD 2014, 111).

The economic capacity of NGOs is a relatively new phenomenon. In 1980, for example, private groups and NGOs provided less than $6 billion in grants for development assistance; just two decades later, development assistance by this expanded group of actors had grown to more than $32 billion.[14] The U.S. Agency for International Development (USAID) estimates that more than three-quarters of the resources flowing into the developing world now come from private sources (rather than public sources), with international NGOs and American foundations leading the way.[15] More importantly, international NGOs manage even more money, implementing development programs for governments in excess of $20 billion (OECD 2014, 115). The economic power of NGOs is particularly apparent within certain countries; one study of "the civil society sector" in thirty-five countries, which included nongovernmental organizations operating both across national boundaries and within countries, estimated that this sector was a $1.7 trillion industry, making it the seventh largest economy in the world (Salamon, Sokolowski, and List 2003). In the United States alone, international nonprofits in 2010 were worth about $30 billion (Schmitz, Raggo, and Bruno-van Vijfeijken 2012).

Larger budgets and more economic resources provide NGOs with ample opportunities to create programs, influence individuals, and shape policies, but so too does the in-kind support of Western governments and international organizations and their consistent urgings to targeted countries to support NGO growth and include NGOs in decision-making. Thus, in addition to money, Western governments, international organizations, and international NGOs all support what Kim Reimann (2006) calls pro-NGO policies with norms "from the top" that seek to push weaker, poorer governments to incorporate NGOs into policymaking at the local, regional, and national levels. The International Center for Not-for-Profit Law (ICNL), for example, was created in 1992 to support "the development of civil society and the freedom of association on a global basis" (Reimann 2006, 61). By the end of the decade, the ICNL was assisting countries all over the world to draft NGO legislation to ensure a favorable and accountable legal structure in which NGOs could flourish. Given some governments' reactions to international NGOs as well as the support given to local NGOs, the ICNL also monitors NGO laws in forty-eight countries and eight international organizations.[16] The ICNL serves an important function, and it is a good example of how powerful Western governments are propelling the NGO boom, encouraging weaker, less developed, and poorer countries to adopt pro-NGO policies and practices.

More and wealthier NGOs translate into more activities, while pro-NGO institutions and practices backed by Western countries provide NGOs with an even greater ability to individually and collectively influence governments and shape peacebuilding outcomes, making them powerful forces to be reckoned with.

Relationships That Matter

The growth of NGOs and their expanding budgets are certainly signs of growing NGO resources, but scholars like David Baldwin (1989) believe that power in international relations is best understood by looking at relationships rather than numbers or resources. Since the Cold War's end, scholars have certainly acknowledged the changes in the relationships between states, international organizations, and civil society, even proclaiming that an important "power shift" has occurred (Mathews 1997). In this new world order, states have not necessarily lost power to the large numbers of NGOs and other nonstate actors, but instead they are increasingly sharing power. As difficult as it is to measure these changes, this is exactly why NGO research needs to adopt a relational approach to understanding how resources, attributes, and interactions shape perceptions and practices as well as outcomes (Anderson 2015, 41–64). Since it is impossible to demonstrate how NGOs actually share power with states in post-conflict peacebuilding, I merely highlight some of the mechanisms and practices that the United Nations has adopted as evidence of the growing influence of NGOs on UN decisions and behavior. Given the United Nations' central role in peacebuilding, its policies have far-reaching consequences on the actions of other actors. To be clear, although the United Nations has made many important changes in how it treats and sees NGOs, it rarely defines who the NGOs are or how power is actually shared.

The UN family is a complex system that includes "a bewildering alphabet soup of semi-autonomous programs, funds, committees, commissions, and agencies" (Forsythe 2007, 270). It is thus impossible and unnecessary to detail all of the United Nations' multifaceted and often longstanding relationships with NGOs, but it is worthwhile highlighting some recent developments that have a bearing on peacebuilding and the NGO bust that inevitably occurs in post-conflict environments. The United Nations reached out to NGOs formally in 1946, granting consultative status to forty-one NGOs through the Economic and Social Council (ECOSOC). During the Cold War period, NGOs were more caught up in East–West rivalries than they were in shaping UN policies. The ECOSOC changed significantly with the Cold War's end, and by 1996 it had given consultative status to more than one thousand NGOs. A decade and a half later, the number of NGOs with consultative status in the United Nations had more than tripled to about thirty-five hundred. Other changes were also evident. A larger percentage of the NGOs with consultative status were based in Asia and Africa, though the majority of those organizations with this "specific relationship" were still international NGOs based in North America or Western Europe. But in addition to granting this privileged position to many more NGOs from different regions, the standing itself evolved. NGOs with consultative status now have more access to UN bodies, agendas, and decision making than ever before.

International humanitarian law provides the legal context in which NGOs operate within the United Nations, and this was clarified long ago with The Hague Conventions of 1899 and 1907 and then The Geneva Convention of 1949. International law also governs the responsibilities and behavior of the International Committee of the Red Cross (ICRC), perhaps the most well-known private humanitarian organization. In the 1990s, international laws related to NGOs were reinforced and supplemented by a series of formal and informal mechanisms that encouraged the United Nations and even Security Council members to solicit the help of NGOs, especially in post-conflict situations. Toward this end, the status of the ICRC changed in 1990, and it became an official UN observer. This made perfect sense from the perspective of the United Nations, because by this point in time the

ICRC was active in nearly ninety countries in Africa, Asia, Europe, Latin America, and the Middle East, providing protection and assistance to the victims of armed conflicts.

Although this new relationship was limited to the ICRC, this was the first time that the United Nations recognized that a private actor was essential to the success of its mission to promote peace in the world. The United Nations also admitted that no other organization public or private had the ICRC's reach, experience, and legitimacy. Moreover, the tasks of ICRC and the United Nations increasingly complemented one another, and cooperation between the two institutions was closer, both in their field activities and in their efforts to enhance respect for international humanitarian law. The United Nations' relationship with the ICRC is unique, but this evolving relationship is symptomatic of broader shifts within the United Nations as it has restructured its relationships with NGOs and other private actors. As Peter Willets (2010) explains in his book *Non-Governmental Organizations in World Politics: The Construction of Global Governance*, in the last two decades, the United Nations went from tolerating nongovernmental organizations to acknowledging them as coveted partners that are essential to the United Nations' goals for the twenty-first century.

Although more obvious, it was not only in humanitarian affairs that the United Nations embraced a different relationship with NGOs; in a range of other issue areas, NGOs were acknowledged as crucial allies and partners because of their experience and expertise. Building on the momentum that started in the 1980s, UN conferences held ever since have been besieged by NGO participation. And by the mid-1990s, NGOs were not only participating at UN conferences but they were hosting their own international conferences, playing a significant role in defining the UN's agenda and policies. Whether in the area of the environment, women's rights, development, or peace, NGOs were increasingly represented and involved. It is still the case that NGOs are prohibited from becoming members of most UN bodies, but important institutional changes within the entire UN family signal shifts in how NGOs are viewed, what is expected of them, and the authority given to them. As Chadwick Alger (2005) confirms, the United Nations' statements were not just rhetoric because crucial institutional changes took place throughout the 1990s and in the beginning of the 2000s that affected when and how NGOs participated in UN bodies, how they interacted with member states, and how they were treated by UN agencies. Put differently, NGOs were not only convenient partners; they were increasingly regarded as key agents of post-conflict reconstruction and peacebuilding.

The Cold War's end prompted the United Nations to emphasize what it called "responsible sovereignty," which meant that when a state cannot protect its citizens, the United Nations has a responsibility to step in and lend a hand. In acknowledging this, the United Nations stated clearly that it did not believe that it could protect people all over the world by itself, and while it wanted to strengthen its capacity for post-conflict responses by changing its policies, it also needed to make sure that those on the ground with first-hand knowledge were involved in making and implementing policies.[17] In other words, practicing responsible sovereignty meant giving more responsibility and authority to NGOs as well as other actors with knowledge and capacity. In an impactful demonstration of the United Nations' newfound enthusiasm for nonstate actors in 1992, a Security Council member invited a Bosnian priest to talk about the war in the former Yugoslavia. Over time, this simple gesture evolved into the Arria Formula, or the practice of Security Council members holding informal, confidential meetings with nonstate actors and individuals, opening the door wide for private organizations and particularly international NGOs to provide input on conflict zones and post-conflict peacebuilding.

Another instance of the expanding access afforded NGOs started later in the 1990s when a group of NGOs gathered to organize the NGO Working Group on the Security Council. In 1997, but only after hearing its first official testimony from an NGO, a permanent mechanism was established to institutionalize regular conversations and input from NGOs, providing opportunities to a group of about thirty major international NGOs to interact with Security Council members (Hill 2002, 27). The first one-hour meeting between Secretary General Kofi Annan and the NGO Working Group turned into a half-day session that included all of the Security Council members (Lindenberg and Bryant 2001, 93). Ever since, Security Council members have met regularly with the Working Group for off-the-record meetings because of the valuable field information this group has and the United Nations lacks. The meetings serve four main functions: to inform NGOs about the work of the council; to provide ambassadors with information and analyses from NGOs; to offer NGOs an opportunity for advocacy and pressure; and to introduce diplomats to NGO representatives in the hope that wider contact and advocacy can take place.[18] These meetings are informal but can include Security Council ambassadors as well as foreign ministers, but regardless of who attends, such face-to-face conversations, which average around forty a year, provide at least some NGOs with opportunities to influence UN policies and even member states.

Mission Creep

By the mid-1990s, the NGO boom was well under way. These actors had more money, and the United Nations, other international organizations, and Western governments were consistently, if not eagerly, working through and with NGOs. More importantly, NGOs themselves had changed, specifically their attitude about what they ought to do in conflict-ridden countries. The NGO mission creep discussed here implicates NGOs in both the problems and unintended outcomes that occur in post-conflict countries. Without denying the incredible diversity of these actors, I suggest that large, Western-based NGOs intentionally used their numbers, financial resources, and connections with governments to become intensively and extensively involved in post-conflict reconstruction and peacebuilding. In other words, NGOs made the most of the post–Cold War environment and states' desire to find cheaper actors to advance their interests by not only "lobbying governments and the United Nations for funds, but also for political commitments" (Rieff 2003, 26). And their boldness paid off. As the decade progressed, NGOs enjoyed unparalleled access and influence.

By the beginning of the twenty-first century, Western governments and international organizations were involved in peace operations all around the world, and NGOs were pervasive fixtures in post-conflict environments. This was not necessarily the plan of governments, and long-term engagement in conflict zones was certainly not a goal for all international NGOs. This was, nonetheless, the reality that started to take shape, and in some of the world's most dysfunctional places, it was international NGOs—and not Western governments or international organizations—that were leading efforts to keep conflict-ridden and fragile states from falling apart. Dubbed by some the "new colonialists," international NGOs provided an array of services and support, essentially imposing their will on weak and poor states (Cohen, Figueroa Kupcu, and Khanna 2008). The journey from powerless, marginalized actors to new colonialists is a perplexing one, but not in uncertain times when governments are pressed to keep risks low. NGOs also started to envision a larger role for themselves, creating new expectations for who should be involved in reconstructing countries and how peacebuilding would unfold.

The history of NGOs in international politics is described in various ways, and their evolution is often divided into phases or generations based on their predominant strategies and activities.[19] NGO strategies are not always clear-cut but depend on the country and sector, but the following phases nonetheless suggest shifts in how NGOs behaved and viewed their roles. So-called first generation NGOs, like the ICRC and Oxfam, were established in the late nineteenth and early twentieth centuries during or after wars or natural disasters to provide emergency relief and assistance to victims. In part to address their predecessors' shortcomings, second generation NGOs shifted from just providing relief and assistance to promoting development and emphasizing self-reliance and the importance of creating small-scale initiatives that would remain beyond the period of the assistance. The Freedom from Hunger Campaign, for example, was initiated in the 1960s and it worked with thousands of local NGOs and organizations on development projects related to health and nutrition, hoping to make lasting changes in communities around the world.

There is no agreement on exactly when third-generation NGOs started to emerge, but by the early 1980s there was a realization that small, community organizations were not very effective if they acted alone. NGOs, instead, needed to work with public and private actors to foster enduring change. Some regard third-generation NGOs as radical and confrontational actors, because they tended to challenge the status quo and called for a restructuring of social relations. Many of these NGOs were also clear that they did not want to merely respond to situations and crises; they wanted to prevent them by becoming involved in building different, sustainable systems at the local, national, and even regional levels (Korten 1987, 145–59). To be sure, NGO behavior varied significantly, and these organizations focused on a broad range of issues, but they increasingly adopted a community-based or a human rights-based approach that put people at the center of their activities.

Changes in strategies and tactics, along with more access and new international challenges, set the stage for the NGO boom in the 1990s, where NGO numbers increased dramatically alongside expectations about what nonstate actors ought to be doing in international politics. As purportedly nimble actors that were gaining the ear of governments, fourth-generation NGOs did not focus on a single issue or sector. Instead, they used their work in one area as an entry point for other activities and larger, more encompassing roles. As Fiona Terry (2002) explains, after years of cleaning up the mess of war, humanitarian groups simply grew tired of acting only after the violence ended and largely in the margins. And because of their years of experience and expertise, many of the largest and most well-known NGOs decided they wanted to take on a more active role, beginning involvement even before violence started and continuing long after short-term needs were met. Out of necessity, but also choice, so-called new humanitarianism was born.

New humanitarianism allowed NGOs to continue providing short-term relief and assistance while they also engaged in long-term projects aimed at restructuring and reengineering societies. Modeling the aspirations and be-havior of Western governments and international organizations, but also carefully following the money trail, NGOs gravitated from managing and responding to violent conflicts to trying to change the very conditions within countries that gave rise to violence in the first place. Although not without controversy, large international NGOs like World Vision, Oxfam, Catholic Relief Services, and the International Rescue Committee (IRC) broadened and deepened their activities, engaging in a continuum of projects that started with traditional humanitarian relief but shifted to reconstruction, civil society development, and to peacebuilding. As David Rieff (2003, 130) puts it, after the Cold War's end, NGOs acted differently; they wanted to "become something larger" and part of a broader political process that would transform institutions and reconstruct societies. Mirroring the discourse and policy changes of governments and international organizations, scores of new NGOs sprung up to focus specifically on post-conflict countries and to assist with international peacebuilding, spawning even more local NGOs in the process.

Certain aspects of the NGO story did not change, and some of the oldest and most well-known members of the humanitarian club, such as the ICRC, CARE, and World Vision International, still provided most of the humanitar-ian assistance to conflict-ridden countries. Representing "a citizen's response to political failure," these groups addressed the immediate, short-term needs of the population in war-torn and fragile countries (Lindenberg and Bryant 2001, 65). The notion of "new humanitarianism" was a bit overstated because, by the early 1990s, many international NGOs had already shifted their funding and strategies, and were intimately involved in civil society development, engaged in various projects aimed at restructuring political, economic, and social institutions. Yet, something was noticeably different in the focus and attitude of many NGOs, to say nothing of their larger budgets, as they increasingly aimed to promote themselves as the best and most legitimate repository for building local capacity, strengthening democratic participation, and advancing local concerns.

In the 1990s, "multi-mandate NGOs" were becoming the norm, with Oxfam, for example, devoting only about 10 percent of its budget to emergency relief while more than 50 percent of its money went to long-term development activities (Chandler 2001, 683). These changes essentially allowed NGOs to step in to provide emergency relief and development, but instead of going home once this work done, they had the resources and mandate to address sociopolitical goals like human rights and gender equality. By operating on what Pamela Aall (2005) calls a "relief to development continuum," NGOs could be responsive to immediate needs while linking any kind of international assistance to grassroots change. Put simply, new humanitarianism allowed NGOs to descend on a country to provide much-needed relief and services that the government could not; it also encouraged them to stay put—for as long as funding allowed.

New humanitarianism and the changes that went with it were not easy on the NGO community, because it meant a parting of the ways for some of its members. NGOs like Médicins Sans Frontières (MSF), Catholic Relief Services (CRS), and Mercy Corps focused more on sociopolitical change, moving away from traditional humanitarianism, while the ICRC and others remained committed to humanitarian principles of universality and neutrality and focused on providing assistance to all. Other NGOs, particularly newer ones with political objectives, thoroughly embraced a broader, larger agenda that incorporated democracy promotion and the advancement of human rights into their missions and projects. What new humanitarianism did was transplant the traditional model of depoliticized charity with "a new model of moral triage based on charity, human rights and good governance" (Rieff 2003, 317). NGOs were no longer just in the business of helping the needy; they were, instead, working alongside governments and international organizations to transform environments and advance liberal peace.

This blurring of humanitarianism, political development, and conflict resolution became the standard way of approaching international peacebuilding. This new formula was based on three assumptions. First, aid and the work of NGOs should address the root causes of conflict as well as deal with large structural issues like poverty and inequity. Second, since violent conflicts were caused by misunderstandings, rather than evil, NGOs could play an important role in changing the attitudes and behavior of domestic actors. Finally, since aid is never neutral and NGO work has important political consequences, NGOs should use their power toward a greater good rather than engage indiscriminately. Although based on untested beliefs, by the beginning of the twenty-first century, these ideas so dominated international politics that NGOs themselves were afraid to advocate for the prioritization of emergency aid over other longer-term political priorities. The benefits of receiving more money and responsibility meant that NGOs were no longer stuck with cleaning up after a conflict ended; new humanitarianism provided them with authority and power.

New humanitarianism and the NGO game that was generated as a result were becoming so entrenched that, if governments responded to a crisis with relief alone, NGOs complained that this was "an excuse to avoid more rigorous responses" and was a substitute for broader, more comprehensive involvement (Chandler 2001, 699). According to this view, traditional humanitarianism merely gives the appearance of doing something, but it does not address why the violence happened or the conditions that gave rise to the problem. The consensus that was emerging promised something more: NGOs would not just respond to violence, they would help transform post-conflict states by preventing conflict in the future and creating more democratic and peaceful societies.

Rhetoric about the power of NGOs was facilitated, if not wholly endorsed, by Western governments that were committed to downsizing government programs and wanted to hand things off to actors they hoped could address situations more cheaply and more effectively. Fearful of becoming too involved in complex internal conflicts, states hoped that NGOs would not only implement their projects but also advance their interests. But it was NGOs themselves and their mission creep that intentionally put their agendas and organizations at the center of peacebuilding. The justifications for involving NGOs in post-conflict peacebuilding were numerous and understandable, but they were not entirely new. NGOs have been involved in conflict and development for decades, if not longer. However, the NGO world changed in important ways in the 1990s; NGOs were more numerous, they had larger budgets, and they increasingly had more access to governmental decisions and policies.

NGOs were also behaving differently, engaging in a continuum of activities and seeking a bridging role between international, national, and local actors. By doing these things, NGOs produced a hive of activities and spillover effects, allowing them to exert "an influence above and beyond their weak formal status" (Gordenker and Weiss 1996, 35). Many of the largest humanitarian NGOs intentionally cultivated networks of public organizations that worked in separate but overlapping ways. In this way, the NGO sector enjoyed significant power, influencing decisions and the policymaking process, even at the governmental level (Fitzduff and Church 2004, 7).

All of this sounds good and even noble, but much is still overlooked or misunderstood about these NGOs and their activities. Promises and rhetoric aside, international NGOs were not, in fact, bridging different interests and actors, partnering with local groups, or empowering those on the ground. Instead, they were reflecting and reinforcing international interests and the agendas of Western countries.[20]

NGO Realities

United Nations–led peace operations always include a large assortment of governments and international agencies that work in different ways with NGOs, but certain actors like the UN Development Program (UNDP), the UN High Commission for Refugees (UNHCR), and the World Bank have traditionally had extensive and deep contact with NGOs. During the 1990s, interactions with NGOs expanded and intensified for all UN agencies, with very specific promises to encourage more and better contact with groups on the ground to promote long-term peace and development. As a UNDP report explained, NGO input pervades many areas of their work, but in the twenty-first century, "the growing influence of local, national, and global civil society organizations is evident as the United Nations has called upon these actors for help with policy making, implementing programs, and monitoring governments" (UNDP 2003, 23). Evaluations of these and other UN efforts toward NGOs, however, expose how international promises about peacebuilding fell short and the NGO game was created.

The UNHCR certainly increased its financial and in-kind support for NGOs and civil society in post-conflict and transitioning states, establishing the NGO Partnership in Action Process (PARinAC) in 1994. These steps and subsequent programs were intended to create a new framework for co-operation and partnership between the UNHCR and some eight hundred national NGOs from around the world. The UNHCR also recognized the important but often overlooked differences between NGOs, stating that although it was committed to providing more access to international NGOs, it was intent on strengthening the capacity of national NGOs. This is because national NGOs were "closer, more acceptable to and effective with refugees and affected populations" in addition to being more flexible and less costly; thus, in the twenty-first century, the UNHCR needed to work with both national and international NGOs (Telford 2001, 11–12). Acknowledging what other UN agencies either missed or intentionally ignored, the UNHCR clarified the situation and the crucial differences between NGOs, noting that empowering international NGOs is not the same as working with national NGOs and groups on the ground.

To help locals and encourage genuine partnerships with local organizations, the UNHCR admitted that it needed to offset the power of international NGOs, which had grown in both number and wealth. Nonetheless, the evaluation of UNHCR policies and its efforts to develop collaborative relationships with national NGOs is sobering. Despite the UNHCR's plans and promises, by the beginning of the 2000s it was still largely unsuccessful in working with and sharing power with national NGOs; instead, resources and influence were still going to international NGOs. On paper more of the UNHCR's projects were working with and supporting national NGOs, but this is also misleading. Although the number of UNHCR "national implementing partners" had indeed increased, the percentage of UNHCR money funneled to local implementing groups had actually declined (Telford 2001).

Although this evaluation of the UNHCR's framework for cooperation and partnership with NGOs does not explicitly state so, it reveals the deceptive practices that international actors engaged in with their embrace of NGOs. That is, promises to reach out to NGOs, because of their expertise and connections, in fact meant more money and access for international NGOs but little for national, grassroots organizations. The UNHCR's NGO plans fell short, in part, because of a failure to make collaborative relationships with locals more of a priority. It was also because of unrealistic expectations placed on national NGOs since they lacked the capacity to work with UNHCR. This meant that the UNHCR recognized the importance of local NGOs and the need to connect with domestic actors in a meaningful way, but it did not necessarily do so.

Similarly, the World Bank changed its institutions and practices to include a field presence, and thus provide more and better access for local organizations, and it expressly acknowledged its desire to involve local NGOs and build partnerships with them (Hassan 2004). Despite important institutional and policy changes within the Bank, its efforts to reach out to local actors were not always successful, particularly in countries like Rwanda and Haiti where the Bank did not effectively coordinate with groups on the ground. A 2007 report specifically criticized the World Bank's civil society development policies in peacebuilding (World Bank 2007). Part of the problem, it acknowledged, was rooted in the confusing terms that the Bank uses and the adoption of policies that call for the Bank to work with and develop civil society and NGOs without, however, explaining who these actors are or acknowledging that civil society and NGO mean different things in different places.

In the post–Cold War period, World Bank documents consistently mention the importance of working with civil society groups and the need for local involvement, but assessments of its programs conclude that civil society is an elusive and contested concept that is interpreted differently, even within the World Bank institutions, but especially in the countries in which it works. Consequently, the Bank's attempts to change its relationships with NGOs often failed to give local actors more of a say. Moreover, international NGOs played a critical role in delivering services in post-conflict environments and helping with infrastructural development, but this did not mean that the international NGOs were connecting with or partnering with local NGOs. As a World Bank report put it clearly, future research on the World Bank's peacebuilding programs need to examine—rather than assume—the importance of NGOs, as well as better understand what civil society actually means and what NGOs actually do in post-conflict reconstruction and peacebuilding (World Bank 2007).

Research by international NGOs confirms some of these same unfortunate NGO realities. For example, a 2013 study commissioned by five UK-based international NGOs focuses specifically on partnerships with national and local actors, because this had been identified as a troubling aspect of international aid (Ramalingam, Gray, and Cerruti 2013). What the study finds is that despite the rhetoric of international NGOs to reach out to locals and build partnerships, efforts to work with national and local organizations do not, in fact, play a central role in the majority of international work. This does not mean that international NGOs do not understand the importance of connecting to local NGOs to enhance the appropriateness of their initiatives, to be more efficient, and to promote better long-term outcomes. Indeed, they do; nonetheless, the report concludes that the majority of international humanitarian responses are still "reactive, driven by emergency, and shaped by ad hoc interactions that take place at the point of crisis" (Ramalingam, Gray, and Cerruti 2013, 4). In other words, there is little time to identify appropriate local actors, and efforts to cultivate meaningful partnerships have largely failed.

A focus on the number of NGOs, their economic power, or even their institutionalization within the UN structure are not perfect ways of measuring the relational power of NGOs in peacebuilding, but they do suggest the growing importance of NGOs in international politics. During the 1990s, in fact, every UN agency went from tolerating NGOs to embracing them, making changes at the top and bottom. Yet, evaluations of UN policies and research that specifically examines funding point to often overlooked problems with the embrace of NGOs: resources and power are not shifting to actors on the ground. While perceptions and funding for NGOs indeed changed in the 1990s, by failing to specify *who* the NGOs were and *how* relationships would evolve, most of the benefits went to international NGOs rather than to groups on the ground.[21]

Scholars writing about specific cases of post-conflict peacebuilding do not make the same assumptions about NGOs or international actors embrace of them, and they certainly do not conflate international NGOs with grassroots organizations. Even if they do not examine the role of NGOs closely, scholars of development and humanitarian assistance often mention the numerous problems associated with international NGOs. In countries as diverse as Rwanda, Cambodia, and East Timor, for example, consistent themes emerge. First, after an explosive growth in the number of NGOs, both international and local NGOs stagnate, their numbers shrink, and many become paper NGOs (Fitzduff and Church 2004, 11–12). In post-conflict countries, writers observe that NGOs that come and go, emerge and disappear, often without leaving much behind. For example, international NGOs have been operating in and around Afghanistan for decades, but the dramatic outpouring of international assistance after 2001 had an obvious but unfortunate effect. The NGO invasion and the mushrooming of Afghan NGOs was not surprising given as Barnett Rubin sarcastically put it, the "billions of dollars in the pipeline and the armies of expatriates waiting like some tribal militia to get into Kabul," but it did not necessarily do much (Rashid 2008, 179). Afghan NGOs were funded by foreign donors and internationals' fancied that they could change the country overnight. They appeared dramatically and were full of assurances, but INGOs disappeared or withered away just as quickly.

Second, regardless of the country, scholars criticize international NGOs for committing the same sins: arriving with set goals in mind, failing to listen to their local partners, and "jockeying for a place that enhances their own legitimacy, position, and fundraising capacities" rather than focusing on those they claim to serve (Strand 2005, 89). Thus, scholars with experience in the field recognize the obvious disconnect between international and local NGOs. In Rwanda, for example, peacebuilding after 1994 resulted in an explosion of NGOs. The participation of these international actors was obvious, but their effect on society was decidedly mixed. On the one hand, international NGOs greatly helped the hundreds of thousands of war-weary Rwandans in countless ways, because they moved fast and they were flexible. Yet, the involvement of so many international NGOs pushed these actors to compete with each other for money and attention. Pressured to demonstrate results quickly, international NGOs had little time to cultivate relationships with local groups. Consequently, a year after international NGOs arrived in Rwanda, the government started to expel them, because local groups claimed that these organizations were doing what they pleased, creating a culture of dependence, and injecting too many Western policies and ideas into Rwandan society (Pouligny 2005).

Finally, despite initial excitement over international involvement and the promise of NGOs, scholars lament how quickly enthusiasm wanes as certain realities set in. The NGO bust means that the frenzy of activities and international attention pushes local actors to behave in uncooperative or dysfunctional ways toward each other. And it ultimately opens the door to organizations that are unconnected to local structures and lack domestic support. For example, international actors arrived over the course of several decades to Sri Lanka, but the country only experienced its NGO boom in the 1990s as international actors became fixated on the idea of post-conflict peacebuilding. This international involvement not only had an obvious impact on the number of local groups that emerged, but anthropologists studying Sri Lanka maintain that this intervention also shaped the behavior and relationships of local organizations. In the medium- to long-term, the boom of NGOs distorted the development of the local NGO sector and negatively affected Sri Lankan society and peacebuilding (Orjuela 2004, 158).

These NGO realities emerged clearly in my fieldwork in the Balkans. The presence of well-heeled international NGOs that promised to engage civil society produced lots of local groups, and NGOs were initially celebrated and naively embraced. Yet, faith and optimism did not last long, because the relationships between international actors and locals did not fundamentally change. The realities of liberal peacebuilding, the desire of Western donors to restructure society in particular ways, and the self-interested behavior of NGOs created surprising and unfortunate effects. Instead of creating domestic partners in peacebuilding, the environment created the perfect conditions for the NGO game and for locals to become disillusioned with international policies and promises.

At first glance, Mostar's recent history is a good example of the promise of NGOs and their overlooked power in post-conflict peacebuilding. The story I initially relayed about this Bosnian city and the inspiring people and organizations involved in the country's reconstruction is often the only one that is reported about NGOs, especially by governments and other agents of international peacebuilding eager to celebrate their achievements. It no doubt captures the moving aspects of the NGO story, of internationals investing in conflict zones and of locals who devote their lives to building peace in their country, believing that NGOs are crucial to its future.

Yet, my initial discussion of the nascent NGO community in Mostar was an incomplete and somewhat misleading account of the NGO reality in Bosnia. Focusing on a single organization at one particular point in time, it did not track the NGO over time. It did not monitor its activities. The story also did not explain how this NGO, like most other Bosnian NGOs, had to engage in a desperate scramble for funds from international donors, jealously regarding other NGOs that had received attention and money. Importantly, my initial statements about the power of NGOs in Mostar left out crucial details about the inactivity and corruption of NGOs, of well-equipped offices that had few constituents and no active projects. In fact, the NGO boom I witnessed in the early 2000s also included many stories of NGOs closing their offices because of a lack of funding or little domestic support. In actuality, in every visit to the region, I witnessed heated discussions that reflected the complications, unintended effects, and disappointments of NGOs. The problem was simple: too many public and private peace builders arrived in Bosnia, each with their own plans for how civil society should develop, and there was little consultation with local groups who were treated largely as implementing agents or employees. As a government official in Sarajevo explained, internationals came to "Bosnia without knowing enough about our country but pretended that we didn't know anything either."[22]

A year after my initial trip to Mostar in 2000, I could find no sign of the woman I had met or the NGO I encountered. While others told me that the NGO was still active elsewhere in Bosnia, its mission had changed; it disappeared from sight in Mostar, as did most of the other Bosnian NGOs I had encountered in my first trip to Bosnia. Yet, these are just a few of the details that I failed to relay about the NGO promise in Bosnia. I also did not elaborate on how frustrated locals were, even in 2000, because they felt like they were animals in a zoo with Westerns visiting only to gawk at their country and its misfortunes. Bosnians resented many of these Westerners, who talked like all-knowing parents and expected Bosnians to act like well-behaved children following their every command. However, by telling just one part of the NGO story, it is easy to mistake and exaggerate the role of NGOs or engage in wishful thinking about their effects on peacebuilding.

In 2004, when the Old Bridge was reconstructed, Lord Ashdown, the top international representative in Bosnia, claimed that the bridge's reconstruction "proves that hope triumphs over barbarism."[23] For locals in the crowd, the sentiment was far less buoyant, if not equivalent, because most felt that, in fact, too little had changed in Mostar and throughout Bosnia. Even a decade after the bridge was rebuilt, Mostar remained divided and embittered, with Croats laying claim to the west bank of the Neretva River, and Muslims sticking to the east bank. The city of about seventy-five thousand still supported segregated hospitals, postal services, fire stations, and educations systems because the people were so polarized (McMahon and Western 2009, 74). The tensions in Mostar actually grew so intense, that in 2013, the city had to postpone local elections, and then it failed to adopt a budget, further aggravating its divided population.[24]

The disappointing and dysfunctional situation in Mostar was replicated throughout Bosnia. Of the scores of NGOs that once existed, with the goal of promoting peace, reconciliation, and development, only a handful remained. Most of the international players had moved on, leaving little more than distaste and disillusionment for NGOs and international peacebuilding. The NGO reality is complicated and messy; it includes lots of groups working in different ways in various sectors. It also changes over time, experiencing periods of growth, activity, and promise, but also decline, disappointment, and decay.

Chapter 3

Bosnia

Much Ado about NGOs

In 2011, a Bosnian official from Catholic Relief Services (CRS) reminded me of something I had heard expressed in different ways on numerous occasions: Bosnia was a big experiment.[1] The remark was not necessarily meant as a criticism of any particular government or international donor. These NGO officials were merely stating how many Bosnians felt, particularly those who have worked in civil society and watched dozens of governments and international organizations come and go. Instead of investing in organizations and programs that were mutually reinforcing and that advanced the country's development, representatives of governments, international organizations, or private foundations landed in Bosnia with their own agendas and good ideas for putting the country back together. They resisted coordination and long-term planning and, when interest dried up, the internationals merely closed their doors and went home. After more than two decades of projectification, Bosnians are eager for the experiment to end.

Academics frequently use the term *international community* to discuss international peacebuilding in Bosnia, suggesting that this group of actors had the same priorities and ways of doing things. Nothing could be further from the truth. At the same time, international interveners faced their own pressures; they needed to be spontaneous and flexible while also behaving deliberately and consistently. By necessity, but also by choice, peacebuilding in Bosnia meant shortcuts were taken and tough decisions were deferred. And when international ambitions fell short, the default option was to turn things over to locals, emphasizing the importance of civil society development and investments in NGOs. For Bosnians, the contradictions of the international experiment are not abstract or hard to pin down; they have been part of their daily reality for almost two decades.

For David Rieff (2003), who covered the wars in the Balkans, Bosnia holds a special place in the record of humanitarian action. Unlike in other countries and crises, international NGOs in this country were "better funded, more political, and more admired by the public at large than in any time previously" (Rieff 2003, 134). Working on behalf of dozens of governments, international organizations, and private donors, who wanted desperately to do something without, however, getting pulled into the country's ethnic tangle, NGOs of all sizes mushroomed in the second half of the 1990s. Whether it was World Vision, the Missing Persons Institute, or Medica Zenica (a local women's group devoted to women's health and empowerment), the conflict in Bosnia was a defining moment for the NGO world, especially those intent on moving beyond traditional humanitarianism.

The NGO turn in Bosnia was based neither on solid evidence nor careful planning but was rooted in the simple idea that "civil society is a crucial agent in influencing the political system and in providing a more solid foundation to democratization, the rule of law and respect of human rights" (Belloni 2001, 163). Faced with conflicting pressures, limited time, and dwindling budgets, convictions quickly became convention, and civil society was confused and conflated with the presence of NGOs.[2] Overnight, large amounts of funding and unmonitored support flowed to all sorts of nonstate actors, and unexpectedly, their very existence became a proxy for the strength of civil society, as well as a demonstration that liberal peacebuilding was on track. Both were a grave mistake.

Experiments are rarely a complete success, and the international community's efforts in Bosnia were no exception. Although international intervention in Bosnia is regularly touted as "one of the most positive examples of international concern and commitment to a post-conflict country," this is not the same as saying that international peacebuilding produced the desired or promised effects (Hertic, Sapcanin, and Woodward 2000, 315). What is clear is that the assumptions made about NGOs and their ability to both provide relief and help lay the foundation for democracy and long-term peace were misplaced and exaggerated. After years of trial and error, the NGO game that was once played with vigor and excitement has largely ended, but not without lingering effects. The large troupe of internationals has gone home, and most of Bosnia's NGOs have either disappeared or have languished from little funding and support. In the wake of these policies and practices, Bosnians do not feel supported, empowered, or transformed; instead, they are discouraged, disappointed, and disillusioned, having spent too much time on initiatives that amounted to little.

This chapter looks at how liberal peacebuilding, with its reliance on civil society development and NGOs, shaped the country's domestic NGO sector and everyday life from roughly 1996 to 2011. The thick, descriptive analysis relies on primary and secondary sources, many of which are policy reports. I also include insights gleaned from dozens of semistructured interviews with Bosnian policymakers, academics, and NGO officials, as well as internationals working in Bosnia over the course of several years.[3]

Priorities and Policies

International involvement in Bosnia over the last two decades has been multifaceted and multileveled. The interveners included numerous public and private actors and countless civil society projects. Obviously, it is impossible to detail all of these organizations or their activities, but certain characteristics and patterns are clear. When the violence started in the early 1990s, international actors wanted to help this Yugoslav republic and its largely Muslim population, but it lacked the tools and the time to develop a comprehensive and coherent plan. What set Bosnia's conflict and then reconstruction apart was the deluge of international NGOs and other private actors that appeared even before the violence ended, allowing both international and local NGO to become a defining feature, if not fixture, of post-conflict peacebuilding. Of the 123 countries that recognized Bosnia as an independent country in 1992, at least 34 provided some kind of humanitarian relief, and all relied on NGOs in some way to distribute their assistance (Maglajilic and Kodzic 2008, 317). A few international NGOs played a high-profile role during the conflict, but their involvement, like that of the United Nations, was not without complications. At different points, in fact, UN peacekeepers and NGO officials were not only bystanders to injustice, but their presence may have encouraged the violence they sought to mitigate (Brown 2009, 8).

The presence of the United Nations and international NGOs during the war complicated some situations, but it was the contradictory policies and in-action of Western governments that put these international actors in harm's way. This was a trend that continued even as Western governments and in-ternational organizations got more involved in Bosnia's war. Since Western governments initially failed to step in to halt the violence, international organ-izations used their limited resources to try to protect the Bosnian people. Writing a field report of his impressions of the conflict, Mark Duffield (1994, 16–17) lamented the demise of military humanitarianism, how lack of "politi-cal will" left the United Nations in retreat—and only NGOs to fill in the gaps.

International NGOs responded in different ways to the West's indecision over Bosnia's unfolding drama. The International Committee of the Red Cross (ICRC), for example, retained its focus on providing relief to all parties, while other international NGOs, clearly frustrated by the West's inaction, abandoned humanitarian principles of neutrality and universality. Their frustration led some international NGOs to use their position and resources to try to punish perceived aggressors, providing aid selectively and only when certain conditions were met. The Bosnian conflict not only inspired a more activist, political approach among some international NGOs, but it contributed to a growing divide within the humanitarian community over the appropriate role of NGOs in conflict zones. Should NGOs be neutral observers, doling out relief to all? Or, was it their job to act as the conscience of the international community, helping victims, but also trying to transform the very environ-ment that gave rise to violence in the first place? The debate over the proper role for NGOs was not resolved in Bosnia, but activities there were a water-shed for future NGO involvement in post-conflict reconstruction. Implicitly, NGOs were acknowledged and embraced as unique actors that could help states and other international actors restructure Bosnian society.

After more than three years of fighting, Western governments finally in-tervened with significant military force, producing a comprehensive peace agreement in late 1995. The Dayton Peace Accords provided a clear sense of what many hoped were the international community's goals in Bosnia: restoring peace, restructuring the political system, and reconstructing the country.[4] The job of restoring the peace was assigned to troops from thirty-six countries. On many levels, this multinational military presence was impressive and successful. There were more foreign troops in Bosnia per capita in the first years after the conflict than in any other internationally led post-conflict reconstruction exercise, with the exception of Germany after World War II and Kosovo in 1999.[5]

A strong military presence bent on stopping the violence and restoring peace was linked directly to the goal of restructuring the political system to manage the country's ethnic diversity within a single political unit. The Dayton Peace Agreement did this by creating a federal state that both divided the country and kept it together. On the one hand, the Dayton Agreement solidified the territorial gains wrought by ethnic cleansing and violence by dividing the country into two fairly autonomous, but largely ethnically homogenous, entities: the Federation and the Republika Srpska (RS). At the same time, the new constitution included provisions for joint political institutions, power sharing practices, and the right of return for refugees. In theory, the Dayton Agreement addressed the contradiction between postwar military realities and the international community's promise to create a unified, multiethnic state. In reality, it left tough decisions for later and naively assumed that international commitment was both unified and long-lasting (McMahon 2004). Dayton separated the country into two, if not three, mono-ethnic units, while top-down and bottom-up mechanisms were created in the hope that they would eventually bring the country and population together. NGO activities were a significant part of the bottom-up plan.

Within a year of the peace accords, a Bosnian government was up and running. Yet, behind the scenes, power was still firmly in the hands of nationalist parties. Political structures were proving problematic and there were, in fact, several governments running different aspects of the country. In 1997, the international community increased the power of the Office of the High Representative (OHR), which had been established to coordinate the activities of international actors and help implement the peace agreement. By the end of the decade, the OHR had become such an integral institution of governance that there was barely a role for Bosnian institutions (Bieber 2002, 321–37). Consequently, in the years since, governance, restructuring, and reconciliation have been pushed and prodded from above rather than emerging organically from Bosnian actors. Moreover, the tensions and contradictions involving governance and the international community's role in supervising this process have had a lasting impact on society and the (under)development of Bosnian NGOs.

The success of military efforts, alongside the international community's ambitious but highly contentious power sharing arrangement, encouraged significant financial resources to flow into the country to help with liberal peacebuilding's third priority: reconstructing the country, which explicitly and confidently included reconciling Bosnia's multiethnic society. It was in this third area of reconstruction and civil society development that NGOs assumed their most central and coveted position. From 1996 to 2007, at least $14 billion poured into this country.[6] From 1993 until 2010, the United States government alone provided roughly $2 billion in aid, with the highest levels coming right after the war ended (CAS report 2009, 9). Although American aid to Bosnia declined significantly after 2000, even in 2011 the U.S. government gave over $40 million of assistance to the country, most of which went to political and economic reforms.

International assistance helped turn the country around, and within a few years, the reconstruction of Bosnia was deemed "remarkably successful" (Reshaping International Priorities in Bosnia and Herzegovina 2002). Reconstruction was funded largely by Western governments and international organizations, but as with the provision of humanitarian assistance during and after the war, the main implementing agents were international and national NGOs that calibrated their activities and missions to match donor priorities (Devine 2011, 3). International NGOs worked in different and diverse ways, but they were on the ground, ready to rescue and transform the country, engaging in a continuum of activities that usually started with relief provision but quickly seeped into areas like refugee returns, education, and human rights.

The International Rescue Committee (IRC), for example, was the first relief organization to airlift medicine into the country in 1992. After the peace agreement was signed and basic humanitarian needs were met, new funding streams emerged that shifted the IRC's activities to restoring the country's physical and social infrastructure. By 1996, $230 million was made available for reconstruction, and NGOs were asked to put in bids to help implement specific objectives. In the end, money for reconstruction was channeled through thirty international NGOs. Two years later, and as needs expanded, the total envelope available for reconstruction and refugee return more than doubled to approximately $520 million. Again, NGOs were asked to help with these tasks (Devine 2011, 3–4). As international priorities continued to shift, NGOs were regularly recruited to help fulfill the international community's mission. In fact, these more nimble actors would become crucial to an important international pastime: encouraging what was vaguely called civil society development to empower locals and build long-term peace and regional stability.

The Civil Society Connection

Rebuilding Bosnia's infrastructure was an important priority, but promoting democracy and reconciling Bosnian society, through what was universally but nebulously called civil society development, received even more attention. This was particularly true as other international efforts were either achieved or proved elusive.[7] As a 2001 UN report put it, strong civil society institutions are necessary, because they "are important vehicles for strengthening local perceptions of new rights and how to exercise them" (UN Office of the Resident Coordinator for Development Operations 2001, 9). This report, like others, lays bare the importance, but also the idealism, associated with reconstructing civil society in Bosnia. It also exposes how often international actors conflated terms and actors, regularly referring to NGOs as civil society organizations. Both NGOs and civil society development were regarded as essential for countering nationalist politicians and transforming the country's divided society; yet, the difference between these actors and the exact nature of their relationship was rarely explained or explored in much detail. Instead, and at least on paper, the two went together seamlessly.

As David Chandler (2000, 235) observes, in Bosnia, hopes were increasingly pinned on NGOs, believing that they could somehow create "a democratic culture of tolerance, moderation, and compromise." In time, strengthening civil society, which would apparently be evident by the presence of NGOs alone, was not only crucial to the prospects for democratization and long-term peace, but it became necessary to Bosnia's viability as a country. As appealing as the civil society narrative had become, these policies and practices glossed over complexities about the actors involved and what it takes to transform post-conflict societies and foster trust and compromise. It takes time and persistence, but as governance and peacebuilding proved difficult, and as other international crises developed, Western governments and international organizations grew increasingly impatient with the Bosnian experiment. In response, peacebuilders turned to the promise of NGOs, allowing international NGOs to provide services, and investing in domestic groups to ensure that peace and reconciliation would move forward. And somehow the power of NGOs would "trickle down," changing local attitudes and behavior.

The Organization for Security and Cooperation in Europe (OSCE) and the U.S. Agency for International Development (USAID) together led the international community's efforts in this area, emphasizing the urgency of having international and local NGOs participate in restructuring the country's political and social institutions. In fact, in 1996, the OSCE's Mission to Bosnia-Herzegovina (BiH) was reorganized to focus on democratization and civil society development, with the goal of bringing the "international community into a closer relationship with grassroots groups and associations which could provide a counterpoint to the politics of the governing authorities and nationalist parties" (Chandler 2000, 229). Regrettably, it did not distinguish between international NGOs and grassroots community associations, and it failed to probe carefully the activities that were most effective in empowering local groups and countering nationalist politics. In other words, policies tended to be aspirational not realistic.

Given the ethnic nature of Bosnia's conflict and the outcome of the Dayton Peace Agreement, which left the country split into mono-ethnic units, strengthening and transforming civil society was not just desirable, it was deemed necessary to unifying the country. For these reasons, the OSCE developed an expansive civil society agenda, with two of its departments focused solely on enhancing civic engagement and social activism.[8] As the OSCE's senior coordinator for democratization and NGO development explained, establishing NGOs is the first principle for democratization, and NGOs are vital for the reconstruction of civil society. This is why the OSCE is committed to the creation of an active and engaged civil society, able to act as an equal partner to the government.

Similarly, USAID looked to both international and Bosnian NGOs to strengthen society and develop closer relationships between international and national groups. To achieve these goals, in the second half of the 1990s, USAID reoriented its funding priorities and programs. During the conflict, the majority of its money went to international NGOs to provide humanitarian assistance and relief, but once the conflict ended, the U.S. government focused on promoting Bosnian NGOs, because "in the long term, a pluralistic civil society will be essential and thus the role of nongovernmental organizations, as advocates for citizen interests and avenues for citizen participation, must be strengthened" (FY 1998 Congressional Presentation 1999).

By this point in time, the U.S. government had established the Center for Democracy and Governance to support American NGOs working with NGOs in Eastern Europe. The New Partnerships Initiative "focused significant resources on strengthening civil society and helping to restructure the relationships between states and civil societies."[9] For the United States, civil society development and support for NGOs were tightly linked, and by 2000, USAID had established a comprehensive democratic agenda in Bosnia to encourage a pro-democratic political leadership and a vibrant civil society. In January of 2001, the Trust for Civil Society in Central and Eastern Europe (CEE Trust) was established with money from U.S. and European private grant-making foundations with the explicit goal of supporting nonprofit organizations in the region.

By the beginning of the twenty-first century, the European Union (EU) was the single largest contributor to peacebuilding in Bosnia, and like the OSCE and USAID, it also claimed that, as the voices of "the people," NGOs were important vehicles for promoting peace and good governance (Fagan 2012, 13). The European Union never developed a civil society agenda comparable to the OSCE or USAID, but it still adopted a range of policies and practices that linked NGOs to civil society development, democracy, and peace. EU offices also linked NGO development and a strong civil society to Bosnia's future membership in the European Union. As various EU reports put it, a strong civil society in BiH is a European Union priority: to build democracy from the grassroots level, to eradicate discrimination, to reconcile ethnic tensions, and to improve human and civil rights. And all of these are critical to fulfilling the Copenhagen political criteria for EU membership (Bosnia and Herzegovina, "Progress Report" European Commission, October 2014). As the largest donor to Bosnia's government and to Bosnian NGOs in the 2000s, the European Union has been clear about the broad areas it wishes to support, seeing the development of the NGO sector, in particular, as necessary for stability and democratic development.

This "civil society through NGO development" strategy was not limited to the OSCE, the U.S. government, or the European Union. Other donor governments adopted a similar approach in their engagement in Bosnia. The Irish government, for example, through its nonprofit group, Development Cooperation Ireland, moved away from providing humanitarian assistance to working with and supporting Bosnian NGOs, ostensibly to build bridges with local groups in society. At one point, Development Cooperation Ireland was funding over twenty Bosnian NGOs as well as promoting the exchange of information and knowledge between international actors and Bosnian NGOs. International organizations, such as the World Bank and NATO, adopted a similar method and narrative, if for different reasons. The World Bank, for example, championed Bosnian NGOs because they promoted economic growth and encouraged sociopolitical change, while NATO looked to NGOs as "implementers" and "partners" in its expansive political mandate in the Balkans.[10]

As government and donor thinking evolved, so did international NGOs, shifting their focus and rhetoric to strengthening civil society and promoting grassroots changes. The International Rescue Committee (IRC), for example, which had started off providing humanitarian relief and then switched to infrastructural development, jumped on the civil society bandwagon. By the late 1990s it was supporting community-building activities, which included local NGOs that promoted reconciliation across ethnic and religious boundaries. Catholic Relief Services (CRS), the International Refugee Committee, and CARE, three of the largest international NGOs that started working in Bosnia during the war, also decided to stay put, transitioning away from the provision of humanitarian assistance to funding "local agents" that would help determine the country's fate.[11] As a CARE International report explained, since the humanitarian mission is largely over, one of its primary goals is to strengthen a pluralistic and diversified civic foundation in Bosnia, enhancing the social welfare of the community (Smillie and Todorovic 2001).

By the beginning of the twenty-first century, an exciting and important consensus had emerged among the throng of international actors muddling their way through Bosnia: successful peacebuilding not only included top-down assistance, but it necessitated bottom-up investments to open channels of communication and build trust with the local population.[12] Yet, the so-called bottom-up efforts often lacked grassroots support and were, in fact, top-down strategies to create certain kinds of organizations that could implement Western projects and agendas. Many of Bosnia's NGOs, in fact, grew out of international projects that provided assistance and services to the victims of violence, while others were created by Western governments and international NGOs as part of an explicit effort to support cross ethnic cooperation and democratization (Pickering 2007, 115). Western donors were particularly interested in funding NGOs that worked on political accountability, rule of law, and civil engagement. The international community's investments in NGOs became important principally because other strategies, like restructuring political institutions, proved unsuccessful. Thus, in the absence of better benchmarks, the mere presence of NGOs became an easy, if superficial, way of measuring the success of international peacebuilding.[13]

Investments in Bosnia's society were not insignificant, but compared to money spent in other areas, support for social reconstruction and civil society development were a small fraction of the international community's overall budget for the country. An Open Society Fund report indicated that during the 1995–2000 period about $5–6 billion (out of an estimated $22–24 billion) was spent on democratization, civil society, media, and other types of bottom-up assistance, most of which was likely channeled to the country's burgeoning NGO sector.[14] Given the crosscutting nature of initiatives that could be interpreted as civil society development, more precise figures on the actual amount of international support that went to funding this sector and Bosnian NGOs do not exist (Papić, Ninković, and Car 2007). What can be corroborated is that while investments in civil society development did not come close to the rhetoric attached to its importance, it was an issue that featured prominently in the agendas and rhetoric of governments, multilateral agencies, and international NGOs operating throughout the country.

The Big Experiment

As a former republic within communist Yugoslavia, Bosnia had almost no independent organizations before 1990. This changed suddenly and dramatically, and by the middle of the decade, the new country was literally flooded with international actors, international NGOs, and private foundations, but also with newly formed local NGOs, associations, and other nonstate actors working in dozens of sectors. In this superficial way, it is easy to point to the short-term effects of liberal peacebuilding on the creation of groups, the development of projects, or what some call microlevel outputs (Brouwer 2000, 21–48). The Union of International Associations (UIA) confirms that liberal peacebuilding, starting officially in December 1995, coincided with a dramatic increase in registered international NGOs. After having no international NGOs registered with the UIA in 1990, by 1996 there were already about 350 registered organizations in Bosnia.[15] UIA data can confirm the growth of registered international NGOs, but it is still woefully incomplete when it comes to explaining what these organizations were doing or their effects on everyday life and people in Bosnian society.

Different reports on Bosnia's NGO sector observe that most of the international NGOs were active for only a brief period, but there is little documentation on their activities or impact (Sterland 2006, 16). By examining several websites that list the international NGOs working in Bosnia in 2006 and again in 2010, I was able to get some sense of, at least, who some of these international actors were and their country of origin (see table 3.1).[16]

Based on what appeared on these websites and the information NGOs themselves provided, I then sorted their activities into two basic groups: service delivery or civil society development. At a basic level, and not without shortcomings, this examination of NGO activities demonstrated the dramatic decline in the number of international NGOs within a few years. It also suggests that most of the international NGOs that operated in Bosnia, at least according to their websites, were involved primarily in service provision rather than what can be called civil society development (see table 3.2).

Table 3.1 International NGOs and country of origin

Country	Year	Total NGOs	United States	Europe	Domestic	Other
Bosnia	2006	230	151	67	12	0
	2010	38	35	3	0	0

Sources: Compiled from the following websites:
InterAction: http://www.interaction.org/taxonomy/term/150; ReliefWeb: http://reliefweb.int/rw/rwb.nsf/doc214?OpenForm&rc=4&cc=bih;
USAID: http://www.pvo.net/usaid/pvo.asp; and
Charity Navigator: http://www.charitynavigator.org/index.cfm?bay=search.map.

In some respects, this information is not that surprising, but it does confirm an NGO pattern in Bosnia. After international actors arrived in large numbers to provide various services, most went home or disappeared from sight. The pattern is clearer when compared with other countries where international peacebuilding also took place (see table 3.3). This information

Table 3.2 International NGOs by deliverables

	Service Delivery		Civil Society		Both	
	2006	*2010*	*2006*	*2010*	*2006*	*2010*
Bosnia	191 (83%)	27 (71%)	20 (9%)	0 (0%)	19 (8%)	11 (29%)

Sources: Compiled from the following websites:
InterAction: http://www.interaction.org/taxonomy/term/150; ReliefWeb:http://reliefweb.int/rw/rwb
.nsf/doc214?OpenForm&rc=4&cc=bih;
USAID: http://www.pvo.net/usaid/pvo.asp; and
Charity Navigator: http://www.charitynavigator.org/index.cfm?bay=search.map.

Table 3.3 International NGOs by deliverables

	Service Delivery		Civil Society		Both	
	2006	*2010*	*2006*	*2010*	*2006*	*2010*
Afghanistan	61 (78%)	150 (73%)	1 (1%)	2 (.98%)	16 (21%)	53 (26%)
East Timor	29 (52%)	37 (84%)	8 (14%)	1 (2%)	19 (34%)	6 (14%)
Kosovo	48 (71%)	17 (50%)	11 (16%)	4 (12%)	9 (13%)	13 (38%)
Bosnia	191 (83%)	27 (71%)	20 (9%)	0 (0%)	19 (8%)	11 (29%)

Sources: Compiled from the following websites:
For Afghanistan: USAID: http://pvo.usaid.gov/usaid/;
ReliefWeb: http://www.reliefweb.int/rw/dbc.nsf/doc104?OpenForm&cc=afg; and
InterAction: http://www.interaction.org/taxonomy/term/197.
For Bosnia: InterAction: http://www.interaction.org/taxonomy/term/150;
ReliefWeb:http://reliefweb.int/rw/rwb.nsf/doc214?OpenForm&rc=4&cc=bih;
USAID: http://www.pvo.net/usaid/pvo.asp; and
Charity Navigator: http://www.charitynavigator.org/index.cfm?bay=search.map;
For East Timor: InterAction: http://www.interaction.org/taxonomy/term/233;
ReliefWeb: http://reliefweb.int/rw/rwb.nsf/doc214?OpenForm&rc=3&cc=tls;
USAID: http://www.pvo.net/usaid/pvo.asp; and
Charity Navigator: http://www.charitynavigator.org/index.cfm?bay=search.map.
For Kosovo: USAID: http://pvo.usaid.gov/usaid/; and
InterAction: http://www.interaction.org/taxonomy/term/167.

demonstrates the profound disjuncture between what was said about new humanitarianism in the 1990s and what international NGOs were actually doing. If anything can be concluded from what international NGOs put on their websites, it is that most of the international NGOs in Bosnia maintained a focus on relief and service provision and gave little attention to sociopolitical activities in civil society.

Estimating the effects of what these international actors actually accomplished is even more difficult. It is clear, though, that international intervention created large numbers of Bosnian or local NGOs. The research on Bosnian NGOs uses different terms to document the growth of local independent organizations, referring to them as NGOs, associations, civil society organizations, and nonstate actors, often without distinguishing whether they are international or domestic organizations. Thus, only rough estimates on this aspect of Bosnia's NGO boom are possible. In 2005, for example, the European Union reported that there were over eight thousand nonstate actors registered in Bosnia—at the state and entity levels, and in the Brčko District, and this included international NGOs as well as domestic actors (Papić, Ninković, and Car 2007, 62). A 2006 USAID report, however, indicated that there were only about 230 NGOs registered at the state level, but as many as 7,000 associations, foundations, and civil society organizations working throughout the country.[17]

Research on Bosnia's NGO sector not only acknowledges the problems in estimating the size of the country's nonprofit sector, but it discusses the even more difficult task of assessing the relative importance of these actors to sociopolitical developments and on the lives of ordinary people. In other words, what do these NGOs, associations, and civil society organizations mean for people in Bosnia, particularly their understandings and perceptions of international peacebuilding? USAID could only confirm that nonstate actors were registered and existed at one point in time in Bosnia but could say little about their activities and nothing about their impact on domestic groups, policies, or Bosnian society, or what are referred to as meso- or macro-level outputs (Brouwer 2000, 21–48).

The very few evaluations of Bosnia's NGO sector that do try to look beyond numbers and focus on outputs and outcomes are not positive, confirming that many Bosnian NGOs existed only on paper, and few produced obvious changes or had a noticeable impact on policies. The United Nations, for example, acknowledges that although there is still not a single or reliable database of the registered NGOs working throughout the country, as many as twelve thousand civil society organizations existed in Bosnia, though only about six thousand or fewer were believed to be active (*Civil Society in Bosnia and Herzegovina* 2011, 8). Other reports use different terms and produce other totals, but the only point on which there is broad agreement is that liberal peacebuilding in Bosnia produced large numbers of NGOs that relied heavily, if not exclusively, on external support for their existence.

International actors did not create all of Bosnia's NGOs, but in most cases they provided substantial funding or in-kind support. The Helsinki Committee for Human Rights in Bosnia, for example, is one of the country's oldest local NGOs. Forming officially in 1998 with the assistance of the Norwegian Ministry of Foreign Affairs, the Helsinki Committee Bosnia has worked ever since to support individual human rights.[18] International actors did not create this organization, but foreign donors and organizations provided immeasurable in-kind support and expertise, helping strengthen the organization's strategy and development by advising its staff.

For members of the Helsinki Committee, international assistance was both important and beneficial, ensuring that issues like minority rights and gender were not ignored.[19] This organization's positive experiences with international actors may have been because of its leadership or due to the Helsinki Federation for Human Rights' philosophy for working with local chapters and its emphasis on cultivating partnerships with individuals in countries and developing appropriate strategies and tactics based on a country's culture and experiences. Most likely, it was some combination of domestic and international factors. It is also the case that this NGO started as a narrowly focused group committed to human rights, and it has not changed its course. Despite temptations to expand or alter its mission, Helsinki Committee Bosnia has not given in to these enticements. In other words, it has not experienced the same boom as many other Bosnian NGOs; its numbers and budget never grew significantly, and it has retained a constant, if low-key, presence in the country that remains to this day.

This is not the typical NGO story, and discussions of Bosnia's NGO sector regularly describe the "mission creep" of NGOs—how the influx of foreign money changed local NGOs and broadened their missions and activities. Consequently, Bosnian groups have suffered a high attrition rate, and very few that started in the 1990s were operating a decade later. The NGO life cycle, however, is not uniform but depends on both international and domestic factors. Bosnians often point to the important work of Catholic Relief Services (CRS), explaining how this international NGO initially provided relief and assistance, but over time it transformed successfully into an active, domestic organization that is funded by outside sources but run by Bosnians. The International Organization for Missing Persons (IOMP) is also distinguished for its important forensic work, focusing on a very specific issue and cooperating with locals to identify missing persons as well as helping to draft a Law on Missing Persons.

It is certainly true that locals acknowledge the important work of particular NGOs; yet, they are often more interested in talking about the pitfalls and shortcomings of the country's NGOs turn and the behavior of many of the international actors that intervened in Bosnian society over the years.[20] Many stressed that, despite the money that once flowed from international actors, it has always been difficult to get financing for training, education, and capacity building for Bosnian organizations. Changing priorities and inconsistencies in funding and leadership created fundamental problems for the stability of local NGOs, even those that were active and strongly supported at one time. The money appeared, but usually with strings attached, and then it disappeared suddenly, which made it almost impossible for local groups to stick to a particular agenda or plan for the long term. This was the real problem with NGOs and international peacebuilding: much was promised but little was delivered.

Bosnians do not deny that, in obvious ways, the big experiment helped certain groups and it focused attention on overlooked and neglected issues, but after years of testing and experimentation, they saw things differently; they saw how international peacebuilding actually unfolds and the limits of foreign generosity. Many different kinds of international donors arrived to help, but they were interested in funding specific kinds of projects that conformed to their predetermined goals of what Bosnia needed (and what their groups would fund). Others arrived with the specific goal of developing "a new breed of NGOs" in Bosnia that did not have prewar ties and that represented liberal ideals (Praxis Paper 2006). This support indeed helped certain individuals and specific groups, but it rarely lasted long or proved beneficial.

Muhidin Mulalic (2011) explains how international policies supported the growth and trajectory of women's groups in Bosnia. The first independent women's organizations in Bosnia were formed by volunteers in Sarajevo and Tuzla, where women came together during the war to help victims of the violence. Throughout the war, women's groups worked with numerous international organizations, governments, and private foundations, and the earliest and most active groups were indigenous organizations responding to domestic needs. After the war ended, and because of the assumption that men make war and women make peace, a lot changed for Bosnian women's groups. Western donors and international NGOs intentionally and specifically reached out to women and women's organizations, funding scores of new organizations and countless projects to work on trauma, ethnic reconciliation, and legal reform.

By the end of the 1990s, the proliferation of women's groups was palpable, with almost three hundred Bosnian women's organizations registered, most of which received all of their funding from international sources (Walsh 2000). As an NGO activist who has been involved in women's organizing since the early 1990s explained, international donors provided incalculable support for Bosnian women and emerging women's NGOs. At least at first, this international intervention helped Bosnian women connect with each other, and it provided numerous opportunities for them to connect with women from all over the world.[21] Over time, though, the dynamics changed and interests morphed, but foreign money continued to pay for conferences, research, and it helped publish books and manuals on a variety of issues related to women's empowerment, feminism, and violence against women. For international donors, the importance of funding women's NGOs was obvious, and donors and locals alike benefited from this mutually advantageous relationship—at least for a while.

The Difficult Truths

For many good reasons, it is hard to get beyond NGO numbers and sort out the broader impact of these organizations on policies and lives. Independent evaluations of Bosnia's NGO sector and secondary sources as well as fieldwork do, however, provide some sense of the impact of the NGO experiment. While not conclusive, there is little evidence that the boom of the 1990s translated into many long-term benefits for the local NGO sector or the country more generally. In fact, because local NGOs depended on external donors for support and direction, Bosnian NGOs remained weak and unconnected, failing to develop a strong identity. And instead of cultivating a network of public and private actors committed to transforming Bosnian society and advancing peace, international policies and practices resulted in the "NGOiza-tion" of society, or the creation of NGOs that were disembedded from local structures and needs.

International NGOs arrived and domestic NGOs grew, and some of these groups engaged in important and inspiring projects. They also employed thousands of Bosnians over the course of many years; yet, these facts aside, it is still difficult to garner much evidence that points to how NGOs impacted specific policies, let alone advanced broader sociopolitical outcomes like de-mocracy, peace, or reconciliation. In different ways, scholars have acknowl-edged some of these difficult truths, describing how the NGO boom of the late 1990s went bust, leaving behind "paper NGOs" and groups that did little more than respond to international agendas (Bieber 2002, 26–28; Pickering 2007, 124). The situation however had other, less obvious effects on Bosnian society and peacebuilding which were even more distressing.

As one EU evaluation put it, because so many Bosnian NGOs were weak or marginalized from sociopolitical processes, new mechanisms needed to be established to activate NGOs and get them involved in policymaking (*Mapping Study of Non-State Actors* 2005, 8). Yet, even these new mechanisms were created "because of the pressure coming from international actors" and not because of the strength of the organizations themselves. While this in-ternational pressure may appear to be positive, it only continues to simulate real changes within Bosnia. By the early 2000s, several informal NGO net-works were established to coordinate the activities of the numerous women's organizations, youth groups, or transitional justice groups, providing some with evidence of the society's maturation and movement toward democracy. Unfortunately, the NGO networks were not well coordinated, the exchange of information was poor, and, like the NGOs themselves, the networks emerged only because of pressure coming from outside the country instead of through internal, organic processes (*Mapping Study of Non-State Actors* 2005). In both cases, it was still international actors and not domestic ones that were pushing for change.

Not all Bosnian NGOs were weak or ineffective. Some have, in fact, adapted well to changing international goals, but the NGOs that did sur-vive, and even those that thrived, were often not the ones that international peace builders tended to support. Two basic kinds of NGOs emerged in post-Dayton Bosnia: mutual or member benefit organizations (MBOs) and public benefit organizations (PBOs) (*Civil Society in Bosnia and Herzegovina*

2011). Mutual benefit organizations are focused on activities like sports, hobbies, or veterans' issues while public benefit organizations provide public goods and work on behalf of the welfare of the country, filling in for a weak government or advocating for certain causes. In Bosnia today, MBOs are quite active and fairly strong, even though these were not the groups that donors funded or international peace builders maintained were essential for Bosnian peace and stability. With every passing year, however, the public benefit organizations that were created to monitor the government or advocate on behalf of certain interests or actors are fading away.

In specific areas, international intervention in civil society has had a big impact, and issues like women's empowerment have been "well covered and appear to be the strongest organizationally and financially," while other issues, such as economic development and education, were largely neglected by international peace builders (*Mapping Study of Non-State Actors* 2005, 75). As one NGO official explained, this is because international donors like to fund programs that show short-term, tangible effects, and this is why they are less eager to fund education or training programs, because their effects cannot be measured easily.[22] They also cannot point easily to their unique accomplishments, which is important to donors. Bosnians have come to believe that an important part of the international experiment is funding what foreign governments and international organizations want and prioritize, putting money behind projects and groups that they believe are important, regardless of what locals say or need. Consequently, Bosnia's NGO sector is often characterized by duplication in some areas (like women's issues), while other areas receive little funding and attention, like training and economic development (*Civil Society in Bosnia and Herzegovina* 2011, 9).

International actors' interest in transitional justice is a good example of how good intentions can go awry and interfere with what some Bosnian NGOs want and need for peace to advance (Irvine and McMahon 2013). Victims associations have existed since the war's end throughout the country; they are ethnically defined, and most are primarily interested in identifying family members and holding individuals accountable.[23] Reconciliation may be one of their goals, but this is not their top priority. Consequently, international donors have tended to ignore victims' associations and their priorities, even though they are, in fact, committed to justice and accountability. The problem is their projects rarely cross ethnic lines, and they do not conform to donors' visions for how Bosnian NGOs should look and what they ought to focus on. Rather than working with existing, indigenous organizations and supporting their activities, international donors instead funded new NGOs and projects that aimed to bring together "moderates" and emphasized peacebuilding and reconciliation.

For many Bosnians, the international community's attitude toward transitional justice was patronizing, misplaced, and impatient. It was also symptomatic of the way international actors approached civil society development and peacebuilding in Bosnia. By creating new actors and demanding interethnic accommodation, largely by holding funding captive, international actors, in effect, minimized the suffering of victims and the participation of local groups. In other words, peacebuilding discouraged process in favor of predetermined outcomes, inadvertently preventing locals from grieving or presenting their own perspectives.

International involvement in this issue area not only hindered dialogue and debate, but it failed to provide locals with the resources, time, and space to come up with their own ways to come to terms with their difficult past. By neglecting victims' associations and other local initiatives that had not approached transitional justice in a way that international actors deemed appropriate, this only encouraged local groups to turn to politicians who were eager to exploit ethnic grievances.[24] In the end, international experiments and preconceived ideas created obstacles for transitional justice, the development of local NGOs, and reconciliation.

Women's groups, by contrast, have been significantly and positively affected by international involvement, as several authors make plain.[25] Yet, international involvement is rarely one-dimensional, and in this issue area as well, the international community's meddling contributed to a striking and unfortunate dynamic: the failure of many women's NGOs to communicate and cooperate with each other, despite common interests and long-term goals. A well-respected leader of one Bosnian women's organization, who has been involved in women's organizing since the early 1990s, had much to say on the topic of the international community's "interference" in Bosnia's civil society.[26] Although she readily acknowledged the benefits of foreign funds to help Bosnian women and establish women's organizations, she could not hide her disappointment and frustration with what she called "the Western project" in her country: "The so-called experts came, but they didn't know anything about Bosnia or the people who lived here . . . they brought their experience from other places, but they should have also listened to local people."[27]

Such comments about the international community's unwillingness to listen and inability to accept, let alone appreciate, the activities and experience of local groups are sadly not limited to transitional justice or women's empowerment. This is because locals and internationals alike acknowledge a similar imperialist dynamic as international actors engaged in civil society development in Bosnia. As one international official put it, international actors pay lip service to helping Bosnians, but they just do not get what civil society is or how it is built.[28] Instead, internationals do what they think is appropriate to support their goals, changing priorities and strategies as they see fit, knowing that locals have little choice but to follow their lead. International groups also have "their favorites," funding the same local groups over and over again, regardless of whether the local NGO is supported or has been able to achieve its objectives (*Mapping Study of Non-State Actors* 2005, 74).

Bosnia's NGO sector has changed in important ways since the mid-1990s, but even after years of money and support, intractable problems with the country's NGO sector are evident, PBOs, if they exist at all, are weak and still depend on external funding for their support and direction. To an unfortunate extent, these NGOs also remain project-based and must respond to the whims of their international donors. As a European Union report put it, although Bosnia's NGO sector was improving by the middle of the 2000s, there was still little evidence to conclude that, with more time and less international funding, local NGOs will ever become important domestic actors (*Mapping Study of Non-State Actors* 2005, 80). In fact, NGOs face even more difficulties in maintaining their long-term sustainability, because they exist only as long as the projects exist, which means they advocate for issues as long as they get paid.

USAID, which evaluates countries' NGO sectors according to seven criteria, arrived at a similar conclusion. Although a lot has happened in Bosnia in the last two decades, the NGO sector is still not mature or self-sufficient. USAID's most recent evaluation of the country's NGO sector, in fact, highlights some of the achievements, including signs of cooperation and networking among certain NGOs as well as government interest and reliance on choice NGOs. Yet, it ultimately concludes that Bosnia's NGO sector remains in "mid-transition" (as it was in 1999), with NGOs only beginning to play a role in making policy (2008 NGO Sustainability Index, 2008). For the Olaf Palme International Center, part of the problem with NGOs in Bosnia, like other parts of the Balkans, is that these organizations do not enjoy the trust of the people or the government. Unfortunately, Bosnian NGOs lack experience and they are perceived as income generators for those who are lucky enough to be employed by them (Evaluation of Support to the Civil Society in the Western Balkans 2010).

There have been notable success stories, where Bosnian NGOs have been active and coordinated on certain projects, particularly in places like Sarajevo and Tuzla. Unfortunately, there are far more examples of bad practices, corruption, and NGOs that exist only to receive international funds with few outcomes to report. This is because most Bosnian NGOs lack domestic roots and legitimacy, and thus they are unable to engage in effective advocacy or outreach (Živanović 2006, 39–53). Even Bosnians who have been involved in this sector have a hard time listing the concrete achievements of the NGO boom or concluding that NGOs have, in fact, strengthened civil society or contributed in some tangible way to building peace or democracy in the country.[29] International involvement in this area has produced an unfortunate dynamic; Westerners come to Bosnia wanting to make a difference, but what has happened is that NGOs—both international and national—have kidnapped civil society and they have instead pursued their own interests.[30]

The central justification for civil society development through NGOs is clear and perhaps unassailable: nongovernmental organizations could provide much-needed assistance, particularly to marginalized and vulnerable groups. At the same time, because of their status as nonstate actors and their connections with Western actors, NGOs could bridge many gaps: between the state and antagonist elements of society, between domestic and international groups, and between public and private groups. The hope and promise was that, in time, civil society development through the creation of NGOs would provide services that the government could not, and that NGOs' practices and spirit would trickle down and transform Bosnian society. Democracy, ethnic moderation, and stability would follow naturally from the NGO boom and the international community's experiments in Bosnia.

Without a doubt, it takes a long time for such changes to occur, but primary and secondary sources as well as fieldwork over the course of many years provide little evidence that the power of Bosnian NGOs is starting to "kick in," proving important to these outcomes, or even that NGOs have modestly improved everyday life. After almost two decades of money and support, the NGOization of Bosnia is coming to an end; most of the internationals have gone home, and the NGOs that remain are either unable or unwilling to engage in the kinds of sociopolitical activities international actors once promised. The frenzy of activities and promises, which heightened expectations as well as the hunt for funding, however, has left something behind: disconnected groups and mistrust. As one report put it, NGOs and civil society organizations in Bosnia are viewed with indifference and are disengaged or mistrusted by the public (*Civil Society in Bosnia and Herzegovina* 2011). A 2011 report was equally pessimistic about the future of NGOs in Bosnia, concluding that the country suffers from "a high level of social apathy, reflected in low levels of civic engagement. Both the linkages between ordinary citizens and civil society (as advocates of citizens' interests) and the level of interaction between civil society and government are underdeveloped, leaving the majority of citizens unconnected to political processes" (*Strategy for Western Balkans 2012–2015* 2011).

From Savior to Something Else

International peacebuilding has achieved a great deal in Bosnia. Violence has not returned, and stability has become the norm. At the same time, even in 2015 politicians regularly threaten to unravel the country.[31] The 2006 elections, once deemed the most important since the war's end in 1995 because of the planned departure of the High Representative, were instead fraught with nationalist rhetoric and divisiveness. With some Bosnian leaders still calling for the country's division, no date has been set for the High Representative's departure. For years, official unemployment has hovered around 40 percent, almost 20 percent of the country lives in poverty, and another 30 percent is in danger of falling into poverty.[32] Although Bosnians engage in many forms of remembrance and reflection, there is little sign of reconciliation or genuine reunification. NGOs are rarely involved in policymaking, and civil society remains weak and divided. What happened to the NGO activities, and why did involvement in this sector fail to help transform the country?

Domestic factors, including the country's multiethnic nature and its history as well as its fragile political environment, are certainly most responsible for the country's weak NGO sector and the persistence of nationalism in Bosnian society. However, international peacebuilding has also contributed to the problems that have unfolded, specifically why Bosnian NGOs have failed to become embedded in local structures and agents of progressive change. Institutional theories, particularly rational institutionalism, focus on material structures and incentives and constraints, while historical and sociological institutionalism emphasizes identities, ideas, and understandings in shaping behavior. Using insights from different institutional approaches, the following highlights how Bosnia's unique setting and actors' interests, as well as ideas, unintentionally but decisively fueled Bosnia's NGO bust. International actors, including international NGOs, arrived wanting to help, but as the processes unfolded, there was no consensus among the international peace builders on how to move the country forward, particularly in the area of civil society development.

One of the most important take-home points from Bosnia's reconstruction is that more is not necessarily better. The presence of so many international actors in peacebuilding discourages even the most committed actors from following through on promises. This is particularly true when it comes to the ambitious but vague notion of strengthening civil society. Within a year of the war's end, at least two hundred international NGOs, eighteen UN agencies, and twenty-seven intergovernmental organizations, as well as seventeen different foreign governments were actively involved in putting Bosnia back together (ICVA 2000). And these numbers only include larger organizations, because many groups failed to register themselves with any international body. Despite a large number of public and private actors involved in reconstruction, many still referred to the "international community's work" in Bosnia as if the community was a single entity that acted in a coherent and planned way to achieve a common goal. In reality, nothing could be further from the truth, and this was the case even when the Dayton Peace Accords were signed in 1995.[33]

Three categories of organizations have been involved in reconstructing the country: Western governments, primarily those on the steering board of the Peace Implementing Council (PIC), intergovernmental organizations like the United Nations and NATO, as well as all sorts of international NGOs, from relief organizations to private foundations to for-profit contractors.[34] At best, the international community has been a conglomeration of somewhat like-minded organizations with different and even contradictory objectives. The director of a Sarajevo-based NGO explained it this way: "The international community made a big mistake in Bosnia; it basically threw a lot of money at the country's problems without agreeing on the solution."[35] International actors descended, and soon thousands of Bosnian groups emerged, but little thought was given to *what* these organizations were doing, *how* they should approach civil society development, or even *whom* they were supposed to serve. What was undeniable was that international players arrived; the involvement of so many public and private actors helped to legitimize international peacebuilding efforts, but this did not guarantee that peacebuilding would be successful. It simply means that no actor is in charge and that no single organization can be held accountable. Good, bad, or irrelevant, no one can be blamed when things do not go as planned or promised.

The big experiment in Bosnia not only included lots of different actors, but the environment created by the Dayton Peace Agreement left many issues intentionally vague, open-ended, and internally inconsistent. As Ambassador Richard Holbrooke once remarked, Dayton sought to please everyone without satisfying anyone; the Dayton "solution," however, left crucial issues about the country's future up in the air, to be determined over time but reliant solely on the goodwill of international actors (Holbrooke 1998). In other words, the peace agreement and the institutions created by Dayton exacerbated an already fragile environment, which rational institutionalists flag as contributing to surprising and dysfunctional outcomes.

The annexes of the Dayton peace treaty explained what international bodies were tasked to do, but no part of the agreement specified how these objectives would be implemented. And nothing was said about what would happen if international organizations failed to carry out their assigned responsibilities. From the outset, Dayton and the peacebuilding mission in Bosnia suffered from an "enforcement gap" in the event that promises were not kept (Daalder 1999, 174). As institutional theories predict, so many different organizations, operating in an uncertain environment, allowed actors to shirk their responsibilities and pursue their own goals and narrow organizational imperatives. Put differently, because of the structure of peacebuilding and the country's tenuous institutions, international actors could attend to their own mandates and missions, ignoring their promises to advance peace and strengthen civil society. And often they did.

The Office of the High Representative (OHR) was created to establish a framework to address the problem of so many actors and to coordinate, oversee, and implement the so-called will of the international community. The OHR was supposed to be the voice of the international community, but it actually represented fifty-five members of the Peace Implementing Council (PIC) and other members of the international community. Despite the creation of this office to centralize and coordinate international policies and priorities, Western governments and international organizations still had—and acted on—their own priorities, adopting different strategies and tactics for operating in Bosnia (Jarstad 2008, 31). After 2002, the OHR also represented the European Union, giving the office even more responsibility.

Despite this office's expanding duties and the obvious need to coordinate international and domestic activities, the OHR was never given the authority or the resources to manage its responsibilities or the conflicting priorities of international actors. Over time, the OHR's responsibilities grew and its staff and budget ballooned. Then it shrank substantially, but all the while, the OHR's authority remained ill-defined, subordinated to NATO and military objectives, and vulnerable to the personality and leadership style of the High Representative. Even in 2012, the OHR was alternately praised and blamed, because its role was not clear and it lacked enforcement capability to carry out necessary reforms.[36] Because of Dayton's structure, no single organization was in charge, and thus there was no way to monitor how closely international promises corresponded with Bosnian reality.

Civil society development was certainly identified as an international priority, but the process and policies adopted to implement it were vague and open-ended, allowing different organizations to support the actors and projects each thought were most crucial. In hindsight, this was a serious mistake, because the proliferation of so many initiatives and international actors involved in civil society hindered communication and coordination, even among the most experienced international players. An official from the OSCE remarked that, when he first arrived in Bosnia (after working in Kosovo), he was genuinely surprised that the international community's approach to civil society development was still so "up in the air," and that there were so few mechanisms in place to connect international and local organizations or to monitor their activities.[37] Even the OSCE, which had worked continuously with NGOs in Bosnia since 1996, did not have what he called a "global approach" for working with international and local actors.

Since the OSCE had no comprehensive list of its NGO partners in Bosnia, it had no way of knowing what this sector did, let alone estimating the particular and unique contributions of NGOs. All of this made it impossible to take stock of lessons learned or to avoid duplication, and even like-minded

Bosnian NGOs found cooperation with other local NGOs difficult and somewhat unnecessary given the proliferation of international actors (and their money) engaged in civil society development. Acknowledging the ongoing problems with coordination in 2008, a Department for Cooperation with NGOs was created within the Bosnian government. Even after a few years and despite the obvious need for such an office to give the sector more cohesion and organization, the Department was not functional. The NGO world in Bosnia has become less cluttered with every passing year, but it is still unorganized and suffers from a lack of transparency and accountability.

In addition to an uncertain environment of too many actors to coordinate and monitor, civil society development was implemented by international groups with particular ideas about the role and function of NGOs. In the city of Brčko, for example, which was once the site of intense ethnic violence, international actors funded lots of NGOs as part of a broader campaign to develop civil society as a way of promoting ethnic reconciliation. It was clear, though, that internationals and locals saw the role and importance of NGOs differently. After several years of reconstruction, Brčko was rebuilt, and examples of ethnic cooperation were evident. However, successes in Brčko were not attributed to NGOs or to any real changes in society. Interviews with international and domestic officials over the course of several years confirmed that neither international nor domestic NGOs played much of a role in interethnic cooperation or the city's development.[38] OSCE officials admitted, that although the OSCE spent a lot of money and time promoting and investing in Brčko's NGO sector, working hard to make NGOs both self-sustaining and multiethnic after several years, they were neither.[39]

Interviewing the director of a Brčko office that was created specifically to assist and coordinate NGO activities, it was clear that, although the "civil society development through NGOs" message had been received in this city, NGOs had not taken root. In fact, the local groups did not emerge organically at all but were created because of international interests and investment. In general, residents of, Brčko, regardless of ethnicity, were skeptical of the NGO craze that had engulfed other parts of Bosnia. "Before I worked here, like most people here, I had a negative impression of NGOs . . . some (NGOs) might be working in an aggressive way, but they were not really grassroots organizations."[40] The director went on to explain that "Here [in Brčko] we have around four hundred NGOs, but maybe there are no real NGOs, because in Brčko people prefer politics and politics pays better. I once asked young people why are there no NGOs working on environmental issues. They answered that there are no NGOs working on this because there was no funds for that."[41]

Not everyone in Bosnia is this cynical about NGOs and their role in the country's reconstruction. The director of the Nansen Dialogue Centre in Sarajevo who works on peace, for example, maintains that international involvement in the country's NGO sector has overall been quite positive. However, she stressed that the outcomes depended on the motivations of both international and domestic actors, which are diverse and hard to simplify.[42] The Dialogue Centre was created in 1994 with the help of the Norwegian government. The Norwegian government has continued to provide financial assistance, training, and other support for the Centre's activities, but they have had a "hands off" attitude, allowing Bosnians themselves to develop and implement projects without setting the agenda or limiting their choices. It is, however, well known that most other international players are not this flexible about the kinds of projects that are created or how they are implemented. Too often, international actors set the agenda by presenting local groups with a call for proposals containing priority areas and funding interests. In the end, the groups chosen for funding must have a certain level of capacity, specifically language skills to interact with donors.

NGOs are not all the same and neither are the interests of international and local NGOs. The international community's interest in supporting local NGOs provided some of these nonstate actors with unprecedented opportunities to carry out certain activities, but in this complex setting, driven by different and changing interests but also a need for measurable outputs, the result was "a constant withering and replenishment of local organizations and the growth of a large but nonspecialized, short-term oriented and financially insecure sector" (Praxis Paper 2006, 17). Put differently, international interest funded certain organizations and activities, but this did not mean that they responded to grassroots needs or that the organizations necessarily reflected local interests. Moreover, the structure of international peacebuilding, particularly the large assortment of actors with diverse and, in some cases, unknown interests, made it almost impossible for local NGOs to build a local constituency or plan for the future. And as aid money decreased, uncertainty, divergent interests and declining interest created a perfect storm for gaming the system.

In 1996, for example, the European Union spent over 440 million euros in Bosnia; by 2000 the amount dropped to 100 million euros, and by 2006, it was down to 64 million euros (EU assistance to BiH 2007). U.S. assistance followed a similar pattern, dropping from a high of $300 million in 1998 to around $70 million in 2006 (U.S. Overseas Loans and Grants 2007). As this international assistance continued to decline, both international and local NGOs were pressured to do more while remaining flexible to respond to new international priorities and funding opportunities. At the same time, donors increasingly emphasized the importance of NGO cooperation, even though dwindling international funds militated against them doing so for fear that they would receive even less money.

As important as international involvement has been to saving this country, Bosnians regularly complain about the complications and counterintuitive effects associated with its interventions into civil society. It is not just local actors' dependence on funding that is problematic; it is also a problem of how international actors behaved, saying one thing and doing another or failing to follow through on what they promised. All of this made Bosnians lose faith and interest in NGOs and their potential, especially the organizations and issues prioritized by international actors. When I asked about the specific effects of international intervention in Bosnian society, an official of the Human Rights Center in Sarajevo replied, "I think the situation is much worse now than it was in years past . . . people are simply tired. Before there was a lot of energy and spirit . . . but now we're stuck."[43]

After years of toiling away and chasing international money, Bosnians are worn-out and overwhelmed, appreciating now that NGOs are only a very small part of the solution to the country's problems. NGOs may be able to fix things at the margins and in specific circumstances, but peacebuilding takes commitment and leadership. It also takes certain domestic institutions, consistency, and focus—all things that international actors have neglected. As one Bosnian NGO official put it, "International involvement has helped Bosnian society in ways, but because donors' interests changed all the time, and most were not interested in funding overhead or supporting capacity building for Bosnian NGOs, there have been lots of projects but the country has no real civil society."[44]

The NGO bust in Bosnia is also due to a clash of understandings between internationals and locals over how the country should develop. The anthropologist Steven Sampson (2002), whose ethnographic research mapped civil society in the Balkans, has much to say about how different histories, identities, and ideas informed and misinformed the policies and practices of international actors in this region. His research concludes that misunderstandings between internationals and locals were, in fact, evident shortly after peacebuilding began, because of actors' experiences and worldviews but also because of power differences. Emerging from years of conflict and decades of Tito's independent brand of communism, many Bosnians were understandably wary of foreign involvement. After reluctantly intervening, and well after the violence began, representatives of international organizations on the ground proved to be ignorant and insensitive to the country's history and experiences. Nonetheless, Bosnians had nowhere else to turn for money and support, and even if international actors did not understand what they had experienced or shared their beliefs, at least they showed up and claimed that they wanted to help.

Asserting that Bosnia suffered from a weak (or even nonexistent) civil society, Western actors engaged in "benevolent colonialism," exerting their power in ways they believed were helpful but, in fact, were condescending and self-interested. Resources, people, and practices created "embedded interests" for international and local NGOs which suddenly had an important role to play in peace and development (Sampson 2002). Put differently, international peacebuilding was based on ideas and practices that included lots of funding for international NGOs and particular liberal projects. But this made international actors, rather than local NGOs and indigenous ideas, irreplaceable to the country's development. In the process, international actors did not address problems by allowing locals to solve problems on their own; instead, they relied on their own so-called experts, underscoring the importance of projects and partnerships all the while creating new interests and ways for Bosnians to behave (if they wanted to rebuild their country and receive Western assistance). Although guided by good intentions, international actors still treated Bosnia as a backward country; it was a problem to be fixed and not people to be empowered.

For Bosnians, rebuilding after the chaos of war and during a period when jobs were scarce and conditions were hard, the NGO game provided both resources and opportunities. Not only was money available for certain kinds of projects and to create organizations, but the NGO world offered useful contacts, chances to travel, and even long-term stays in Western countries. To be clear, international peace builders did not impose or coerce Bosnians, but the relationships were not devoid of power or an explicit agenda. Bosnian elites understood this well, recognizing that to continue receiving money and support from Western donors, they needed to listen and heed the advice of internationals. Yet, despite a discourse that focused heavily on civil society development, partnership, and democracy promotion, many Bosnians perceived these policies and practices to be foisted on them or at least done to them, and on many issues, mutually agreed-on strategies and goals were elusive.

The NGO game that accompanied international peacebuilding in Bosnia was different for all the players involved. For a while, everyone benefited from the money and ideas that were available in generous amounts. The benefits, however, did not last long before dwindling budgets, different international priorities, and certain realities set in. As NGOs came and went and proved extraneous to domestic change, Bosnians became increasingly suspicious and disillusioned with these actors and their policies. At best, NGOs were seen as a source of income and a well-intentioned distraction. At worst, they were regarded as symbols of the West's mission and another obstacle to genuine peace and development. As one Bosnian scholar lamented, "Civil society development is mission impossible; despite large doses of international assistance being injected into Bosnian society, only a few hundred NGOs are active in the country, and far fewer have succeeded in playing any role in promoting good governance" (Živanović 2006, 39).

The NGO frenzy is over in Bosnia, but international and local NGOs are still sprinkled throughout the country. Most of them are local NGOs, and while they may be active, it would not be fair to say that they are not important agents of liberal peacebuilding. There is also little reason to believe that these particular organizations will someday play an important role in shaping policies or advancing peace. Indeed, most of the evidence presented suggests that just the opposite is true. At the same time, the international community's reliance on NGOs was not wholly negative, and a thin version of peace prevails. This is not, however, the same as saying that the NGO boom in the 1990s has helped build democracy or promoted peace in this country. In fact, most of the NGOs proved to be temporary; they were dependent actors that did not enjoy much grassroots support, and most were unable or unwilling to engage in broader activities.

By necessity, I had to streamline a lot of what transpired in Bosnia over the past two decades. However, the goal was to explore how international peacebuilding, with its attention to NGOs affected the country's NGO sector and to see whether promises made about NGOs lived up to expectations. Given the NGO realities after years of investment, international actors have acknowledged many of their mistakes. For the United States, disappointment with Bosnian NGOs has meant working more with contractors and for-profit organizations that promised to work toward certain liberal goals and agreed to specific, measurable deliverables.[45] In fact, all international actors have focused more attention on the Bosnian state and entity institutions, making assistance to NGOs conditional on cooperation with government bodies or other NGOs.[46] The European Union has also shifted away from funding NGOs and civil society to focusing squarely on helping the Bosnian government as it prepares for the country's accession in the European Union. The European Commission, for example, now focuses most of its assistance on strengthening government institutions, rule of law, and economic development, and since 2005, it has made funding for NGOs contingent on their cooperation with other NGOs and with the government (Fagan 2006).

Some international donors, like the Swedish government, continue to support local NGOs and encourage them to develop their capacity by building NGO networks, creating umbrella organizations, and conducting research that takes stock of the lessons learned since international intervention began.[47] Similarly, in the mid-2000s Catholic Relief Services overhauled its international assistance programs, making domestic capacity building a priority and taking specific steps to empower Bosnian NGOs and locals. In other words, mistakes have been acknowledged, and changes have been implemented. The NGO game is largely over in Bosnia; unfortunately, there is no clear victor in sight.

Chapter 4

Kosovo

Copy, Paste, and Delete

The changes in Kosovo were subtle, but they were unmistakable and not positive. As a journalist at *Koha Ditore*, one of Kosovo's main newspapers, put it, once international actors intervened and started supporting civil society, social actors looked and behaved differently. With money and attention being thrown at them, "The locals themselves transformed and no longer seemed to focus on what was important to locals; instead, they suddenly dressed differently, talked differently and acted differently. They didn't live in [Kosovo's] civil society."[1] Kosovars may have indeed noticed these changes after NATO-led intervention began and international actors descended on the region, but research on reconstruction in this southern Balkan country rarely pays attention to what happened to Kosovo's once vibrant society. Perhaps this is because donors and peacebuilding agents assumed that civil society did not exist in Kosovo before the West intervened. In truth, Western actors just failed to notice domestic realities and they were indifferent to how their actions affected everyday life.

In 1999, when NATO-led interveners landed in this part of Serbia, the situation differed significantly from Bosnia's reality at the end of 1995. Nonetheless, international engagement in Kosovo was regularly compared to and modeled on its neighbor to the north and even to post-conflict situations elsewhere. This is why Kosovars joke that when it came to international peacebuilding, Western governments and international NGOs had Bosnia, Rwanda, or some other far away country on their mind, adopting a "copy, paste and delete" strategy in their policies and practices. Projects and strategies from other post-conflict countries were not just modeled on those elsewhere, they were blatantly copied and then thrust on Kosovars, who were treated as if they did not know how to do things on their own. The problem was that neither did international actors, who often appeared to care less about Kosovo's history or its precarious political status. Apparently, money and good intentions were more important than policies tailored to the peculiarities of the conditions on the ground.[2]

In one very important respect, this slice of Serbia differed from other post-conflict environments because, by the time international intervention began, Albanian Kosovars already had a vibrant, and even effective, civil society. In fact, for almost a decade, numerous civil society organizations had provided a range of services. Theoretically, these indigenous organizations could have provided a solid foundation for Western donors interested in partnering with local organizations. International peace builders certainly identified civil society development as an important goal, but this did not mean the strengthening of existing organizations. Instead, local groups became "paid suits"; they "put on ties and got on TV" and advanced the priorities and strategies of international actors, rather than the agenda of locals.[3] After more than a decade and a half of investment and engagement, Kosovo's once vibrant society remains fragmented and doubts about the success of international peacebuilding remain. As a 2012 USAID report observed, constituency building by civil society organizations remains in its infancy, and the priorities of these organizations often do not reflect the international community's goals in Kosovo (*The CSO Sustainability Index* 2013). The question is: What went wrong?

International intervention paved the way for Kosovo's independence in 2008, but it also altered Kosovar society, changing the incentives for social organizing and reducing the need for social solidarity and entrepreneurship.

Since international donors were initially opposed to Kosovar independence, many of the strongest and most active civil society organizations were not funded, opening the door wide for international NGOs to do what they pleased. There were many reasons that both the spirit of self-reliance and social mobilization were not sustained during reconstruction, including the financial, socioeconomic, and political calculations of locals.[4] But Kosovars realized quickly how the NGO game was played and that only certain kinds of social activism and organizations would enjoy the support of foreign donors.[5] An NGO boom indeed took place, but the new organizations and networks materialized because of donor interests and funding, not because liberal peacebuilding and democratic change had taken root.

This chapter looks at the effects of international peacebuilding from approximately 1999 until 2012, but it also provides some background on the history of this troubled region during the 1990s.[6] It relies on primary and secondary sources, including reports written by the United Nations and think tanks based in Kosovo, as well as on insights gleaned from semistructured interviews in 2011.[7] It argues that international actors were "vast and richly endowed and full of capabilities"; and despite the fact that many Kosovars, Albanians, and Serbs alike did not agree or support many of their goals, internationals were determined to reconcile society and create a multiethnic democracy in Kosovo. In the process, however, international actors and specifically the scores of NGOs that descended on the region crowded out, rather than complemented existing institutions. As Francis Fukuyama (2004, 103) warns, the dynamic between international actors and locals unintentionally weakened, rather than strengthened, the capacity of Kosovar civil society, and local organizations suffered as a result.

International Priorities and Policies

In March 1999, NATO intervened in the Balkans for the second time in Kosovo, the Albanian-dominated enclave nestled within southern Serbia. As an autonomous province in the Yugoslav federation, Kosovo once enjoyed a high degree of self-governance. This changed suddenly in 1989 when the Serb leadership rescinded its autonomy, and for almost a decade, Albanians were excluded and repressed by the Yugoslav government. Despite attempts by Albanian leaders to seek a peaceful resolution, civil war broke out in 1998. Between the actions of Yugoslav forces and NATO's short but effective bombing campaign, as many as ten thousand people were killed and about a million Kosovars were on the move.[8] By the summer of 1999, the UN Security Council created the United Nations Interim Mission in Kosovo (UNMIK) as a transitional governing authority, and international peacebuilding officially began. In the years since, the international presence has shrunk considerably, but to this day Western governments and international organizations still play an important role in governing Kosovo.[9]

International peacebuilding in Kosovo was fashioned closely on activities in Bosnia, even though the situation in these two places differed considerably. Not only was Kosovo legally part of Serbia in 1999, but a final resolution on the territory's future was not agreed upon when the international protectorate was established under the United Nations' leadership in June. Leaving many important political and economic decisions up in the air, international actors agreed on a set of principles to address Kosovo's status. First, there would be no border changes to accommodate ethnic differences. Second, there would be no union of Kosovo with Albania. Finally, there would be no reversion to the status quo, and Kosovar Albanians would not be subjected to the authoritarian policies of Serbia in the future.

Based on experiences and lessons learned in Bosnia, international actors settled on what seemed to be a clear leadership structure and agreed-on international mission. As important as its peacebuilding priorities were, however, international actors did not support the creation of an independent Kosovo. As UN Security Council Resolution 1244 made clear, once the withdrawal of Yugoslav and Serb militaries was complete, the United Nations would be in charge of establishing an international civil presence and supervising the interim administration. UNMIK created four thematic pillars for engagement to coordinate activities. "Unprecedented in scope and capacity" and led by the United Nations' special representative, the international community's agenda in Kosovo was carried out by an extensive network of public and private actors that sought to stabilize the region, reconstruct institutions of governance, promote democracy, and reconcile the people of Kosovo (Richmond and Franks 2009). Unfortunately, within a short time these pillars became muddled and the international community's mission expanded, encompassing a broad range of activities from providing humanitarian assistance to promoting stability to governing the country. International actors tried hard to avoid the mistakes made in Bosnia, but the assortment of public and private actors involved lacked a clear and comprehensive plan for how it wanted to accomplish its goals in Kosovo.

Officially, NATO intervened in this part of Serbia to halt the "humanitarian catastrophe" and to restore stability to the inheritors of the former Yugoslavia (NATO 2005). After two months, NATO's bombing campaign ended and the NATO-led Kosovo Protection Force (KFOR) was established. At its peak KFOR included some fifty thousand foreign troops from thirty-nine NATO and non-NATO countries. In addition to helping with the return of refugees and internally displaced persons (IDPs), KFOR provided internal security and protected minorities, paying close attention to ethnic reprisals against Kosovar Serbs. Despite international promises and KFOR's impressive size, whose foreign troops' presence was one of the largest in a peacebuilding mission on a per capita basis, about half of the prewar Serb population fled, and those who remained were isolated in KFOR-guarded areas.[10]

Tensions between ethnic Albanians and Serbs, did not disappear, especially in northern parts of Kosovo and in the divided city of Mitrovica. International efforts to provide security were not accomplished immediately, but most accounts of KFOR's mission were quite positive and violence reoccurred only briefly in 2004. Even after Kosovar leaders unilaterally declared the country's independence in February 2008, which many feared would lead to violence, stability increased and NATO-led troops were able to withdraw. By the beginning of 2012, fewer than ten thousand foreign troops remained in Kosovo.

Stopping the violence and creating a stable environment were both necessary to allow the international community to accomplish its secondary goal of rebuilding Kosovo's damaged and outdated infrastructure and establish institutions of governance. Kosovo's political future was not clear, but the international community still committed itself to creating a modern democratic entity in this part of the Balkans. Almost immediately, UNMIK created Provisional Institutions of Self-Government (PISG), and elections were held. According to UN Resolution 1244, the United Nations and other international actors had final authority over the region, and domestic institutions would be "supervised" by international actors. International supervision effectively translated into directing and controlling many decisions, because regardless of the sector or issue area, decisions both big and small were ulti-mately funded and addressed by the United Nations' special representative and other international officials. Frustrated with the international commu-nity's unwillingness to take a stronger position on its political future, in 2008, Kosovo's leaders declared that, although they were committed to protecting and promoting the rights of all peoples, Kosovo would no longer be part of Serbia and was an independent sovereign country. After indepen-dence was declared, UNMIK handed over most aspects of governance to Kosovo's Albanian leadership. However, the United Nations and members of the contact group as well as other international actors continued to be cen-trally involved in governing the newly independent country.[11]

Reconstructing Kosovo's infrastructure and its institutions of governance was directly linked to the third priority: transforming civil society and recon-ciling Kosovo's different ethnic groups, specifically the dominant Albanian population and the Serb minority. This final objective would be accomplished in various ways, though much money and rhetoric emphasized the impor-tance, if not the urgency, of strengthening Kosovo's civil society by supporting and cultivating grassroots organizations. As in Bosnia, it was in this area that both international and local NGOs received the most attention and financial support. Kosovo's status as an autonomous region within Serbia, however, made this task far more complicated. Since ethnic Albanians had been ex-cluded and repressed by the Yugoslav government after the Serb leadership rescinded its autonomy in 1989, local groups were created to fill in for re-treating state institutions and to help Kosovar Albanians.

The oppression and exclusion of Albanians from public life meant that the Kosovo's majority Albanian population spent almost a decade organ-izing independently of the government, and numerous, effective civil so-ciety organizations (CSOs) existed by the time UNMIK was established. However, if international actors were not careful, strengthening civil society and reconciling the population through the support of indigenous organ-izations would result merely in money and backing for Kosovar Alba-nians. Regardless of what international actors said and promised, they could not allow this to happen; they needed to support Serbian groups. Better yet, international actors would support brand new organizations that were committed to advancing liberal goals and transcending ethnic differences.

Strengthening and Transforming Civil Society

After Serbia revoked Kosovo's autonomous status in 1989 and reasserted direct rule on the region, the Yugoslav government withdrew all financial support for Kosovo and stopped providing public services. Left to fend for themselves, Kosovar Albanians created their own schools, health care centers, and governing institutions. In many ways, Kosovo's "parallel institutions," which formed spontaneously and were run almost entirely by volunteers, provided fertile ground for the international community to engage domestic partners and empower local nongovernmental organizations. Kosovo's civil society organizations were even considered to be quite effective, because they reflected the needs and interests of most of the population.

The Mother Teresa Society (MTS), for example, started in 1990 and provided health care and humanitarian aid to as many as 350,000 people at one point in time. MTS was independent and tried to remain above politics, but most of the other civil society organizations (CSOs) were, in fact, closely tied to Kosovo's civil resistance movement and reflected ethnic divisions. Given the Serbian republic's treatment of the majority Albanian population, it is not surprising that most of Kosovo's CSOs provided assistance and services to Albanians only. However, some of the CSOs were human rights and advocacy organizations, like the Council for the Defense of Human Rights and Freedom, and monitored and reported on human rights abuses against both Albanians and Serbs. Other organizations that developed later, including the Kosovo Action for Civil Initiative, Riinvest, and the Kosovo Foundation for Open Society also encouraged interaction across ethnic lines and were committed, at least in principle, to creating a multiethnic, democratic society.

But it was not only local NGOs in Kosovo that were divided, serving different groups and pursing different goals; this was also true of international NGOs that competed to be the leading voice of the international community's interests in Kosovo. By January 1999, about a dozen international NGOs formed the International NGO Council of Kosovo (INGO Council). NATO bombing from March to June of that year forced most of these international groups to relocate to the former Yugoslav Republic of Macedonia. From Macedonia, the INGO Council tried to lobby the United Nations and other international actors to help the refugees fleeing Kosovo and to respond more actively to the unfolding humanitarian crisis. However, during the summer of 1999, and because of a sudden and dramatic increase in international attention and donor money, the number of international NGOs working on Kosovo grew significantly; some operated in Kosovo directly but many were still located in Macedonia and other neighboring countries to avoid violating Serbia's sovereignty.

To collect and disseminate information about humanitarian activities and organizations based in Kosovo proper, a group of international NGOs created the NGO Focal Point. While the INGO Council and the NGO Focal Point were each taking shape, both pledging to work on behalf of Kosovars, the situation within the republic was changing rapidly. When the NATO campaign ended, even more international NGOs descended on the Balkans, creating an even more pronounced, but also more chaotic, NGO boom. Meanwhile, although the INGO Council and the NGO Focal Point each claimed to represent the NGO community working on Kosovo, the NGO boom meant that, even though only a few months had passed, there was no way any external group could say that they represented anyone in Kosovo, except perhaps themselves. In other words, even before UNMIK was established, the NGO game was being played with various international NGOs and other private actors competing with each other, claiming to work on behalf of Kosovars and their interests.

The United Nations, the OSCE, and the European Union were the dominant intergovernmental organizations in Kosovo in 1999, and each had different responsibilities and approaches to achieving their multiple, if overlapping, objectives. They were united, however, in the great significance they attached to strengthening civil society, explicitly relying on NGOs to rebuild and reconcile. As in other parts of Central and Eastern Europe, investments in this area were viewed as indispensable to creating a healthy, participatory, and modern democratic state. Shortly after UNMIK was established, in fact, a UN report noted that, despite the numerous organizations involved in the country's reconstruction, there was consensus on the priorities, including the need to assist the people of Kosovo in strengthening the capacity of local and central institutions and civil society organizations, as well as working with "the over 250 international NGOs and 45 local NGOs" (UN Security Council 1999).

The United Nations led the peacebuilding mission, but the OSCE and its mission in Kosovo were given the primary duty of institution and democracy building. For its part, the OSCE focused special attention on civil society development, particularly on supporting marginalized groups, such as women and minority populations. It also linked civil society development to democracy promotion, because "civil society plays an important and influential role in voicing citizens' interests and concerns before government" ("Supporting Democracy in Kosovo" 2002). Building the capacity of newly established NGOs and civil society groups was necessary to encourage citizens to participate in the democratic process. It was also inevitable for region's development. Working with the Kosovar Civil Society Foundation (KCSF), the OSCE tried to ensure that local NGOs were able to play an active and effective role in society.

Over time, the OSCE's involvement in this area was overshadowed by the European Union, which became Kosovo's largest donor. The European Union's policies and priorities for transitioning and candidate states in Central and Eastern Europe had long focused on civil society, and it too supported the development of local NGOs in Kosovo, largely for the same reasons.[12] In fact, many of the European Union's core objectives for post-communist countries involved building the capacity of local NGOs to work on a range of social, political, and economic issues. This was especially the case in post-conflict states in the Western Balkans, where the European Union was working with new states that had little experience with democracy (Fagan 2012, 9).

Before Kosovo's independence in 2008, the European Union was just one of many powerful international organizations operating in the region, and its most visible office, when it came to civil society development, was the European Agency for Reconstruction (EAR). Since Kosovo's provisional institutions did not have the capacity to manage and administer EU assistance, EAR programming and delivery followed what Adam Fagan (2012) calls a "centralized de-concentrated model"; this essentially allowed the European Commission to establish priorities and be directly involved with local groups. Put differently, during this period when it was supposedly strengthening Kosovar civil society, the European Union was instead creating civil society because of its influence over which groups were funded and the activities that were supported.

Initially, the European Union focused most of its money and efforts on providing humanitarian relief and services, but by 2005, it shifted to what it vaguely called civil society development, emphasizing capacity building and the sustainability of local groups. Working with the Agency for Coordination of Development and European Integration, but consulting different European organizations and member states as well as the United Nations and the World Bank, EAR programs relied heavily on NGOs. The aim of these programs was to strengthen "the capacities of key local NGOs that were deemed to have sufficient initial capacity and potential to manage the allocation of EU assistance and running training and capacity building workshops for smaller and weaker organizations" (Fagan 2012, 172–73). After Kosovo's independence in 2008, however, the European Union's funding strategy shifted again, and like other international donors, it started to channel most of its aid and technical support to government institutions, ensuring that these bodies were in line with European standards.

Since 2008, the most visible arm of the European Union's reach has been the Rule of Law Mission in Kosovo (or EULEX), which focuses on the rule of law and reforming the police, judiciary, and customs. Yet, the importance of supporting civil society did not disappear entirely, and the European Union regularly invited local organizations to meetings to provide assessments and to present their concerns. Nongovernmental organizations were also encouraged to work closely with national and international institutions, including the National Council for European Integration, the European Integration Task Force, the Kosovo Assembly Committee for European Integration, and the Ministry for European Integration. Although it is difficult to estimate just how much foreign money has gone to supporting Kosovar society and its nascent NGO sector, scholars maintain that policies and priorities in this area did not merely seek to strengthen Kosovar civil society or empower local actors. Instead, they aimed at fundamentally changing Kosovar society and transforming peoples' attitudes, and this "necessitated a radical shift of focus for civil society organizations from the politics of resistance to a politics of reconstruction and state-building" (UNDP 2008, 39).

To ensure the creation of a multiethnic Kosovar society, rather than a society that gave preference to Albanians, international actors actually avoided working with many of the already existing civil society organizations, promoting what one author called "the hitherto unfamiliar idea of the NGO" and stimulating the development of an NGO-based civil society to instill and create a culture of participatory democracy (Sterland 2006, 3). For a long time, the United Nations, the European Union, and the U.S. government, as well and other international donors, had framed their post-conflict reconstruction aid in terms of support for civil society, but in reality the policies and practices were often aimed at changing and restructuring society and grassroots organizations (Fagan 2012, 166). A strong and participatory civil society was deemed essential to the success of international peacebuilding for many reasons, including teaching citizens the habits and norms of participation and stimulating the economy. More importantly, civil society development was helpful for constructing EU-complaint frameworks and societies, which allowed European states to dominate agendas and influence the issues that were addressed in Kosovo. In other words, building civil society was both a means and an end for international actors committed to advancing global projects, primarily through local NGOs. These international investments moreover needed to be structured appropriately, because of the international community's overriding need for stability and thus the reconciliation of Kosovar Albanians and Serbs.

The Humanitarian Circus

Before UNMIK was established in 1999, international NGOs were involved in the work of feeding, housing, and caring for victims of repression and violence. But once UN offices opened their doors, Kosovo transformed rapidly. The NGO boom was fast and impressive. Although exact numbers are hard to find, one source estimated that within a matter of a few months, as many as four hundred international NGOs or other private international actors were on the ground working in Kosovo (Currion 2010). The overwhelming response of so many public and private actors was a clear demonstration of international interest, as well as the ability of international NGOs in particular to mobilize quickly. With so many actors arriving and NGO emerging within such a short period of time, events confirmed the popularity, if not the power, of engaging nongovernmental organizations in post-conflict reconstruction. At the same time, the influx of so many foreign actors, each with their own pet projects, created "a humanitarian circus," with humanitarians virtually stepping on each other to be part of the action (Rieff 2000, 26). So many actors, wanting desperately to demonstrate to their own governing bodies and the world that they were making a difference, not only set the stage for the NGO game in Kosovo, but it ensured the inevitable bust that occurred as international actors each promoted their own agendas and local groups competed for funds and attention.

If Bosnia was a watershed for NGO involvement in post-conflict settings, Kosovo was the heyday. International NGOs in Kosovo enjoyed even more financial support, access, and influence. As in Bosnia, international priorities not only attracted huge numbers of international NGOs but these organizations, in turn, supported the creation of local groups. As the following makes clear, however, the circus of humanitarian actors that set up shop in Pristina did not necessarily produce local actors able or willing to carry out international objectives. Most accounts, in fact, make the point that while scores of new organizations were created, and some occasionally influenced policies, this aspect of international engagement was detrimental to Kosovo's nascent NGO sector and to everyday life more generally. As the president of Kosovo's American University observed, international money created a strange and unintended situation, where "every bright person with a good idea doesn't form a business but instead creates an NGO, and then goes around asking for money."[13] This was not always the case, nor was it the intention of international peacebuilders, but this is exactly how the NGO game took shape in Kosovo.

In the 1990s, Kosovo was home to a large number of indigenous civil society organizations, most of which did not have ties to international donors or international NGOs. After 1999, new nonstate actors of all kinds, from large international humanitarian aid agencies to private foundations and local citizens' associations, either set up shop in the region's capital city, Pristina, or expanded their efforts to assist the United Nations in its peacebuilding mission. Many of the international NGOs had worked in Bosnia or other post-conflict countries, and they followed a standard pattern, delivering emergency assistance, providing an array of services, and finally engaging in broader sociopolitical and development activities. The Union of International Associations (UIA) confirms that after 1999 there was a dramatic increase in registered international NGOs in Serbia.[14] In 1996, for example, no international NGOs were registered in Serbia, which Kosovo was still a part of at the time; by 2000, UIA recorded that Serbia had more than fifteen hundred registered INGOs, and by 2006 the number jumped to almost twenty-five hundred.

It is difficult to know for sure, but given the date of UNMIK's creation, the dramatic growth in registered international NGOs is likely linked to the policies and practices of international actors. UIA data, unfortunately, cannot tell us what the INGOs did, but different websites that list the NGOs working in

Kosovo provide some interesting details. If thousands of international NGOs were registered in Kosovo in 2006, they certainly did not share their activities with organizations like USAID or InterAction, both of which tried to provide comprehensive information on NGOs working in Kosovo. According to information from various websites, fewer than one hundred international NGOs indicated that they were still active in Kosovo in 2006, and just a few dozen were left in 2010 (see table 4.1).

Moreover, a small number of the international NGOs stated on their websites that they were focused on civil society development, while the vast majority indicated that they were engaged primarily or exclusively in providing services, as table 4.2 shows.

International donors provided lots of money for NGOs to thrive in Kosovo, but their growth was facilitated by UNMIK's policies, which made it easy for international and local NGOs to register and receive money from abroad. Given the tremendous response by such a large assortment of inter-

Table 4.1 International NGOs and country of origin

Country	Year	Total NGOs	United States	Europe	Domestic	Other
Kosovo	2006	68	33	15	7	13
	2010	34	33	1	0	0

Sources: Compiled from the following websites:
InterAction: http://www.interaction.org/taxonomy/term/150;
ReliefWeb:http://reliefweb.int/rw/rwb.nsf/doc214?OpenForm&rc=4&cc=bih;
USAID: http://www.pvo.net/usaid/pvo.asp; and
Charity Navigator: http://www.charitynavigator.org/index.cfm?bay=search.map.

Table 4.2 International NGOs by deliverables

	Service Delivery		Civil Society		Both	
	2006	*2010*	*2006*	*2010*	*2006*	*2010*
Kosovo	48 (71%)	17 (50%)	11 (16%)	4 (12%)	9 (13%)	13 (38%)

Sources: Compiled from the following websites:
InterAction: http://www.interaction.org/taxonomy/term/150;
ReliefWeb:http://reliefweb.int/rw/rwb.nsf/doc214?OpenForm&rc=4&cc=bih;
USAID: http://www.pvo.net/usaid/pvo.asp; and
Charity Navigator: http://www.charitynavigator.org/index.cfm?bay=search.map.

national actors, UNMIK created an NGO Liaison Office within Kosovo's provisional government structure. The office was charged with helping NGOs receive money from abroad and providing a basic way for the government and international authorities to track NGO activities. Initially, most of the new NGOs registered as "Kosovar NGOs," even though they were largely branch offices or implementing agents for international donors, including the UNHCR, UNDP, USAID, and EAR.[15]

The numbers of NGOs that were engaged in Kosovo between 1999 and 2012 vary significantly, depending on the source, and it is impossible to know if they were international or local organizations. According to the Kosovar Civil Society Foundation, for example, by 2001 there were at least one hundred and thirty NGOs and associations registered in Kosovo, while just four years later the numbered exploded to more than three thousand NGOs (Sterland 2006, 25). However, a 2008 UN report suggested that the numbers were much larger, and almost five thousand local NGOs but only about five hundred INGOs were registered with the NGO Liaison Office (UNDP 2008, 24).

Regardless of the exact number, Kosovo's Ministry of Public Administration created a separate Department for Registration and Liaison with NGOs to accommodate and organize these new actors when it became an independent country. The Department retained the same functions and responsibilities as the former NGO Liaison Office, providing a sense of the scope and the nature of the NGOs operating in Kosovo. Nonetheless, there is still no consensus on the exact numbers, and the office itself does not have the capacity to monitor the organizations or evaluate their impact. UN evaluations do indicate that most local NGOs are small, single-project organizations; and about a quarter are located in the capital, with almost half focused on either women or youth (UNDP 2008, 24).

After more than a decade of international investment, three types of NGOs exist in Kosovo. The majority are involved in distributing humanitarian aid or providing services. A second group includes advocacy organizations that tend to work in conjunction with projects that are closely linked with a targeted group, such as women and youth. These groups may have access to the Kosovo government, but they are almost exclusively funded by international donors. It is difficult to separate these into distinct groups, because they engage in activities that transcend the boundaries between service provision and advocacy. The third group of NGOs includes think tanks and research organizations, many of which were created by international organizations or individuals with international experience, such as Riinvest, the Kosovo Institute for Policy Research and Development (KIPRED), the Kosovan Institute for Research and Documentation (KODI), and the Kosovo Action Civic Initiatives (KACI).

The explosion of NGOs in Kosovo has given rise to the creation of NGO networks and coalitions that have particular goals. Both networks and coalitions want civil society organizations to have more influence, but these groupings are slightly different; networks are generally well structured and more sustained while coalitions are usually temporary and issue or donor driven. Two examples of networks that are often cited are the Kosovo Women's Network (KWN), which was created by eighty-five women's NGOs, and the Kosovo Youth Network (KYN), which represents over one hundred youth organizations and centers from throughout Kosovo. The KYN is less a venue for NGO coordination than it is an organization that represents and advances youth interests to the Kosovar government.

NGO coalitions vary quite a bit and appear and disappear more quickly. There are examples of successful coalitions that emerged to address a specific issue or law, such as the Coalition for a Clean Parliament. There is also the NGO Peacebuilding Coordination Group (NPCG), a coalition of NGOs that focuses on peacebuilding and refugee/IDP returns, exchanges information, and coordinates NGOs committed to peace. All of these organizations and structures suggest a certain level of development for nonstate actors that are collectively trying to shape policies and change attitudes.

At least on the surface, there are other positive signs that humanitarian circus produced NGOs that are active and even reflect international liberal goals. Surveys of NGO officials, for example, confirm that many of the leaders of these organizations indicated that their most "highly-regarded value" is democracy, defined as citizen involvement in decision making and the promotion of equal rights and a multiethnic society (UNDP 2008). It is important to note that while some NGO officials are guided by progressive ideas, their ability to shape policies is still dependent upon their relationship to government institutions, and that ability is not strong. In 2003, for example, Kosovar's government reached out to local NGOs for input on its National Action Plan for Gender Equality. Unfortunately, this much cited example of NGO involvement in policymaking in Kosovo did not create a permanent mechanism for government–NGO communication or even significantly more coordination.

In Kosovo, NGO–government relationships still rely on personal connections, and government institutions are often suspicious of NGOs, especially those that seek to monitor its actions or criticize its policies. Cooperation between civil society groups and government offices at the municipal and local levels is better, but for the most part, government officials do not have a well-defined vision of what NGOs do or what their role should be in Kosovar society.

Some research suggests that public attitudes in Kosovo are in line with what the international community hoped for: one in five Kosovars participates in some way in civil society, and most polled in 2008 indicated that they were knowledgeable about or had some experience or with civil society (UNDP 2008, 51). At the same time, Kosovo civil society has many different kinds of social organizations, and NGOs are just one of many groups in this sector, which also includes private businesses, sports associations, and the media. Thus, while international actors may conflate civil society with NGOs that advocate for progressive, liberal causes, Kosovars do not. Awareness of NGOs and their participation in civil society may be important in some issue areas or at specific times, but not many of those polled actually linked civil society and NGOs with democratization or political decision making. In fact, when it came to characterizing the role of civil society in relation to the government and democratization, opinions were split about what civil society actually does, with about a quarter saying that civil society "should offer services which the government does not have capacity to provide while just 20 percent see it as serving a watchdog role" (UNDP 2008). Tellingly, when Kosovars were asked *whom* NGOs report to, almost half of the respondents said that NGOs "report to their donors" and not the people they supposedly serve or help.

Beyond the Spectacle

Exact numbers on Kosovo's NGO boom are hard to establish, but their dramatic growth in the early 2000s is documented somewhat but agreed on completely. Their existence alone, however, provides little sense of their activities or how NGOs shaped groups in society or domestic activities. NGO networks and coalitions, as well as the progressive views of some Kosovars, provide encouraging, if superficial, evidence that international peacebuilding practices have had a positive impact. The more important question is: How did the NGO boom shape Kosovar society and everyday life? In short, the outcomes were not what were expected or promised. As the executive director of Kosovo's Foreign Policy Group put it, after so many years of international engagement, the country is still "in a great crisis over what civil society should or should not do . . . too many of the NGOs are puppets of foreign embassies and not capable of being respected. Kosovar society and local NGOs need the international community, but they also need to be able to criticize and complain."[16]

Kosovo has changed in obvious and positive ways since international peacebuilding began in 1999. Some claimed that these changes happened quickly, and within a few years of international engagement, the protectorate showed signs of becoming a democratic society, using the presence of more than two thousand NGOs as evidence of this fact (Archer 2003, 31–40). Implicitly, observers suggested that these organizations were not only active, homegrown organizations, but they were toiling away to construct a multiethnic, liberal democracy. Some of Kosovo's NGOs were both active and indigenous, but after peacebuilding began, most were not, and it is a mistake to assume anything about these organizations, their goals, or their impact. In fact, Oliver Richmond and Jason Franks argue that the existence of a strong civil society (after 1999) in Kosovo was a figment of the international community's imagination, something that was substantiated solely by the large number of NGOs that have registered in the last decade or so (Richmond and Franks 2009). That is, the NGO boom simulated, rather than reflected, a robust civil society.

The fact is the NGO game hides and distorts what really happens on the ground, because although organizations grow quickly and in great number, their life cycle is short-lived. Forgotten as well in simplistic observations of numbers are details and analysis about what the NGOs were doing or their relationship with foreign donors. After 2004, for example, when the emergency and reconstruction phase ended, international funding for Kosovo decreased steadily, but support for civil society development and local organizations was never offset by local resources. One report noted that while some domestic funding was made available for Kosovar NGOs, only about 20 percent of the NGOs were given some funding, and funds usually went to charitable activities or to sponsor specific public events (*CSO Sustainability Index for Central and Eastern Europe and Eurasia* 2012, 3–4). And despite appearances, many of the NGOs in Kosovo were not active and existed only on paper. In 2011, for example, the government's NGO office reported over six thousand registered NGOs and associations. Yet, this same office could not say whether these organizations were active or not, nor could its director generalize about the sector's activities or accomplishments. Thus, even the government office tasked with registering and overseeing NGO activities has little to say about these organizations. It is simply impossible "to know what they do and if they made a difference."[17]

International policies inadvertently weakened certain NGOs, and the cumulative effect of peacebuilding efforts in this area undermined the strength and potential of the country's entire NGO sector. Characterizing the actors that emerged in the 2000s, one author explained that most of Kosovo's NGOs are relatively new, have an ill-defined identity, and suffer from low administrative and management skills; and without international assistance, "they are rudderless and go from project to project" (Sterland 2006, 25). Some NGO officials, moreover, may claim to be committed to specific goals and to working toward creating a more participatory society, but they are not free to do what they want because they depend upon the good will (and money) of foreign donors. The local population knows this all too well. A few Kosovar NGOs have been involved in orchestrating some successful social campaigns, but Kosovar society is consistently described by observers as fragmented, uncoordinated, and lacking in leadership. A large part of this is due to NGOs' financial dependence, but it also emerged because of how international actors behaved and the strategies they pursued. One humanitarian aid worker describes it this way:

> The arrival of NGOs on the scene was described by some as a 'feeding frenzy' of crisis junkies. Some NGOs arrived to offer help without demonstrating experience or competence to serve the people they intended to help. Instead of defining their own missions and building on prior field experience, some providers sought to promise whatever donors were willing to underwrite. Several hundred non-governmental organizations became involved. The difficulty arose not so much in the need to screen the groups but in the failure to coordinate them.[18]

Almost immediately, the influx of well-funded and well-connected international NGOs upset the local environment, changing the incentives for social organizing. Frustratingly, international groups deemed existing Kosovar groups to be inappropriate and lacking in necessary skills. Thus, instead of working with local partners, many of which had been providing services or advocacy for years, local branch offices of international NGOs were created to carry out internationally funded projects. Since these international groups "brought with them expertise, funds, and projects that required a considerable amount of human resources for implementation," they had little need for or interest in reaching out to local groups (*Mapping and Analysis of Kosovo Civil Society* 2005, 23). By sidestepping local actors and creating hybrid international–local structures in their place, international groups became both the primary providers and beneficiaries of large sums of money going to social services (Llamazares and Levy 2003, 8). These decisions and practices meant that international donors regarded local NGOs as subordinates to instruct rather than partners to empower. Unfortunately, these early missteps had a direct and negative impact on the sustainability and effectiveness of Kosovo's fragile NGOs sector, and once popular civil society organizations decreased in number, alongside perceptions of NGO power.

The harmful effects of the NGO game were not limited to undermining indigenous organizations or treating locals as implementing agents, but these practices, in turn, shaped the willingness and capacity of locals to carry out social projects. Since important questions related to territory, nationhood, and independence loomed large, Kosovar Albanians who were once active in social activities withdrew from civil society, focusing on other issues and essentially letting international NGOs take over. This is why, even after years of investment and support, Kosovo's NGO sector remains so weak and unstable. USAID's NGO Sustainability Index, which assesses the strength and embeddedness of NGOs, observed that most of Southern Europe's NGOs have improved in certain ways. Yet, Kosovo's NGO sector has declined in strength in almost every respect. Similarly, research conducted by the United Nations Development Program (UNDP) confirmed that while the NGO presence in Kosovo was once impressive in numerical terms, when more than four thousand NGOs were registered with the Office of NGO Liaison, these numbers concealed a more uninspiring reality where only a few hundred NGOs were actually active and engaged in projects (UNDP 2008, 131).

Some assessments of the development of Kosovo's NGO sector after 1999, particularly the financial quandary facing local groups, squarely blame international actors. Their lack of a firm vision for what they wanted to support in Kosovo meant that donors and international NGOs jumped from theme to theme, preventing local groups from cultivating their own identity or defining a clear role in society, which makes it almost impossible to receive funds. As a researcher at KIPRED, a Pristina-based think tank, explained, because of the international community's behavior our organization started to be "careful when it comes to accepting donor money," and it has refused the promise of money or support to be sure that KIPRED as an organization was able "to set its own plan and able to deliver on its promises."[19] Often, local NGOs, even though they were aware that international organizations went from idea to idea, were forced to "follow the money" instead of committing themselves to particular issues or principles. This aspect of the game proves fatal for NGOs that genuinely want to develop an identity and following.

At different points, for example, international actors promoted intensive campaigns that it thought were necessary for the country's development, like AIDS awareness or drug abuse. Yet, neither of these were big problems in Kosovo. Nonetheless, because local group were often desperate for funding and needed to keep their organization afloat, they accepted international funds, and for a while, international actors ideas for what Kosovo's civil society needed to address. Often, local NGO officials complained that donors pushed agendas that were artificial and even inappropriate but did disappointingly little to change everyday life in Kosovo. Without a clear and stable long-term goal for what international actors wanted to accomplish and because they sometimes focused on inappropriate or low priority issues, international actors gave the impression that they saw local organizations as mechanisms to promote their own ideas and not partners in their own right. In other words, the international community's top-down approach, which deliberately sought to avoid sensitive issues, effectively froze Kosovar society and prevented it from developing.[20]

UNMIK's "immediate preoccupations" in Kosovo were a function of what foreign governments and donors thought they could get "their constituencies" to support. Thus, this international body had little room to maneuver, and it had even less time to listen to those on the ground. To achieve what foreign governments and donors wanted, they encouraged, if not demanded, local NGOs to adopt certain policies, claiming all the while that Kosovar society needed to be self-sustaining to develop an organizational identity and their own vision for the country's future. Yet, since international funding was distributed in small amounts and for short durations, local NGOs had to be reactive, multimandate organizations to ensure some funding. It was thus not unusual for Kosovar NGOs to list numerous fields of activity, from democratization to women's rights to economic development in their mission statements. However, after years of working in this way and with "the international gravy train drying up, people just don't know what to do."[21] International practices, and specifically the NGO game, not only weakened the ability of local actors to act, but it fueled disillusionment with the promise of NGOs and peacebuilding more generally.

There is some good news when it comes to Kosovo's NGO sector, but after years of investment and attention, "civil society remains weak" and the government does not have a strategic approach for its interaction with civil society organizations (UNDP 2008, 42). Interestingly, the public does not even know what NGOs are doing. Research conducted by Kosovo's Civil Society Foundation confirmed in various reports from 2005, 2006, and 2007 that same basic truth: civil society organizations are weak, no major improvements have been made in the sector's development, and the capabilities of these organizations are quite uneven ("Better Governance for a Greater Impact" 2011). Moreover, these reports recognize that cooperation between authorities and civil society is inconsistent at best.

Focus group participants that were interviewed indicated that, while most blamed the country's leaders and domestic institutions for the country's weak NGO sector and growing negativism toward weak civil society, international donors shared some responsibility. International actors have not, in fact, tried to cultivate local NGOs, seeing them as little more than "dependent vehicles for the delivery of external support" (*Mapping and Analysis of Kosovo Civil Society* 2005, 39). Instead of drawing on and strengthening existing structures and organizations, internationals went to Kosovo with a template that did not fit local needs or expectations. As one Kosovar activist put it, "The main problem is that [the internationals] came and tried to do what they did in Bosnia here. But in Bosnia there was no alternative movement or capable organizations. In Kosovo, people were prepared for reconstruction and peacebuilding. Kosovo did not have a perfect "civil society," but there was a structure and a network of nongovernmental organizations. Instead "of making the old structure better, they went backwards—as if nothing happened here" (Mertus 2004, 340).

International officials working in Kosovo acknowledge some of the problems with the international community's strategy and tactics; "NGO is really a new concept in Kosovo, and international actors really do not understand civil society here or how to get people to become political active."[22] Instead of reaching out to existing local actors, the international community created new organizations and mythologized the contributions of civil society. This kind of behavior, "allows us [internationals] not to do our homework on countries; so people come with no knowledge of the history and traditional structures and basically just say that everything has to change."[23] What ensued was the NGOization of Kosovar society according to the whims of international donors rather than the strengthening of local agents and the cultivation of partners in peacebuilding.

Kosovo changed in obvious ways after its independence in 2008, but there was still the perception that international actors mattered most to governance and to sustaining NGOs. This is because the Kosovar government had little money or interest in NGOs or in strengthening civil society, in part because they tended to see these organizations as competitors rather than political partners in the country's development. As a Kosovar NGO official explained, " I used to remark that if any new country wanted to learn about how to develop a 'third sector' in their country, they should come to Kosovo" (UNDP 2008, 72). However, after more than a decade of international interference in this area, the situation has changed; most Kosovar NGOs are weak and do not mobilize local groups, and the government is suspicious of them, believing they are more loyal to their donors than to the Kosovo government. For these and other reasons, some Kosovars see NGOs as merely employment opportunities for lucky individuals but not social organizations intent on advancing the interests of citizens and helping the public. Perceptions of the NGO sector are not positive in Kosovo, with many considering NGO officials to be little more than well-paid intellectuals. While unfortunate, this sentiment is not that different from perceptions of NGOs in other Balkans countries (Grodeland 2006).

International efforts in Kosovo have had some positive effects, creating scores of NGOs, but when one looks beyond the large numbers, the darker sides of peacebuilding and the NGO reality become more visible and disconcerting. With large numbers of internationals descending on Pristina, the city immediately exploded with expatriates, imported goods, and higher prices. The lingering effects of the peacebuilding economy not only impacted housing costs and taxi fees but prices for everything rose, putting many things beyond the reach of ordinary Kosovars. The post-conflict economy also shaped perceptions of NGOs and, whether people admit it or not, NGOs were seen as a chance for a better life and international connections. Interviews throughout Kosovo suggest that after more than a decade of money and international support, the population is troubled by the changes in society and the effects of the NGO bust. Although every fourth Kosovar family indicated that they benefited from a civil society activity, when asked about the impact of specific organizations, more than half of Kosovar Albanians and almost three-quarters of Kosovar Serbs acknowledged that the overall impact of civil society organizations was both positive and negative, with almost half saying that these organizations did not represent their "interests at all" (UNDP 2008, 82).

From Peace Building to Benevolent Colonialism

International peacebuilding helped Kosovo in numerous ways, and in large part because of international support, Kosovo is now recognized by more than one hundred countries. In 2013, Kosovar leaders even signed a historic agreement with Serbia that normalizes relations between the two states. Yet, Kosovo remains politically weak, economically vulnerable, and corruption is so rampant that the country's future remains tenuous. Its traditionally moderate approach to Islam is also being challenged because of the influence of foreign money, which has contributed to new social divisions and disturbing trends.[24] If international peacebuilding was supposed to help create the foundation for a well-governed, democratic state that could provide economic growth and adequate public services, then the mission has indeed fallen short (Briscoe and Price 2011). To make matters worse, Kosovo's once vibrant society has been replaced with organizations that are weak and fragmented and a population that is exhausted and disillusioned.

On the issue of NGOs in everyday life, the president of the American University of Kosovo was blunt: "Kosovo has an NGO problem."[25] It was not as though NGOs are incapable of doing positive things, and this American university administrator, with many years in the region, could name several international and local NGOs that he felt had made important improvements in the country's education, and in microlending, and anticorruption efforts. Yet, these achievements existed alongside other processes that made local actors too dependent on international donors for their money and ideas. The NGO world thus encouraged instrumental and self-serving behavior, even among those who were intent on doing good things. Institutionalist theories highlight how formal and informal institutions and various structures associated with peacebuilding shape the "rules of the game" and the interactions between international and local groups, creating surprising outcomes. It is also the case that civil society development is a complex, historical process that takes place over time and is shaped by policies, ideas, and critical junctures as well as many actors. The following focuses on certain structural realities and policies undertaken in the aftermath of UNMIK's creation and how uncertainty, organizational interests, and ideas informed behavior as well as reactions to local organizations and activities. Paradoxically, international peacebuilding laid the foundation for both the growth and the demise of Kosovo's NGO sector.

Even among post-conflict environments, Kosovo stands out because the complex political arrangement that existed for almost a decade while the international community dithered over its final status. The UN Resolution on Kosovo reflected some of the compromises and contradictions associated with Kosovo's political status. At its core was the special recognition that both reaffirmed the international community's commitment to the territorial integrity of the Federal Republic of Yugoslavia (FRY) and called for substantial autonomy and meaningful self-administration of Kosovo. The ambiguity associated with Kosovo's status was not just a problem of vague language in the UN Resolution over what "substantial autonomy" and "meaningful self-administration" meant. Uncertainty was reflected in the many years that international actors could not agree on what they were willing to risk if Serbia decided to take retake part or all of Kosovo. This fundamental ambiguity permeated international policies and practices, including how it invested in civil society and worked with local actors. It also made international reconciliation and civil society activities fundamentally flawed.

Liberal peacebuilding in Kosovo was, at the same time, ambitious and ill-defined; consequently, international actors did not establish policies that were predictable or instilled trust among the people. Although Western governments and international organizations claimed to be pursuing the same liberal peacebuilding goals, it was clear from the very beginning this was not a united group of actors intent on the same kind of peace. Some international actors held a "status positive" attitude toward Kosovo's future independence, while others were more "status neutral." This resulted in different, if not conflicting, policies in their approach to civil society development, resulting in varying levels of support for pushing reconciliation, integration, or independence forward. Even after independence, a handful of EU member states did not immediately recognize Kosovo as an independent country and some even tried to limit the integrative policies of the European Commission Liaison Office (ECLO) and EULEX. Thus, despite good intentions and the international community's rhetorical commitment to liberal peacebuilding, which essentially meant reconciliation but no changes in borders, actions were "inadequate, misguided, or perverse," because they did not agree on Kosovo's future status (Call 2008, 365).

International actors certainly tried to avoid the mistakes they made in Bosnia. First and foremost, too many uncoordinated actors undermine rather than help peacebuilding. In Kosovo, specific steps were taken "to avoid the problem of having too many principals with overlapping agendas," and a more streamlined structure was created to define the tasks of international actors with the aim of improving accountability (O'Neill 2002, 75–76). Thus, Kosovo's four-pillar system assigned specific aspects of peacebuilding to different international actors, and the principals, or identified international organizations, were required to meet regularly. On paper, all the agents of peacebuilding reported to one person, the special representative of the secretary-general (SRSG), and thus to the United Nations. Compared to Bosnia, the international protectorate in Kosovo was a vast improvement in both coordination and accountability, suggesting it might do a better job in strengthening civil society and supporting domestic groups.

Nonetheless, UNMIK was still an "unwieldy beast" with several heads and too many limbs. The international principals themselves were still large, heterogeneous organizations that had to contend with their own internal divisions and diverse objectives. Peacebuilding in Kosovo may have been streamlined and better organized than in Bosnia, but there were still lots of organizations with competing interests and different priorities over both *what* the international community would do and *how* it would move forward. Peacebuilding in Kosovo thus also suffered from too many actors and far too little coordination.

Within a year of UNMIK's creation, the United Nations, the UNHCR, the European Union, the OSCE and USAID, as well as hundreds of international NGOs, descended on Kosovo as part of a vast international and heterogeneous coalition. Each of these organizations had their own organizational imperatives and approach to building peace. And this only intensified as time went on and actors changed their mandates. For example, the UN High Commissioner for Refugees (UNHCR) was responsible for Pillar One, which meant coordinating and overseeing all humanitarian assistance programs, but this still required UNHCR to manage and monitor hundreds of international NGOs. Many of these INGOs had been in the region for years, and they were not interested in UN coordination or interference; and they certainly were not planning on answering to this organization. As one author observed, many of the INGOs operating in Kosovo did not always seem to be driven by the needs on the ground but instead were motivated by a desire to beat out their rivals for money, prime locations, and projects (Stoddard 2006, 175).

The actors may have been well-intentioned, but they still had different reasons for being involved in this country and thus several different constituencies to respond to and consider. To make matters even more complicated, on top of, or rather outside of, UNMIK's elaborate civilian structure was the NATO-led Kosovo Force (KFOR), which reported to NATO Command in Brussels but not to the SRSG or the United Nations. Since the legal relationship between UNMIK and KFOR was never clearly defined, it essentially left the military force with a lot of room to do what it pleased, and it sometimes failed to communicate its actions or intentions with other international actors (Gheciu 2011, 95–113).

KFOR itself was not a unitary organization working toward common long-term goals; not only was the KFOR commander in place for six-month stints, which meant that military policies and practices could change substantially, but national military units were not bound to follow the KFOR commander's orders. Troops regularly checked in with their commanding officers in their national capitals first and then informed KFOR's leadership if they were able to follow their "requests." Kosovo's peacebuilding mission was thus not only hurt by the presence of large numbers of international actors with different interests and objectives, but internationals' behavior contributed to the region's uncertainty and the lack of agreement over the international community's chain of command.

Since Kosovo was declared the "first humanitarian war," the fifty thousand members of the Kosovo Force (KFOR) were deeply and extensively involved in providing humanitarian relief and reconstruction activities. They were also uniquely involved in civil society, providing some of the very same functions as NGOs. It is difficult to generalize about how international and local NGOs perceived the military's intimate involvement in civil society, but KFOR's involvement was unique, and its relationships with NGOs were not well established. It is also true that KFOR's blurring of the boundaries between military intervention and humanitarianism undermined trust with both international and local NGOs, hindering the provision of impartial, independent, and effective relief. This behavior and fragile relationships prevented KFOR from developing partnerships with some indigenous organizations. The NGO community in Kosovo was diverse, and while some NGOs approved of NATO's and KFOR's involvement, many clearly did not, and this resulted in "contestation and competition over the production of trust about the nature of problems faced by peace builders" (Gheciu 2011, 101).

There were other, equally important structural issues that international actors either overlooked or completely ignored: international peace builders were not generally seen as part of a post-conflict intervention where the situation was settled and agreed on. Instead, as Flora Ferati-Sachsenmaier (2015, 22–23) concludes, both Kosovar Albanians and Kosovar Serbs appreciated that, since international actors were committed to the long-term goals of reconciliation and democracy, this meant "continuing the conflict over the status of Kosovo by other means." In other words, the international community's policies and intentions were viewed by Kosovars through their own lens, their exclusive ethnic identities, and historical experiences.[26] Thus, although Kosovar Albanians embraced international involvement especially early on, these international actors were also tainted by their interests and long-term goal: to create a multiethnic Kosovar state. Moreover, historical acts of international benevolence in Kosovo's past often ended up being coercive and oppressive. Thus, Albanians' experiences within the Yugoslav federation, but specifically within Serbia, tainted perceptions of liberal peacebuilding, specifically regarding efforts to strengthen civil society through creating and funding new multiethnic groups and NGOs focused on individual human rights.

Traditional European colonialism was violent, repressive, and exploitative, even though it promised to develop Balkan countries and assist people politically and economically. When foreign countries and international organizations intervened in Kosovo at the end of the 1990s, it was hard for locals to view the behavior of Western actors, even though they had rescued them from Serbia's grip, in a wholly altruistic light. As well-intentioned as their rhetoric sounded, their behavior and policies often belied their declared motivations. And sometimes the behavior of international actors differed so wildly from their rhetoric and promise that Kosovars started to see Westerners, and particularly EU organizations, as imperialistic and hypocritical.[27] As promises and money fell short, Kosovar elites started to believe that Serb repression was being replaced by the West's more benevolent form of colonialism. The latter was obviously preferred, but in both scenarios, institutions and practices were undemocratic and failed to treat local actors as equals.

International actors also flaunted their role as the liberators of Kosovar Albanians while simultaneously creating institutions that allowed internationals—and not those who were elected by the Kosovar people—to decide important aspects of the country's future. As one international official explained, "The parallel government [created by international actors] wasn't a good model for democracy," because while elections were held and domestic institutions were established, decisions both big and small were put in the hands of internationals rather than Kosovars themselves (Mertus 2004, 340). The enormous multinational and multiorganizational peace operation led by the United Nations was further evidence of this. As the most complex peacebuilding mission ever planned, UNMIK replaced the functions of the state and gave the United Nations unprecedented authority. As long as this international presence remained, it replaced Serbia's leadership with UN commands and institutions, putting legislative and executive authority, including the administration of the judiciary, in the hands of international rather than Kosovar leaders.

The new "democratic" institutions created by the international community were justified in the minds of international designers, because of Kosovo's unique political situation but undemocratic strategies and practices undermined local support for peacebuilding. Moreover, the everyday behavior of some international peacebuilders suggested that at least some individuals were uninterested in, or at least indifferent to, input from Kosovar society. UNMIK, in particular, was labeled unresponsive to civil society, and in some cases it was known to be outright dismissive of what local NGOs wanted. For example, when the Women's Network called for the implementation of United Nations Resolution 1325 (on the role of women in conflict prevention and peacebuilding), it never even received a response from UNMIK (UNDP

2008, 89). Three other grassroots campaigns that took place in the 2000s (We Are all Missing; Reforma 2004; and Avoko Network), which commanded significant support from civil society, were, in fact, directed toward the behavior and decisions of international actors. In other words, these campaigns emerged specifically because of the inaction and indifference of UNMIK and the special representative—and not as a result of their encouragement or international backing.

International actors regularly criticize Kosovar NGOs and civil society groups for trying to do everything without a central, overriding mission. Locals do not necessarily disagree with this observation, but they explain how the structure of international peacebuilding and the NGO game played by international donors are to blame for this reality. According to interviews conducted by Kosovo's Civil Society Foundation, NGO officials explained why it was so hard to work with international donors. As one NGO official explained, "It is difficult to talk about our organization's vision, because we can talk of it only theoretically, because having a vision depends on human and financial resources" (*Mapping Analyses of Civil Society in Kosovo* 2005, 33). Nonetheless, because international actors demand that they do so to receive grant money, NGOs must construct a coherent vision statement for what they want to achieve. Better yet for the organization, however, is a vision statement based on what they think international funders will like and are willing to support. All the while, international actors regularly change their priorities, making it difficult for local groups to articulate a long-term plan or to follow through on their stated goals. As one NGO official put it, "We have planned so many things, like sustainability programs and strategic planning, but it is impossible to do all this because we don't have stable financing" (*Mapping Analyses of Civil Society in Kosovo* 2005, 53).

NGO dependence on international funding, alongside the absence of domestic alternatives, requires that local organizations adopt a short-term survivalist mentality, accepting funding on a project to project basis. Thus, instead of spending time cultivating relationships with local supporters and working collaboratively, local NGOs end up doing what they can, even if it does not conform to their mission or reflect their constituencies' interests. This is the NGO reality in financially strapped Kosovo. Moreover, the pressures of finding money and the need to demonstrate tangible outcomes make local NGOs even more predisposed to compete, rather than cooperate, with like-minded groups. Given the many problems local NGOs encounter because of the structure of peacebuilding and actors' different interests, the OSCE tried to coordinate all of Kosovo's NGOs under a single umbrella to facilitate communication and improve coordination and outcomes. Local NGOs resisted almost immediately, in part because of competition for donor attention and international funds. Kosovar NGOs, even those that tried to distance themselves from the international community, had to provide some proof to donors that they were doing "something" to receive funding and continued support. Thus, although local NGOs have criticized KFOR, the United Nations, international NGOs, and other members of the international community for doing too little in Kosovar society, local NGOs admitted that they too were engaged in peacebuilding as "performance" rather than undertaking activities that genuinely attempted to transform structures and attitudes (Gheciu 2011, 103).

Certain ideas and historical practices, simultaneously stood in the way of the growth of civil society and the development of Kosovo's NGO sector. As in other post-conflict countries, international peacebuilding has been guided by certain ideas and principles, but these ideas are interpreted differently by international and local actors. International actors, for example, claimed that they intervened in Kosovo largely for humanitarian reasons, and peacebuilding aimed to improve security and human rights. Unfortunately, when it came to civil society development and developing human rights in the region, there was a clash of understandings over *what* human rights are and *who* should be protected (Mertus 2004, 337). With international actors calling for ethnic reconciliation and human rights for all, Albanians started to think that their liberators either did not know what had happened to them at the hands of Serb leaders, or they did not care, unintentionally minimizing their mistreatment and discrimination. At the same time, Kosovar Serbs also did not want to cooperate with international organizations that were bent on transcending ethnic differences and empowering Albanians (Ferati-Sachsenmaier 2015). The result was a collision of different ideas and understandings about human rights, democracy, and self-determination, exacerbated by the fact that Kosovo had little history with independent organizations and a culture of tolerance.

In the 1990s, Kosovar Albanians created a parallel society that was separate from the Serbian state; in some ways, it was an example of the internalization of human rights norms, and these ideas played an instrumental role in bringing Kosovar Albanians together in a common struggle and informing Kosovar Albanian identity. Yet, Albanians' interpretation of human rights was shaped fundamentally by their unique history, particularly their oppressive treatment at the hands of Serbian authorities and thus Serbia's lack of interest in advancing the position of Albanians within Kosovo. As a consequence, after Kosovo was liberated by international actors many Kosovar NGOs and their followers did not tend to emphasize the rights of all individuals, particularly the rights of Kosovar Serbs. The challenge for the international community in interacting with these Kosovar groups was reinforcing the positive aspects of Kosovo's human rights culture while trying to transform its negative tendencies, encouraging Kosovar Albanians to think about human rights in terms of individual rights, not group rights. Yet often, not enough care was taken regarding this problem, and in the process of promoting human rights practices, international actors, unintentionally, discounted the history of Kosovar Albanians and their experiences with repression and violence. That was, at least, how some locals saw it.

As time went on and expectations went unfulfilled, international peace builders were increasingly perceived as heavy-handed and disrespectful of local groups and norms; and instead of working with Kosovar human rights groups, the international community tended toward creating new NGOs to promote Western understandings of human rights. As one international observer explained, "From the social point of view, the creation of high-visibility, public interest NGOs might not be the most productive tool by which to bring about change. In a country where many are still plagued by subsistence problems, it is more difficult to mobilize citizens in the name of the public good rather than in their immediate self-interest" (Mertus 2004, 341). Nevertheless, the international community's strident commitment to protecting human rights for all and promoting interethnic reconciliation and peace solidified an adversarial and violations-oriented understanding of human rights, which was not how Kosovars had defined or understood human rights groups in the past. Put differently, international understandings of human rights, democracy, and reconciliation were pushed and imposed on Kosovars without recognition of other approaches or Kosovar understandings of these concepts.

In other areas as well, the ideas and strategies used by internationals were misunderstood by Kosovars because of their own their experiences and history. English words like *project*, *capacity building*, and *NGO* were adopted and used regularly by Serbians and Albanians alike, but anthropologists argue that these words held very different meanings for people in the former Yugoslavia. Capacity building is a word that is used by internationals to mean a process to strengthen relationships; for Kosovars, capacity building meant an outcome, providing certain training and building technical competencies of an organization's staff with the aim of achieving professional standards. In other cases, it was not just a matter of different words or understandings; it was also that international actors intentionally used words instrumentally to legitimize certain behavior and policies. For example, international peace builders asserted that policies in Kosovo were guided by "partnership" to strengthen civil society. In practice, because of the weakness, immaturity, or unacceptability of local NGOs, international actors did not treat local NGOs as partners but relied on them to perform services. They did not generally encourage their participation in creating agendas or making decisions. In fact, international promises were so different from the reality that was unfolding that locals became disappointed and distrustful of the promise of civil society development and peacebuilding more generally.

In Kosovo, the international community maintained that its strategy to develop civil society through NGOs would advance both peace and reconciliation. International efforts no doubt accomplished a great deal, but there is little evidence that policies were successful either in strengthening domestic groups or transforming societal attitudes. In fact, given the state of Kosovo's NGO sector today compared with the 1990s, it appears that international intervention in civil society hurt as much as it helped. This is not to say that the international community's strategy failed completely or that NGOs did not accomplish anything in Kosovo; however, the outcomes were more complicated and messy. Superficially, the presence of large numbers of NGOs created lots of activities and projects. Yet, many of the NGOs existed only on paper and were compelled to follow the identified interests of international rather than domestic supporters. And once international funding disappeared, so did the NGOs. Kosovars not only lost interest in social activities, but they increasingly became frustrated and disillusioned with international peacebuilding and its promises.

The institutionalist framework used here focuses largely on the structure of international peacebuilding and the interests of the actors involved. It also considers how ideas are understood differently by international and local actors involved in peacebuilding. In many ways, institutionalism simplifies too much of what happened and generalizes about the motivations and behavior of diverse international and local NGOs. However, the realities on the ground and the NGO game that was played between well-intentioned international groups and locals are not that dissimilar to what happened in other post-conflict countries. Thus, in spite of rhetoric about strengthening local actors and sharing power, various factors militated against this and prevented NGOs from becoming strong, embedded partners in peacebuilding.

After more than a decade and a half of international involvement, most of the Western players have gone home, and interest in NGOs has faded. The failures of international peacebuilding are indeed unfortunate, but they are not permanent, and the situation is not without hope. As in Bosnia, disappointing outcomes have led to situations where local actors have refused foreign money in order to carry out domestically driven priorities and garner more domestic support. In fact, the boom and bust cycle of NGOs has been replaced by the slow emergence of local groups that are intent on representing the public's interests rather than fulfilling international objectives (*CSO Sustainability Index for Center and Eastern Europe* 2012). The failure of international peace builders to purchase Kosovo's civil society, along with international crises elsewhere, has actually fueled a sense of genuine liberation as Kosovars recognize their excessive and debilitating dependence on the international community's charity. After years of growth and demise, it is clear that NGOs performed some important tasks in Kosovo that neither governments nor international organizations were able or willing to carry out. The problem, thus, was not only with the NGOs themselves, but that too much was assumed and expected of these actors.

Conclusion

The End of a Golden Era

Greg Mortenson's (2006) now infamous book, *Three Cups of Tea: One Man's Mission to Promote Peace*, tells the story of how Mortenson got lost trying to climb the K2 mountain and was helped by locals, and how he tried to repay the communities in the remote region between Pakistan and Afghanistan for their hospitality. In 1996, he created the Central Asia Institute whose mission was, according to its website, "to empower the communities of Central Asia through literacy and education especially of girls."[1] Or as the founder liked to embellish, this international NGO promotes peace one school at a time.

A few years after the Central Asia Institute was created, Mortenson was being called a liar and a crook for fabricating important parts of his story, and his organization came under investigation (Krakauer 2011). Even more damaging to its reputation and to NGOs all over the world was the disclosure of the Central Asia Institute's financial records. The Institute had used upwards of $4 million on outreach in the United States and $3 million on materials and supplies to build schools in Central Asia, but less than $1 million actually made its way to the people of Central Asia.[2] The revelations were particularly difficult for Americans who had become enamored with Mortenson's persona. They were also sold on the fiction that building peace is a matter of NGOs and pennies.[3]

Mortenson has since been replaced as the Institute's director because of his financial mishandlings and the organization's dismal performance. Despite claims that the Central Asia Institute supports grassroots initiatives that are based on community participation and empowerment of locals, all evaluations found just the opposite to be the case. Most of the Institute's money never made it to Afghanistan, and the international NGO largely relied on a top-down, externally driven approach to interacting with Afghan society and to advancing peace. There was minimal oversight of its activities, and locals had little say in the development of projects or the organization's direction.[4] Put differently, the Central Asia Institute has gone bust, and the damage to this NGO is likely beyond repair. NGOs are certainly not all the same, but clearly in the case of the Central Asia Institute, as with many NGOs, its activities and impact were both exaggerated and misunderstood.

NGOs are involved in a broad array of activities, but they are not inherently effective organizations that develop projects that reflect and advance those they claim to serve, as is claimed or assumed. They are also not necessarily organizations interested in empowering local communities or transforming societal relationships. We assume a great deal about NGOs and the NGO reality in conflict-ridden countries, but hardly ever are these organizations monitored or evaluated objectively, especially in light of their grandiose promises. As the case of the Central Asian Institute makes clear, in the embrace of NGOs, it is crucial to distinguish between organizations based in the United States or any Western country and local, indigenous actors. The game Mortenson played in Central Asia was unfortunate, but it is not that unique. Instead of assisting those in need and bridging international ambitions with local needs, many well-intentioned international NGOs end up advancing their own agendas and organizations and the careers of their staff. Some money and assistance, indeed, may make their way to those on the ground, but rarely is power shared or are promises kept.

To be fair, Mortenson's Institute did help build many schools in Central Asia, and women were often well-represented in its projects. Trying to provide some perspective to this NGO scandal, the journalist Nicholas Kristof points out that Mortenson and the Central Asia Institute have still done more than most governments to promote peace in this troubled region.[5] That peace has not been achieved in Afghanistan or Pakistan and a considerable amount of money has been wasted are discouraging, but we still cannot dismiss this NGO's achievements or blame it alone for the outcome. Kristof generously concludes that this international NGO has, in fact, done more good than harm, raising awareness of the plight of Central Asians and focusing attention on the disadvantaged position of women throughout the region. Like the NGO boom and bust pattern described in this book, the Central Asian Institute's legacy to peacebuilding in Central Asia is decidedly mixed, with some parts educational and inspiring, while other aspects are disappointing, if not downright shameful.

Just as the take-home lesson of Mortenson's "three cups of deceit" is not simple, this book aimed to present a nuanced argument about international peacebuilding and the engagement of NGOs. To recap, I argue that because of changes in how states understand security and their desire to transform conflict-ridden societies quickly and inexpensively, international peacebuilding results in a growth of both international and local NGOs. In the short-term, the NGO boom creates scores of organizations and an untold number of projects. The result, however, is the projectification and NGOization of post-conflict societies instead of the establishment of strong domestic actors that are embedded in local structures and eager to advance liberal peace. A NGO boom is thus followed by a bust, where NGOs decline in number and where locals feel dissatisfied and disillusioned with civil society development schemes and international peacebuilding more generally.

Institutionalist theories help illuminate the structural dynamics of this process and explain how certain policies and practices inadvertently hurt the development of the local NGO sector. This framework reveals why both international and local NGOs are constrained by certain structures and self-interest. At the same time, historical practices and certain ideas contribute to paternalistic behavior by international agents as well as frustration and disillusionment among locals. Thus, although NGOs may exist plentifully in post-conflict countries, their growth and existence are neither synonymous with nor symptomatic of the creation of local partners committed to liberal peacebuilding. Unfortunately, international peacebuilding's embrace of NGOs as a strategy to provide assistance, reach out to locals, and bridge common goals only simulates change, a shift in power to local actors, and the development of strong social organizations.

This book looked at the NGO reality in post-conflict peacebuilding in Bosnia and Kosovo, but this chapter includes evidence from other countries and settings, because NGO booms and busts are not limited to the Balkans or even to liberal peacebuilding. In fact, as I suggested in other chapters, although students of post-conflict reconstruction and international relations have only recently started to consider the importance of NGOs and everyday politics, scholars focused on humanitarian relief and development have observed similar trends and problems with NGOs long ago. As I mentioned in chapter 2, boom and bust cycles and problems with NGOs have also occurred in Rwanda, Afghanistan, and Sri Lanka, where international actors have played an important role in building peace. Although scholars who are focused on individual cases of post-conflict reconstruction have described some of these same dynamics, they have not analytically linked them to problems with peacebuilding, trends in international assistance, or the challenges faced by the local NGO sector.

This concluding chapter first evaluates the future of international peacebuilding, and then it looks briefly at NGO cycles in other post-conflict countries as well as other transitional countries for additional comparative evidence. The shadow cases I identify suggest that this is a common transnational dynamic and the NGO game exists in other settings. Scholars writing about post-conflict development and postcommunist transitions and failing states, in fact, observe similar NGO patterns and outcomes. The problems and paradoxes associated with NGOs in international relations are becoming more obvious and recognized, but this does not mean that NGOs will disappear any time soon. I end the chapter with some reasons for optimism about these international and domestic actors. The NGO world is still dominated by the interests of Western governments, but increasingly NGOs, as well as the governments that fund them, are acknowledging the shortcomings and contradictions of the NGO reality.

Liberal Peacebuilding in Crisis

As with the Central Asia Institute's fall from grace, reactions to the failures of liberal peacebuilding have run the gamut, though most scholars now admit that the liberal peace has been, at best, "troublingly diverted" (Richmond 2011, 226). Why this is and who is at fault remain hotly debated. Western governments and international organizations are not only criticized for failing to create the institutions that are necessary for long-term peace in the Balkans, but efforts in places like Bosnia and Kosovo are confused and conflated with American-dominated efforts in Afghanistan and Iraq.[6] As Roland Paris (2011, 40–41) notes, liberal peacebuilding is at a crossroads, in part because scholars and policymakers consistently fail to make a distinction between different kinds of international interventions, putting together the multilateral and largely humanitarian interventions of the 1990s with the U.S. government's unilateral military interventions in Afghanistan and Iraq. Consequently, it is difficult to judge fairly what international strategies have worked and why this is.

Post-conflict humanitarian interventions, which are *largely* about alleviating human suffering, are different from postconquest interventions, which are driven largely by geostrategic concerns and a desire for regime change. Distinguishing between the two is not easy or obvious, because, as Kimberly Zisk Marten (2005, 6) recognizes, all international interventions contain elements of self-interest and strategic importance as well as elements of altruism. At the same time, there are important similarities between the international actors involved in these different interventions and the strategies and rhetoric adopted in the humanitarian missions in places like Kosovo and Cambodia and in the interventions of Afghanistan and Iraq. Examining these international interventions together may prevent a fair evaluation of liberal peacebuilding, but for our purposes here, it does allow us to compare the effects and challenges associated with international actors reliance on NGOs in post-conflict environments.

Debates over the international community's liberal peacebuilding agenda have in fact become so popular that the criticisms have taken on a life of their own and only vaguely address contemporary policies and practices, which continue to evolve (Campbell, Chandler, and Sabaratnam 2011, 2). The meta-critique of liberal peacebuilding argues that all contemporary projects of international conflict management, regardless of what they are called or the small differences between them, are based on the same logic, self-interested behavior and imperialistic ambitions. Much has changed since liberal peacebuilding began in the early 1990s, but there is still no denying the international community's peacebuilding record: the achievements have been few, the challenges great, and the outcomes unpredictable. Kosovo is case in point; although the region was once an enthusiastic supporter of the West and its intervention, Western actors are increasingly unpopular, and liberal values now compete with radical Islamic ideas.[7] But regardless of the country, it is still difficult to make the case that international efforts to promote liberal peacebuilding have been a resounding success. At the same time, it is plain wrong to conclude that international actors have not achieved anything at all in the Balkans, Cambodia, or East Timor by leading efforts to stop violence, reconstruct countries, and transform societies. In most places, in fact, not only has violence ended and scores of lives been saved, but a fragile peace is holding. Often without considering the paucity and problems with the alternatives, the analytical pendulum has swung from exuberance over liberal peacebuilding to distrust and even antipathy for what is sometimes referred to as humanitarian imperialism.

Again, much of the recent criticism of peacebuilding is linked to American-led misadventures in Afghanistan and Iraq, and in both countries there is no shortage of examples of how the United States failed to plan for these interventions or how it imposed its will, using the banner of liberal peacebuilding to garner support and legitimacy. U.S. officials, in fact, repeatedly maintained that it was doing what was best for Iraq and was what the Iraqis wanted, even though all evidence indicates otherwise. The March 2013 Final Report from the Inspector General for Iraq Reconstruction, for example, makes this abundantly clear, especially at the beginning. Simply put, American-led reconstruction of Iraq was planned and implemented without input from Iraqis. Even the former Ambassador to Iraq, James Jeffrey (2010–2012), admits that "there was never an impression that the Iraqis were included in any decisions about programs or projects."[8] Daniel Serwer (2012) of the U.S. Institute of Peace maintains that while the initial motivations and policies of the United States differed significantly from liberal peacebuilding in the 1990s, over time the United States did learn from its mistakes, shifting its orientation and practices. By 2008, new policies were making headway, though achievements proved fleeting, and Iraq today is bloodier than it had been in years, with sectarian violence and nonstate actors threatening to undo years of U.S. investment and even the Iraqi state itself.

Developments in Afghanistan offer some reason for guarded optimism, but international efforts there have not fared much better than in Iraq. In fact, Western donors and international NGOs are openly ridiculed for their meaningless and expensive peacebuilding activities, which have included balloon giveaways, fashion shows, and projects that provide free bicycles for women. Such projects attract a lot of attention and a flurry of excitement, but how these distractions help the population or further peace is unclear at best. Unfortunately, most assessments of everyday life, Afghan civil society, and the work of NGOs are uniformly negative. As Ahmed Rashid (2008, 179) puts it, the NGO invasion, created by American-led intervention, led to an explosion of Afghan NGOs and countless social projects. The problem was that most of the foreign-supported Afghan NGOs lacked domestic support and suffered some of the very same problems as NGOs in the Balkans. As an American embassy official offered in 2013, international donors—whether they are governments or international NGOs—basically threw "money at anything with a pulse and a proposal" in the hope that something would stick ("Foreign Projects Give Afghans Fashion" 2013). Ironically, with the decline of the American military and shrinking government budgets for peacebuilding and for Afghanistan specifically, there is more interest (at least rhetorically) in investing in local NGOs and other bottom-up strategies. Since international actors are wary of working with the Afghan state, but still want to prevent Afghanistan from going the way of Iraq and descending into chaos, it is not surprising that international actors will likely continue to support civil society development and NGOs in the desperate hope that they will somehow transform the country and deliver peace.

Given the calamities in Iraq and Afghanistan, and also the lingering problems in the Balkans, Asia, and elsewhere, there is either little money or no stomach for extensive international involvement in conflict-ridden countries. Liberal peacebuilding, as practiced in the Balkans, is likely over in the near future. Even those who supported international intervention in Libya in 2011, for example, did not forget the missteps in the Middle East or the dilemmas associated with intensive international peacebuilding elsewhere.[9] At the same time, it is irresponsible and dangerous for powerful Western countries to ignore intrastate violence completely, especially governments that massacre their own people, or failing states that are unable to provide minimal protections or public goods for their populations. These were among the reasons offered by Western governments and international organizations for military intervention in Libya in March 2011 to oust Muammar al-Qaddafi. The international community's response to Libya demonstrated that, although liberal peacebuilding may be in crisis, some form of international intervention and conflict management are still possible.

While few and far between, there are situations when Western governments and international organizations will likely come together to use military force to intervene in the domestic affairs of another country to stop bloodshed, help overthrow a despotic government, or support a failing state. Libya, however, also reminds us that while multilateral, international intervention might happen again in the near future, it will not necessarily be followed by ambitious and extensive peacebuilding by international actors. International intervention in Libya was led by NATO; it was swift, and by most accounts the military mission was successful (Daalder and Stavridis 2012). The international actors, however, departed quickly, leaving the Libyan government in charge of reconstruction and peacebuilding. Fearing mission creep, shortly after Qaddafi was overthrown, members of the international coalition warned that foreign governments needed to balance the needs of the local population with the norms of sovereignty and state rights. Put differently, international actors had limited responsibility and interest in leading post-conflict reconstruction after the military mission was over. Peacebuilding instead needed to be put in the hands of Libyans.

Almost seven months after the international intervention began, the United Nations Support Mission in Libya (UNSMIL) was created to support—rather than to lead—Libya's transition and peacebuilding. As the United Nations' Department of Political Affairs explained, that the Libyans will lead this rebuilding effort is a point the interim authorities have strongly emphasized in their contacts with the international community. The Libyan government reached out to the United Nations for support and its expertise in a number of these areas but also to help to ensure that outside assistance is well-coordinated ("Building the new Libya" 2012, 1–2). Interestingly, without any other big ideas for how international actors could make a difference in promoting peace and stability, foreign aid was channeled through civil society and explicitly earmarked for so-called civil society capacity-building, producing hundreds of local NGOs since March 2011.[10] Thus, the NGO game continues, albeit with a somewhat different constellation of actors in this country.

Libya demonstrates that there are some situations where Western governments and international organizations will come together to provide the military might to stop internal conflicts and even change a country's government. However, this experience suggests that if international intervention occurs, post-conflict reconstruction and peacebuilding will likely be led by domestic actors and only supported by the United Nations, foreign governments, and international actors. Scholars like Roger Mac Ginty (2011) have long advocated for peacebuilding strategies that rely on traditional methods and reflect local customs. Unfortunately, the international community's strategy in Libya is no success story or model to emulate, because less than two years after Qaddafi was overthrown, the country spiraled into civil war with armed militia groups roaming the streets. Given what has transpired since international actors withdrew from Libya, the international community's engagement there may instead serve as an ominous warning of what can happen if international actors use military force to change a political system but then do not assume more responsibilities for building peace. As hard as it is to accept, a hybrid model of post-conflict peacebuilding may be as ineffective and unappealing as internationally-led peacebuilding.

In Libya, Western governments and regional organizations were able to contain liberal ambitions but no precedent was set. This is why international intervention in Libya did not spill over into decisive action in Syria, which has also been in the throes of a bloody civil conflict since the spring of 2011. Given the strength of the Assad regime and lack of international will, Western governments and international organizations have avoided comprehensive military intervention, focusing their efforts elsewhere. A leading strategy has been to aid organizations working within the country and support regional partners who are opposed to Assad. However in Syria, as in other war-torn countries that seem beyond the reach or immediate interest of Western countries, there are few options for international engagement. Since the concerted use of military force has not attracted a significant international coalition, some have actively encouraged Western governments and international organizations to channel money instead to the "far more nimble forces of civil society" within these countries to help them move toward stability in an indirect and bottom-up way.[11] Again, as in the past, the international community may turn to NGOs and civil society development because problems are too complex and time consuming for states to manage on their own. And there are few alternatives.

As in the early 1990s, Western governments and international organizations that lack the will or a way forward in conflict-ridden countries are likely to turn to civil society and to NGOs for easy, quick, and cost-effective ways to help deliver services and advance international interests. Ironically then, the crisis of liberal peacebuilding may result in even more money and support for policies aimed at funding NGOs, developing civil society, and empowering so-called local partners. Western governments and other international donors are understandably reluctant to work with authoritarian governments that are unable or unwilling to deliver humanitarian assistance or who are uninterested in progressive liberal causes. Thus, despite any revelations about NGOs or the failure of international actors to fulfill promises to work with local actors, disbursing aid directly "to the people" and to NGOs is likely to be regarded as both well-intentioned and appropriate. Even as scholars document that much of the money for post-conflict reconstruction and development never gets to those on the ground or goes to a privileged few, it is still hard to change historical practices and resist the powerful appeal of NGOs (Gingrich and Cohen 2015; Barnett and Walker 2015). It is also the case that when it comes to dealing with uncertain, conflict-ridden countries, Western governments and international organizations have few options and a limited toolbox. And it is true that doing something for people on the ground is likely better than doing nothing at all.

Beyond the Balkans

This book looked at a specific kind of intensive and extensive peacebuilding in the Balkans, but research on other post-conflict countries, though limited in the attention generally given to civil society and NGOs, suggests similar NGO booms and busts. In fact, even when international actors have not taken a lead in peace operations, an explosion of NGOs has been documented as international NGOs and other foreign actors descended on conflict-ridden countries. The UIA confirms the sudden and even dramatic growth of NGO activity once international involvement began in Afghanistan, East Timor, and Cambodia. Comparisons of international NGO activity also make plain that NGO booms are not driven by internal factors, a country's size, its location, or even the difficulty of the undertaking. However, only through careful research that focuses on the aftermath of intervention can we know what these organizations did, how they interacted with local groups, and how their presence affected the lives of people on the ground and their perceptions of peacebuilding. Strikingly similar and troubling NGO cycles and patterns as we have seen in the Balkans are however observed by area studies experts.

In Afghanistan, for example, there were about 180 registered international NGOs in 1990. This number declined during the Taliban's rule when Western actors were forced out of the country, but INGO numbers increased immediately after the U.S.-led intervention in 2001, and within a few years, more than 250 INGOs found their way to Afghanistan.[12] In East Timor, UN-led peacebuilding is directly linked to what can only be called a NGO explosion on this small island country. In October 1999, when the former territory of Indonesia became a UN protectorate, there were only a handful of registered international NGOs; within five years, more than one hundred INGOs were registered in the country.[13] Similarly, United Nations-led peacebuilding in Cambodia contributed to such a growth of NGOs that, even a decade later, the Cambodian government could not say how many NGOs were operating throughout the country, let alone provide any meaningful evaluation on what they were doing.[14]

After the Paris Peace Accords were signed in 1991 and the United Nations took over running Cambodia, international NGOs arrived in droves. Within a few years, NGOs were either providing or managing about a quarter of all international aid going to this country (Un 2006, 235). After the horrors of the Khmer Rouge (1975–1979), in which an estimated two million Cambodians were killed or starved to death, followed by a decade of civil war, NGOs had plenty to do. The country's infrastructure was in desperate need of repair, but the United Nations was intent on addressing the roots of the violence and preventing it from reoccurring. Because of its emphasis on conflict transformation, international and local NGOs were encouraged to help rebuild institutions and promote sociopolitical change. International NGOs enjoyed many advantages in Cambodia; they could act quickly, they were willing to take risks, and they had capacity and access that the United Nations simply lacked. The largest and most well-known international NGOs focused on humanitarian relief and economic development, but international and Cambodian NGOs alike engaged in democracy promotion and human rights activities.[15]

As was the case with multimandate NGOs in the Balkans, Cambodian NGOs engaged in a wide range of activities, providing services, educating people on democratic values, and raising political consciousness, all in an effort to promote better state–society relationships. International peacebuilding in Cambodia had an obvious impact on society, and the process created "many groups, political parties and NGOs, the range of which was both impressive and exciting" (Richmond and Franks 2009, 39). However, by 2011, so many international NGOs, aid organizations, and foundations had flocked to Cambodia to clear landmines, implement HIV/AIDS programs, and work on civil and political rights, that it was impossible to evaluate their multiple and varied effects.[16] A certain pattern was nonetheless evident: international NGOs arrived, they multiplied, and policies and practices encouraged the creation of local NGOs that were engaged in a broad range of activities that went beyond traditional humanitarianism.

There are obvious differences between the United Nations-led efforts in Cambodia and peacebuilding in Rwanda in the mid-1990s, which involved numerous international actors but was not a United Nations-led effort. Nonetheless, a similar boom of NGOs took place once the bloodletting stopped, when more than two hundred international NGOs flooded the small African country (Fisher 2005, 183–89). In previous decades, violence in Rwanda attracted relatively little international attention, and only a few international NGOs were active in the country (Musahara and Huggins 2005, 16). By the second half of the 1990s, the situation could not have been more different. The response by the international NGO community was not only tremendous, but as Katrina West (2001, 41) observes, the efforts were "diffuse and their influence striking." International NGOs arrived to attend to the needs of the people who remained in Rwanda, while a significant amount of international aid went to those who took refuge in neighboring countries—many of whom, incidentally, had perpetrated the genocide. Within a year of the conflict's end, at least 180 international NGOs were registered and working within Rwanda, while another 100 NGOs were reported to be working in the Goma region, the site of refugee camps in Zaire (Storey 1997, 387).

Unlike the international NGOs that had worked in Rwanda in previous decades, the international groups that arrived after the 1994 genocide did not return home once humanitarian needs were met. They were different because new humanitarianism principles allowed these NGOs to use their growing resources and access to stay put to provide what they maintained were necessary long-term social, economic, and political services. Their large staffs, moreover, allowed them to make decisions in areas that went beyond traditional humanitarian roles, and some even operated on equal footing with the United Nations. Because of their declared interest in strengthening civil society and building local capacity, international NGOs also provided funding for Rwandan NGOs. As one author put it, in the "gold rush that accompanied all the international money and attention focused on genocide, Rwandans naturally followed the money" and within a very short period of time, scores of new local NGOs appeared (Kelly 1999, 63). The excitement did not last long and the domestic NGO boom did not produce the effects that were hoped for, because the growth of these groups was both driven and directed by foreign donors.[17]

With significant resources and close relationships with the United Nations and donor countries, international NGOs quickly became powerful actors in Rwanda. The NGO game encouraged the development of Rwandan NGOs and supported a variety of projects, but locals felt that they had little say in what was happening in their society and complained that the activities of international NGOs were actually counterproductive, because they ignored local agendas and intentionally pushed indigenous NGOs aside (Fitzduff and Church 2004, 11–12). As in the Balkans, international NGOs contributed to new hierarchies and to what Peter Uvin (2001, 177) calls a new form of colonialism in Rwanda. Tragically, the explosion of Western-supported NGOs proved intensely problematic, because too much aid money was channeled through multilateral agencies and to international NGOs, creating a postconflict agenda that was both totalizing and unchecked (Uvin 2001, 189).

The NGO reality in Afghanistan after 2002 exhibited remarkable parallels, even though international NGOs had been operating in the region for years. International NGOs arrived in Afghanistan in the late 1980s after the Soviet Union withdrew and the United Nations was put in charge. Given its lack of experience but also its dearth of capacity, the United Nations looked anxiously to international NGOs for help expanding its influence while it tried to develop Afghan society. The United Nations claimed that it was encouraging Afghan NGOs as a part of a broader effort to promote democracy and other sociopolitical changes. And as UN operations dragged on, with little success it expanded the role and responsibility of NGOs, having them work on some of Afghanistan's most complex issues, like health care, education, and economic development.

When the Taliban gained control of Afghanistan in the mid-1990s, the United Nations and most of its international partners were forced to withdraw; only the ICRC and a few NGOs stayed in Kabul while the rest either went home or moved to neighboring Pakistan. Western funding for humanitarian assistance decreased during the Taliban period, but the number of international NGOs working on Afghanistan continued to grow, creating what many referred to as a humanitarian shadow state based in Pakistan. Despite their physical distance, the activities of international NGOs were firmly established in Afghan life, and the 2001 intervention only allowed for more NGO engagement. After the 2002 Tokyo conference, in which Western countries pledged upwards of $4.5 billion to Afghanistan's reconstruction, international NGOs arrived in Kabul in record numbers (Rashid 2008, 179).

As in other countries, Afghanistan's NGO boom did as much harm as good. The influx of foreign money and international NGOs certainly created large numbers of Afghan NGOs in the short-term. A 2002 report commissioned by the Norwegian Foreign Ministry, for example, confirmed that within one year of US-led involvement, the number of registered NGOs in Afghanistan grew almost five-fold; of the more than one thousand NGOs that were registered, about a third indicated that they were international NGOs, even though all the NGOs in Afghanistan were funded by sources coming from outside the country (Harpviken, Strand, and Ask 2002). Complications and problems were evident almost from the beginning, because the NGOs were "here today, gone tomorrow" and no one could count on them.[18] When an NGO lost its funding (and this happened a lot), it simply closed its office in Afghanistan and went home or it moved to another international crisis. The appearance and disappearance of NGOs was all too common in Afghanistan, but with so much foreign money flowing into the country, it was not as though anyone was keeping track of what NGOs were doing.[19]

Afghanistan's problems with corruption predate recent international peacebuilding efforts by decades, but since neither the Afghan government nor international agencies were able to manage the large number of actors that arrived in the country after 2001, many suggest that the NGO invasion contributed to the country's corruption and mismanagement. Within a few years, Afghan government representatives started to complain that NGOs, whether they were large and international or small and domestic, were ineffective and corrupt, because they used too much of the money they received from abroad on overhead and staff. Several accounts of peacebuilding in Afghanistan acknowledge that the NGO boom after 2001 was due to both supply and demand. That is, not only did international donors make more money available to and for NGOs, increasingly relying on them in many sectors, but domestic actors were increasingly interested in NGOs and what they promised they could achieve.[20] International donors, Western governments, and international organizations thus channeled even more money through international NGOs and to local groups, including to for-profit contractors to build schools, strengthen government ministries, and foster economic development.

International NGOs were involved in many sectors in Afghanistan, but they were tasked, first and foremost, to work with local communities and cultivate indigenous groups to try to transform attitudes and behavior. US-AID, for example, gave American Christian NGOs more than $55 million between 2001 and 2005 to work in Afghanistan, based on the belief that NGOs, rather than governments, are better able to connect with people on the ground and build peace from the bottom up (Rashid 2008, 176). Many international NGOs have been praised for their work in Afghanistan, specifically their activities involving education, women's empowerment, and marginalized groups. As one international official put it, despite the many shortcomings of international NGOs, they are called on time and time again in Afghanistan because much of the work in the short- to medium-term can only be done by these actors. As Paul O'Brien (2004, 191) reflects, if not NGOs, then who will do the work in Afghanistan?

In surprising ways, the NGO boom and bust in Afghanistan is similar to what transpired in Sri Lanka starting in the late 1990s. Although international actors arrived over the course of several decades to this island country, this post-conflict country only experienced a tremendous growth of NGOs in the mid-1990s, as donor interests shifted and became fixated on the notion of post-conflict peacebuilding. Foreign governments and international organizations thus channeled large amounts of financial and in-kind assistance to international NGOs and a range of local civil society organizations within Sri Lanka. The anthropologist Camilla Orjuela (2004; 2011) notes that the international community's interest in peacebuilding in Sri Lanka produced thousands of community-based organizations (CBOs), NGOs, and other civil society groups that were, at least in name, focused on conflict prevention, peacebuilding, and reconciliation.[21] This international involvement had an obvious impact on the number of groups in Sri Lankan society, but it also shaped the behavior of local groups and their relationships with other domestic actors. In the medium- to long-term, however, this international intervention distorted, rather than helped, Sri Lanka's budding NGO sector.

The connections between Sri Lankan NGOs and other domestic actors were neither deep nor lasting, largely because local NGOs needed to be acceptable to their foreign donors. Thus, despite a virtual army of international,

national, and local NGOs in Sri Lanka that were ostensibly committed to building peace, no peace movement ever emerged. In fact, after the involvement of so many foreign actors and international NGOs, there were not even a large number of active peace organizations left behind. Since most of the local NGOs were created by outside assistance, when the money disappeared, so did the NGOs. The bottom line was that Sri Lankan NGOs were passive toward their funders, and their dependence on external actors for money meant that they were competitive with each other. As in the Balkans and other post-conflict countries, an NGO bust occurred, and while some Sri Lankan NGOs were involved in important activities, they were also "disconnected and disembedded from local society" (Orjuela 2010, 158).

The research on NGOs in peacebuilding in Africa, Europe, and Asia is far from conclusive, but it does suggest that in many conflict-ridden countries, and even when international actors do not lead peacebuilding efforts, NGOs were omnipresent, engaged in the provision of relief and services as well as in sociopolitical efforts to promote peace and stability. In these countries as well, foreign governments and international donors intentionally funded and supported local NGOs as an explicit strategy to connect with the population and strengthen civil society. Counting the number of NGOs may be the easiest way of demonstrating the effects of international intervention, but numbers are perhaps the least meaningful way of approximating NGO power or impact (Belloni 2008a, 206). The existence of lots of NGOs, while important on some level, may tell us more about the international community's strategy and what they want to fund in a targeted country than it does about the strength of civil society or the effectiveness of peacebuilding.

Beyond Conflict and Peacebuilding

For critics of foreign aid, the unintended and negative dynamics associated with NGOs in peacebuilding are not surprising. International assistance, whether it is for a post-conflict, postcommunist, or developing country, often fails to create the conditions necessary to produce long-term positive changes, and aid can contribute to new problems and hierarchies in a targeted country. Thus, the conclusions of developmental economists about the broad effects of aid, as well as why this might be the case, are similar to the observations and analysis in this book about NGOs and post-conflict peacebuilding. As

Christopher Coyne (2013, 21) puts it, "The failure of humanitarian action is due to the constraints and incentives that place limits on what can be achieved in reality, no matter the effort or the resources brought to bear." Others are even more pessimistic, maintaining, as Angus Deaton (2013, 305) recently wrote, "Aid and aid-funded projects have undoubtedly done much good; the roads, dams and clinics exist and would not have existed otherwise. But the negative forces are always present: even in good environments, aid compromises institutions, it contaminates local policies and it undermines democracy."

Without making NGOs or post-conflict peacebuilding the central focus of their analysis, critics of foreign aid implicate NGOs in the problems of foreign aid and the contamination of local policies. Although they are called *non*governmental, NGOs are inherently linked to governments and are dependent upon them in obvious and important ways. This unhealthy relationship only intensified during the 1990s. Given NGOs' newfound power, their dependence on Western governments, and the natural tendency of bureaucracies to be self-interested and to expand their operations, NGOs have an incentive to retain the status quo and to exaggerate the suffering within countries as well as their own achievements (Barnett and Walker 2015).

Developmental economists and critics of humanitarian aid, however, are not the only ones to observe the unintended and negative effects associated with transnational actors and efforts to strengthen civil society and promote liberal change. Scholars of democratic transitions, social movements, and women's empowerment have made similar observations about the surprising and negative dynamic created by foreign attempts to "fund virtue" by supporting local NGOs.[22] Whether it is in South Africa, Romania, India, or Brazil, attempts by international actors to purchase civil society by strengthening domestic NGOs have not been wholly positive, because the outcomes tend to reflect and advance foreign interests and agendas (Jalali 2013). Thus, even when there is no violence but where the state is unable to resist external influences, transnational involvement gives rise to unintended and negative consequences.

The paradoxical impact of transnational activism has been a popular subject for scholars focused on women's empowerment and human rights.[23] Sarah Henderson (2003), for example, writes about how Western donors working in post-Soviet Russia helped, but ultimately hurt, the country's burgeoning women's movement. As in other postcommunist countries where Westerns tried to strengthen civil society and improve women's rights and promote democracy, Western-funded NGOs were ghettoized, left out of policymaking, and did little more than channel money into the hands of urban elites that espoused international goals (McMahon 2002). Tragically, an almost identical dynamic has been observed in Afghanistan with Western funding for Afghan women's groups. International assistance in Afghanistan indeed fueled scores of women's NGOs but the NGOization of Afghan society and lack of accountability of these actors created a backlash, marginalizing and isolating the activities of so-called local women's groups (Wimpelmann Chaundhary, Ashraf Nemat, and Suhrke 2011).

"The NGO Republic of Haiti" is perhaps one of the most extreme examples of the NGO game at play.[24] International NGOs, foreign governments, and an array of international organizations and foundations have been involved in Haiti for decades, but the 2010 earthquake suddenly made billions of dollars available for this troubled island country. The international response to the earthquake was swift and impressive, with international donors committing more than $5 billion to the relief effort over a two-year period. Pledges of assistance, moreover, came with assurances that actions would be taken based on the principles of aid effectiveness and good humanitarian donorship, and they would build on lessons learned elsewhere. The Interim Haitian Reconstruction Commission (IHRC) was created for this very reason: to be sure that international involvement was efficient and that partnerships were made with local organizations. The international community's response to the earthquake opened the door wide to hordes of international NGOs, and within a few years, an explosion of Haitian NGOs was evident. But Haiti's NGO reality was anything but efficient nor was it characterized by partnerships. As one report criticizing the international community's efforts put it, the NGOs are simply not that helpful in Haiti, in large part because only about 1 percent of foreign donations actually went to support government infrastructure—and even less went to help develop local Haitian organizations (Kristoff and Panarelli 2010).

None of this means that NGOs have done nothing in Haiti or that they have been totally irrelevant to the country's development, because there are many documented cases of international and local NGOs providing much-needed relief and carrying out important community projects. Still, the structure of international assistance and actors' interests and ideologies created tons of NGOs that existed only on paper or merely channeled money to urban elites, ignoring those in most need. Meanwhile, money going to NGOs undermined the strength of the Haitian public institutions, encouraging the best and the brightest in Haiti to work for international NGOs instead of for the government. Haiti recently beat out Rwanda for having the largest number of NGOs per capita than any country in the world except India. In spite of Haiti's recent NGO boom, the population remains impoverished, unemployed, and stuck in a dead-end cycle of underdevelopment. Haiti is, unfortunately, not that unique among the poorest countries, which represent as much as 12 percent of the world's population. In these NGO republics as well, international NGOs are more numerous and extremely powerful, for better and for worse.

The NGO Future

NGOs have made a dramatic journey in international politics from insignificant, tiddlywinks to crucial agents of peacebuilding, delivering most humanitarian assistance, engaging in economic development, and promoting human rights and political change. The growth of NGOs in post-conflict countries is due, in large part, to changes in the structure of the international system. Certain ideas about post–Cold War threats, *who* is needed to address international challenges, and *how* to go about addressing them has helped to make NGOs allies in security and development. For many reasons, governments and international organizations have turned to NGOs and other nonstate actors to transform troubled countries and help individuals. Both the uncertainty and the optimism created by the Cold War's end was addressed by the embrace of NGOs.

Yet, the largest and most powerful NGOs are still created by Western governments and reflect only certain interests in global civil society. National and local NGOs, particularly those based in post-conflict and transitioning states, receive little money and are minor actors; they are ignored by governments and often distrusted by the population. Although NGOs will not disappear any time soon, the "golden age" of NGOs in international politics, where funding, rhetoric, accountability and intention were assumed and exaggerated, appears to be ending. Increasingly, NGOs both international and local are criticized for how they interact with the people on the ground; their instrumentalization by Western actors is taken for granted, and their collusion with international agendas is increasingly identified as a fundamental flaw of many NGOs. There are many reasons why the golden age of NGOs is ending; it is also important to note that members of the global aid regime and NGOs themselves are increasingly aware of the need for change. A recent report by Oxfam stated the problems clearly: the efforts of NGOs, as an important part of the global aid regime, are often too little, too late, and inappropriate for the situation and needs of the people on the ground (Gingrich and Cohen 2015).

Despite the recognition of the problems, there are at least four gaps that unfortunately continue to create the conditions for the NGO game, undermining their work in conflict-ridden countries. These are significant problems, but they are not permanent and will inform NGOs in the future. First, there is the "funding gap" and how much international assistance actually gets to local actors in post-conflict and transitioning countries, particularly to local NGOs. For example, between 2007 and 2013, less than 2 percent of all humanitarian assistance actually went to national or local actors (Gingrich and Cohen 2015, 14). Funding will not change overnight, and powerful international NGOs will not give up their large budgets and power easily, but there is increasing recognition of this problem and its consequences especially for local NGOs (Barnett and Walker 2015). The good news is, as this publication by Oxfam suggests and other reports by international NGOs more directly state, many of the largest and wealthiest international NGOs recognize the need to shift resources, responsibilities, and power to local actors. Moreover, since 2007, some forms of international assistance have increasingly targeted and reached out to national actors, specifically local NGOs. One report noted that local NGOs received a larger percentage of UNHCR's funds, increasing from 9 percent in 2004 to 14 percent in 2012 (Poole 2013, 18). Documenting the severity of the funding gap and how it affects outcomes, trust, and perceptions on the ground is an important first step to genuinely empowering local actors rather than International NGOs.

Money going to international groups is only part of the reason for the NGO game and why NGOs rarely live up to expectations and promises. There is also the "empowerment gap," which is rooted in the disingenuous rhetoric coming from governments and international organizations about support for national NGOs, civil society development, and local capacity building to allow new actors to share responsibilities and influence. In reality, Western governments and international organizations have only simulated a power shift, and, like funding, most decisions and authority still rest with Western governments and powerful, rich organizations. Tracking financial flows is easier than discerning changes in relationships, but by failing to give more authority and decision-making power to national governments and local actors and treating them like implementing agents rather than partners undermines trust. It also undermines international peacebuilding and development.

The global aid regime is seemingly aware of the "accountability gap" and the importance of working closely with beneficiaries, or the people they claim to serve. The accountability gap created by international actors and their policies prompted what some call the accountability revolution, or the recent push to get international NGOs to develop common standards and better tools to monitor their activities. The accountability revolution has led to important reforms in the NGO community; it has also, ironically, created a cottage industry of initiatives and networks aimed at improving outcomes and developing better partnerships. Progress, however, has been slow, and some complain that accountability has been implemented in "technical, de-politicized ways," ignoring broader political and social effects, but at least accountability and transparency are becoming clear, achievable goals.[25]

International actors, in general, and international NGOs, specifically, are doing more to track and evaluate their work, but as a 2010 report on the *State of the Humanitarian System* concluded, it is still hard to monitor the activities of the large number of public and private organizations involved in conflict-ridden countries, humanitarian assistance, and development, and "lessons are more often identified rather than learned."[26] The creation of the Global Humanitarian Platform (GHP) and the endorsement of its "Principles of Partnership" in 2007 indicate that international actors clearly recognize that equality, transparency, and complementarity, among other issues, are still lacking in the current way that Western governments and international organizations engage with post-conflict, developing, and transitional states.

These gaps, which exist alongside other problems with how international actors provide assistance, point to the fourth and perhaps most revealing reason for the NGO game: the "motivation gap," or the reluctance or unwillingness of Western governments, donors, and international NGOs to change the current system despite its problems. The benefits and advantages of forming genuine partnerships and empowering local actors are clear and increasingly documented, but these lessons have not translated into formal policies that shape how donors and governments engage in conflict-ridden, transitional, and weak countries (Ramalingam, Gray, and Cerruti, 2013, 6). The question, then, is not: Do international peacebuilders understand the problems and the gaps in providing assistance and embracing NGOs, but are Western governments, international organizations, and international NGOs really interested in changing the system to improve outcomes and advance peace?[27]

After many years of dramatic growth, the NGO boom has started to level off in the twenty-first century, and with every passing year the number of newly registered international NGOs has declined. This is perhaps because of the shortcomings and unintended consequences associated with the NGO game. NGOs are certainly criticized by governments around the world, and many countries have adopted stronger legislation and regulatory frameworks to monitor NGOs and to study more closely their activities and effects. Since the attacks on the United States in 2001 and the U.S. government's subsequent war on terror, which directly impacted which NGOs the United States supported in other countries and why, many governments have become suspicious of the NGO world and are rethinking their assumptions and expectations of NGOs. This is true for both international and local NGOs. NGOs' fall from grace and the backlash against these actors is increasingly evident, specifically in countries that have been the target of international peacebuilding. After years of naively celebrating NGO involvement and assistance, governments and people are realizing that NGOs are not always what they seem (Carothers 2006; Howell et al. 2008).

The NGO reality in post-conflict peacebuilding is difficult to study and hard to characterize simply. This is why more research is needed to know what these organizations do and what they achieve, but do what is also promised to understand peoples' perceptions and expectations of them. NGOs are constantly changing and adapting, developing standards, introducing new technology, and creating various mechanisms to increase accountability and transparency. NGOs must do all of this and more if they want to "stay ahead of the game, lest they risk becoming outdated and irrelevant, because they are failing the very people and partners they intended to serve" (FSG 2013, 6). It may not be obvious, but it is important to remember: the NGO game and the myth that funding for these organizations inherently "does good" and results in new relationships and shifts in power is not without victims or consequences.

Notes

Introduction

1. See, for example, Paris 2004; Call and Cousens 2008; McMahon and Western 2009 and Richmond and Franks 2009; Paris and Sisk 2009.

2. Others mention how difficult it is to generalize about NGOs or their activities. See Smillie 1995; Hilhorst 2003; DeMars 2005; and Ahmed and Potter 2006.

3. David Rieff, 2010, "How NGOs Became Pawns in the War on Terror," *New Republic*, August 2. https://newrepublic.com/article/76752/war-terrorism-ngo-perversion.

4. There are some exceptions. See, for example, Chandler 2000; Pickering 2007; and Fagan 2012; Toal and Dahlman 2011.

5. Here, too, there are some exceptions. See Campbell, Chandler, and Sabaratnam's (2011) edited volume *A Liberal Peace*; Richmond and Franks 2009; and Richmond 2011.

6. I thank Mary Anderson for reminding me that the neglect of NGOs was not universal, especially among practitioners and those working on international development and peace in other parts of the world.

7. On the effects of the war on the population, see Stiglmayer 1993; Rieff 1995; Maas 1997; and Mertus 1999, 2000; Burg and Shoup 1999.

8. Interviews with the Association of Citizens "Women of Srebrenica" in September 2000 and July 2001, Sarajevo, Bosnia.

9. Sejfija is quoting the research of the local democracy agency in Tuzla, *Lokalna samouprava je vase pravo* Tuzla: Agencja lokalne demokracije, 2002.

10. Interview, July 2008, Sarajevo, Bosnia.

11. To mention just a few who describe the role and effects of NGOs in peace building, see West 2001 on Afghanistan and Rwanda; Orjuela 2004 on Cambodia; Un 2006 on Cambodia; Rashid 2008 on Afghanistan; and Goodhand and Walton 2009 on Sri Lanka. Richmond and Franks 2009 discuss several countries.

12. Janine R. Wedel, 2011, "Will Foreign Aid Dollars Help or Hurt Democracy in the Middle East? *The World Post*, June 2, updated August 2. http://www.huffingtonpost .com/janine-r-wedel/will-foreign-aid-dollars_b_870131.html.

13. There was, however, a growing literature about NGOs in transitioning and developing countries by scholars of comparative politics and development studies. See, for example, Lindenberg and Bryant 2001 and Hilhorst 2003.

14. Keck and Sikkink 1998; DeMars 2005; DeMars and Dijkzuel 2015; Murdie 2014; and Wong 2012 to name a few.

15. On liberal and neoliberal institutionalists, see Keohane 1984, 2005.

16. For some of the seminal works, see Nye and Keohane 1971 and Huntington 1973.

17. On the methodological challenges associated with studying civil society development and NGOs, see Carothers 1999.

18. For more on field research, see Manheim and Rich 1995, especially 155–70.

1. Uncertain Times

1. Istvan Deak, 1993, "A World Gone Raving Mad," *The New York Times*, March 28. https://www.nytimes.com/books/98/12/06/specials/kaplan-balkan.html.

2. For a discussion of how Kaplan's piece was received by the White House and others, see Dabelko 1999.

3. For a similar analysis, see Stephenson and Zanotti 2012.

4. For a discussion of these changes, see Brown 1993 and Brown 1996, especially chapter 1 in both volumes.

5. For more on balance of power and the security dilemma and how it was used to explain ethnic conflict, see Posen 1993.

6. For different causes of ethnic and civil war, see Snyder 1993; Fearon and Latin 2003 and Bowen 1996.

7. See, for example, David 2008.

8. Boutros-Ghali 1992, para. 11.

9. Ibid.

10. Boutros-Ghali 1995, para. 10.

11. See Clinton 1993.

12. See Clinton 1994.

13. Warren Christopher, 1993, "New Steps toward Conflict Resolution in the Former Yugoslavia," U.S. Department of State, New Conference on Former Yugoslavia, Office of the Spokesman, February 10. http://dosfan.lib.uic.edu/ERC/briefing/dossec /1993/9302/930210dossec.html.

14. See "Redefining Security" 1994. A Report to the Secretary of Defense and the Director of the Central Intelligence. http://www.fas.org/sgp/library/jsc/chap1.html.

15. Ibid.

16. OSCE, 1992, *Challenges of Change.* http://www.osce.org/mc/39530?download=true.

17. For similar changes in NATO during this period, see Edstrom et al. 2011 and Henriksen, 2007.

18. For more on these trends and the reasons for them, see the Human Security Report Project 2012, particularly chaps. 5–8.

19. As I mentioned in the introduction, there is no consensus on what these international activities are called. The Rand Corporation prefers the term *nation building* whether it is referring to the United States, the United Nations, or the European Union. See Dobbins et al. 2001, 2003, 2008.

20. UN General Assembly and Security Council, 2000, "Report of the Panel of United Nations Peace Operations" A/55/305-S/2000/809, August 21. http://www.un.org/documents/ga/docs/55/a55305.pdf.

21. Ibid, (the Brahimi Report).

22. Kofi Annan, 2000, *We the Peoples. The Role of the United Nations in the 21st Century.* New York: United Nations. http://www.un.org/en/events/pastevents/pdfs/We_The_Peoples.pdf.

23. World Bank, 2014, *Practical Guide to Multilateral Needs Assessment in Post-Conflict Situations: A Joint UNDG, UNDP, and World Bank Guide*, Geneva: The World Bank. http://siteresources.worldbank.org/INTCPR/1090494-1115612329180/20482303/PCNA+Supporting+Material.pdf.

24. UN Security Council, 2005, Resolution 1645, New York: United Nations. http://www.un.org/ga/search/view_doc.asp?symbol=S/RES/1645%20%282005%29.

25. USAID, 2005, *Conflict Mitigation and Management Policy*, April, PD-ABZ-333.

26. UN General Assembly, 1998. "Arrangements and Practices for the Interaction of Non-Governmental Organizations in All Activities of the United Nations System," Report of the Secretary-General, A/53/170, 10 July, sec. 33. http://www.un.org/documents/ga/docs/53/plenary/a53-170.htm.

27. UN General Assembly, 1998. "Provisional Agenda of the Fifty-Third Session of the General Assembly," A/53/150, 10 July, sec 48. http://www.un.org/documents/ga/docs/53/plenary/a53-150.htm.

28. UN General Assembly and Security Council, 2000, "Report of the Panel on United Nations Peace Operations" A/55/305-S/2000/809, August 21. http://www.un.org/documents/ga/docs/55/a55305.pdf.

29. Ibid.

30. Chadwick Alger (2007) takes his title from Johan Galtung, 1975.

31. For more on World Bank policy toward NGOs, see Bojicic-Dzelilovic 2002.

2. Of Power and Promises

1. "The Old Bridge Area of the Old City of Mostar," 2005, UNESCO World Heritage Nomination, July 15. http://whc.unesco.org/uploads/nominations/946rev.pdf.

2. For a good review of Mostar's history and experiences during and after the war, see Moore 2013.

3. Confidential interview, September 2000, Mostar, Bosnia.

4. For an exception, see Donini's 2007 research on Afghanistan.

5. There are exceptions. See Autesserre 2014 and Pickering 2007.

6. OECD statistics are available online at: www.oecd.org/dac/stats/idsonline. Information on the OECD's tracking of NGOs was also informed by email correspondence with Ann Zimmerman in June 2010.

7. Joseph S. Nye, 2004, "The Rising Power of NGOs," *Project Syndicate*, June 24. http://www.project-syndicate.org/commentary/nye10/English.

8. For more information on different kinds of power and on measuring power in international relations, see Baldwin 1989.

9. The Union of International Associations (UIA) is itself an international NGO that was established in 1907 and started publishing reports on international organizations and associations before World War I. The UIA now provides information on more than sixty-five thousand civil society organizations in more than three hundred countries and territories, but it is also a membership organization that requires registration. Thus, even the UIA cannot capture the scores of NGOs that are not paying members. See the UIA's website at http://www.uia.be/yearbook or their *Yearbook of International Organizations* which profiles both INGOs and IGOs.

10. Interview with Bajram E. Ksumi on May 12, 2011, Pristina, Kosovo.

11. Email correspondence with OECD in June 2010.

12. In more recent reports, and because OECD governments use different terms, the OECD uses civil society organization (CSO) synonymously with NGOs, though it recognizes four different types of NGOs: donor-country NGOs; international NGOs; developing-country NGOs; and undefined. See OECD 2013. http://www.oecd.org/dac/peer-reviews/Aid%20for%20CSOs%20Final%20for%20WEB.pdf.

13. See OECD, Query Wizard at http://stats.oecd.org/qwids.

14. OCED, 2016, Grants by Private Agencies and NGOs, doi: 10.1787/a42ccf0e-en. https://data.oecd.org/drf/grants-by-private-agencies-and-ngos.htm#indicator-chart.

15. Ibid.

16. For more on the ICNL as well as the Russian government's reaction to NGOs, see the ICNL website, available at: http://www.icnl.org/research/monitor/index.html.

17. For a list of the main organizations involved in post-conflict situations, and explanation of their work, see Durch 2004.

18. James A. Paul, 2010, *A Short History of the NGO Working Group* (New York: NGO Working Group on the Security Council). http://www.ngowgsc.org/content/short-history-ngo-working-group.

19. There is quite a large literature, especially on development and humanitarian NGOs. See for example Smillie 1995; Anderson 1999; and Terry 2002.

20. For similar arguments, see Duffield 1994; Chandler 2001; Rieff 2003; and Barnett 2011.

21. For more on the United Nations and NGOs, see Martens 2005.

22. Interview with Goran Simic, Ministry of Justice, May 2011.

23. "Mostar Bridge Opens with a Splash," 2004, *BBC News* July 14.

24. Daria Sita-Sucic, 2013, "Politicking Paralyzes Divided Bosnian Town of Mostar," *Reuters,* February 5. http://www.reuters.com/article/2013/02/05/us-bosnia-mostar-idUSBRE9140O620130205.

3. Bosnia

1. Interview with Goran Bubalo, May 2011, Catholic Relief Services, Sarajevo, Bosnia.

2. For more on this, see Brown 2009.

3. I started doing fieldwork in Bosnia in September, 2000, and returned for several weeks at a time in 2001, 2003, 2005, 2007, 2008, and 2011. The interviews took place in the Federation cities of Sarajevo, Mostar, Zenica, and Travnik, and in Brčko. Interviews were conducted alone, or in a group in English, or with a Bosnian translator. In addition, I was also a participant observer at meetings, interviews, and conferences.

4. The Dayton Peace Accords and annexes are available at the U.S. State Department's website. See http://www.state.gov/p/eur/rls/or/dayton/.

5. The other countries that the Rand Corporation examines include Japan, Somalia, Haiti, and Afghanistan. See Dobbins et al., 2003, 151–52.

6. This includes assistance to the country after the war, not money spent during the war. See the State Department's Bureau of European and Eurasian Affairs, September 2007. On EU assistance, see EU Assistance to BiH 2007; Bosnia and Herzegovina 2009.

7. For others who also talk about this priority, see Fagan 2012; Brown 2009; Belloni 2008a, b; Pickering 2007; and Chandler 1998.

8. See Belloni 2008a and 2008b; Ottaway and Carothers 2000.

9. "Core Report of the New Partnerships Initiative," USAID Document, PN-ACA-951, July 21, 1995, http://pdf.usaid.gov/pdf_docs/PNACA951.pdf; after November 2001, the Center became the Office of Democracy and Governance.

10. For more, see Wells and Hauss 2008 and "History of the NATO-led Stabilisation Force (SFOR) in Bosnia and Herzegovina" 2001.

11. For more on Catholic Relief Services (CRS), see Gagnon 2006. The author also interviewed several CRS representatives in 2000, 2001, and 2007, in Sarajevo, Bosnia. On CARE International, see Smillie 2001.

12. For more on this, see Belloni 2008b; Pickering 2007.

13. See Papić 2001 and Fagan 2005.

14. The costs that are financed by international organizations or bilateral donors for the peace implementation, or for the fund designated for the BiH refugees abroad, are not included in this amount. See Srdan Dizdarević et al., Open Society Fund 2006, 397. See http://pdc.ceu.hu/archive/00003187/01/democracy_assessment_in_BiH.pdf.

15. See *Yearbook of International Organizations* 2007, 2001.

16. These numbers were gathered by looking at the websites for InterAction; ReliefWeb; as well as USIAD's website on private voluntary agencies and Charity Navigator.

17. There does not appear to be a difference between an *NGO* and an *association*. It may be that the latter term has been chosen because of a negative connotation associated

with NGOs in Bosnia. See USAID 2006. It could also be that the term *association* was a holdover from the community period.

18. For more on the committee and its work, see: Human Rights House Network, Bosnia and Herzegovina. See http://humanrightshouse.org/Members/Bosnia_and _Herzegovina/index.html, accessed January 10, 2013.

19. Interview with Zivica Abadzic, May 2011, Sarajevo, Bosnia.

20. In 2011 this included the Dialogue Center: Nansen Dialogue Centre Sarajevo, Foundation CURE, the Human Rights Center at the University of Sarajevo, Catholic Relief Services (CRS), and TRIAL.

21. Interview with Duska Andric-Ruzicic, June 2008, May 2011, Infoteka, Sarajevo, Bosnia.

22. Interview with Saša Madacki, May 2011, Human Rights Center, Sarajevo, Bosnia.

23. Interview with officials of TRIAL, June 2011, Sarajevo, Bosnia.

24. Ibid.

25. See, for the example, the research of Irvine (2013) on Croatia, Mulalic (2011) on Bosnia, and Henderson (2003) on Russia.

26. Confidential interview, May 2011, Sarajevo, Bosnia.

27. Ibid.

28. Interview with official from the International Organization of Missing Persons, June 2011, Sarajevo, Bosnia.

29. Interview with a representative of International Council of Voluntary Agency (ICVA), October 2008, Sarajevo, Bosnia.

30. Confidential interview with representative of the Center for Human Rights, October 2008, Sarajevo, Bosnia.

31. Over the years this remains the consistent conclusion. See Woehrel 2013; McMahon and Western 2009; "Ensuring Bosnia's Future" 2007.

32. CIA, "Bosnia and Herzegovina," *The World Factbook,* [online] www.cia.gov /library/publications/the-world-factbook/geos/bk.html, accessed September 5, 2012.

33. See Daalder 1998; Holbrooke 1998.

34. The PIC was created in 1995 to represent the fifty-five countries and various international agencies that were involved in helping to implement the Dayton Peace Accords.

35. Interview with Mirsad Tokaca, 2008, Sarajevo, Bosnia.

36. "Dodik Blames High Representative for Bosnia's Ills," 2012, *Balkan Monitor,* November 12. Available at: http://www.balkaninsight.com/en/article/dodik-blamed-high -representative-for-bosnian-problems.

37. Interview with James Rodehaver, 2008, Sarajevo, Bosnia.

38. Interview with Judith Jones, June 2003, Brčko, Bosnia.

39. Confidential interview with OSCE official, June 2003, Brčko, Bosnia.

40. Confidential interview, May 2011, Brčko, Bosnia.

41. Ibid.

42. Interview officials at the Dialogue Centre, June 2011, Nansen Dialogue Centre, Sarajevo, Bosnia.

43. Interview with Saša Madacki, May 2011, Sarajevo, Bosnia.

44. Confidential interview, May 22, 2011, Sarajevo, Bosnia.
45. Interview with Mark Ellingstadt, January 2007, Sarajevo, Bosnia.
46. Interview with Danille Harms, 2007, Sarajevo, Bosnia.
47. Interview with Lejla Hadzic, 2008, Sarajevo, Bosnia.

4. Kosovo

1. Interview with Avni Zogiani, May 2011, Pristina, Kosovo.
2. This is a point that others note in their interviews in Kosovo as well. See Richmond and Franks 2009.
3. Interview with Avni Zogiani, May 5, 2011, Pristina, Kosovo.
4. I thank Flora Ferati-Sachsenmaier for this point and related ones that follow on the disjuncture between international goals and the goals of both Albanians and Serbs in Kosovo.
5. Interview with Christopher Hall, June 2011, Pristina, Kosovo.
6. In this chapter I only use the term *local NGOs* instead of *national* because of Kosovo's status within Serbia until its independence in 2008.
7. It draws heavily on the following reports: *Mapping Analyses of Civil Society in Kosovo* (2005); the UN Kosovo Human Development Report (UNDP 2008), and "Better Governance for a Greater Impact" (2011). I also conducted forty-six formal interviews in May and June 2011. Although I had a translator, only three of the interviews required translation from either Albanian or Serbian. The civil society meetings I attended in May and June 2011 were in Albanian or Serbian and were translated.
8. The numbers are still contested, but these are taken from O'Neill 2002.
9. For more on international involvement and decisions after 1999, see O'Neill 2012; Pickering 2012; King and Mason 2006.
10. On troop level comparisons, see Dobbins et al. 2003.
11. The members of the Contact Group include the United States, the United Kingdom, France, Germany, Italy, and Russia, as well as representatives of the EU Council, the EU Presidency, the European Commission, and NATO.
12. See Schimmmelfenning and Sedelmeier 2005 and Kostovicova 2008.
13. Interview with Christopher Hall, June 2011, Pristina, Kosovo.
14. Data for "Yugoslavia" was used from the *Yearbook of International Organizations* 2001/2002, ed. 38, and "Serbia-Montenegro" was used in the *Yearbook of International Organizations* 2007/2008, ed. 44 since data for Kosovo was not available.
15. This may explain the differences in the numbers between the UIA and those on the websites of USAID, InterAction, and other international NGOs.
16. Interview with executive director, June 2011, Foreign Policy Club, Pristina, Kosovo.
17. Interview with Bajram E. Kosumi, director of the Department for Registering and Liaison with NGOs, May 2011, Pristina, Kosovo.
18. From Independent International Commission on Kosovo, 2000, *Kosovo Report: Conflict, International Response, Lessons Learned* (Oxford: Oxford University Press), 202–3, taken from Zherka 2013.

19. Interview with Krenar, May 2011, Pristina, Kosovo.

20. Interview with Avni Zogiljami, May 2011, Pristina, Kosovo.

21. Interview with Christopher Hall, May 2011, Pristina, Kosovo.

22. Interview with Paäivi Nikander, Decentralization Adviser, ICO, May 2011, Pristina, Kosovo.

23. Ibid.

24. Molaeb, Amjad, 2014, "The Changing Face of Islam in Kosovo," *The New Context*, July 18. http://thenewcontext.milanoschool.org/the-changing-face-of-islam-in-kosovo/, accessed August 1, 2015.

25. Interview with Christopher Hall, June 2011, Pristina, Kosovo.

26. Ferati-Sachsenmaier discusses the diverging interests of both groups and argues that this structural reality and the fact that neither Albanians nor Serbs were committed to the international community's goals in Kosovo was the main hindrance to international peace building in Kosovo.

27. For more on the European Union's mission in Kosovo, see Lorezo-Capussela 2015.

Conclusion

1. See the Central Asia Insitute's webpage at https://centralasiainstitute.org/.

2. Annie Lowrey, 2011, "Don't Build Schools in Afghanistan: The Real Lesson of the Three Cups of Tea Scandal," *Slate,* May 5. http://www.slate.com/articles/business/moneybox/2011/05/dont_build_schools_in_afghanistan.html, accessed September 1, 2013.

3. Pennies for Peace is a service-learning program within the Central Asia Institute. For more on this see http://www.penniesforpeace.org/about-the-program/.

4. Jon Krakauer, 2013, "Is It Time to Forgive Greg Mortenson?" *The Daily Beast*, April 8, http://www.thedailybeast.com/articles/2013/04/08/is-it-time-to-forgive-greg-mortenson.html, accessed September 3, 2013.

5. Nicholas Kristof, 2011, "Three Cups of Tea Spilled," *The New York Times*, April 20.

6. This is a point that others make. See Gagnon, Senders and Brown, 2014.

7. "The Lost Generation: Desperate Parents Reveal Hundreds of Young Men and Women Have Left Kosovo to Fight for ISIS in Syria," 2016, *Daily Mail,* February 1. http://www.dailymail.co.uk/news/article-3426369/The-lost-generation-Desperate-parents-reveal-hundreds-young-men-women-left-Kosovo-fight-ISIS-Syria.html.

8. See "Learning from Iraq: A Final Report from the Special Inspector General for Iraq Reconsruction," Hearing before the Subcommittee on the Middle East and North Africa, July 9, 2013." http:// https://www.gpo.gov/fdsys/pkg/CHRG-113hhrg81868/pdf/CHRG-113hhrg81868.pdf.

9. For more on this, see Western and Goldstein 2011 and Hitchens 2011.

10. The number is unknown because most are still not registered. See Barah Mikail, 2013, *Civil Society and Foreign Donors in Libya*, (AFA, Fride and Hivos), July 23. http://

www.medea.be/2013/07/civil-society-and-foreign-donors-in-libya-part-1/, accessed February 20, 2014.

11. Janine R. Wedel, 2011, "Will Foreign Aid Dollars Help or Hurt Democracy in the Middle East? *The World Post,* June 2. http://www.huffingtonpost.com/janine-r-wedel/will-foreign-aid-dollars_b_870131.html, accessed November 15, 2013.

12. For more on this see *Yearbook of International Organizations 2007.*

13. Ibid.

14. Ken Silverstein, 2011, "Silence of the Lambs: For do-gooder NGOs in Cambodia, accommodation with the regime is very profitable," *Slate.com,* June 20. http://slate.com/articles/news_and_politics/foreigners/2011/06/silence_of_the_lambs.html, accessed July 18, 2012.

15. For more on this, see Richmond and Franks 2009 and Un 2006.

16. Ken Silverstein, 2011.

17. For similar observations, see West 2001, especially chapter 6; also Kelly 1999.

18. Ruth Gidley, 2005, "NGOs Respond to Crackdown from Afghan Government," *ReliefWeb,* April 8. http://reliefweb.int/report/afghanistan/ngos-respond-crackdown-afghan-government, accessed October 10, 2013.

19. Ibid.

20. See Rashid 2008; Chayes 2006; and Johnson and Leslie 2004, especially chapter 4.

21. For more on Sri Lanka, see Orjuela 2010; Goodhand and Walton 2009; Orjeuela 2004; Goodhand, Lewer, and Hulme 1999.

22. For more on this in the context of postcommunism and democratization, see Ottaway and Carothers 2000. On aid more generally, see Sogge and Saxby 1996 and Smith 2014.

23. On the effect of transnational relations on women in Russia, see Henderson 2003; in Central and Eastern Europe, see McMahon 2002; and in Latin America, see Alvarez 1990.

24. On Haiti and international assistance, see Schuller 2012 and Klarreich and Polma 2012.

25. J. Alexander, J. Darcie, and M. Kiani, 2013, *The 2013 Humanitarian Accountability Report* (n.p.: Humanitarian Accountability Partnership), http://www.alnap.org/resource/8758.

26. Ibid, 21–22.

27. Others ask a similar question. See Leo 2013 and Barnett and Walker 2015.

References

Interviews[1]

Abadzic, Zivica. Director, Helsinki Committee for Human Rights. Sarajevo, Bosnia. May 2011.

Abaspahic, Haris. Advisor to the FBiH Prime Minister. Office of the Prime Minister. FBiH. Sarajevo, Bosnia. May 2011.

Appleby, Peter. Deputy Head of Office. Brčko Final Award Office. Office of the High Representative. Brčko, Bosnia. May 2011.

Apriou, Armond. Human Rights/Cultural Preservation. European Commission. DG Enlargement. Brussels, Belgium. June 2011.

Asllani, Mjellma. Manager, American University in Kosovo. Pristina, Kosovo. May 2011.

Batinić, Hrvoje. Civil Society Administrator, Open Society Fund Bosnia-Herzegovina/ Soros Foundations. Sarajevo, Bosnia. May 2011.

Beca, Edin. Lawyer, Coalition for Return. Sarajevo, Bosnia. June 2001.

Berlincioni, Natascia. Quaker Peace & Service. Sarajevo, Bosnia. July 2001.

Biser Association. Various officials. September 2000, July 2001.

---

[1] Individual titles and organizations were current at the time of my interviews.

Blakaj, Bekim. Head of Office, Fund for Humanitarian Law. Pristina, Kosovo. May 2011.

Bomberger, Kathryne. Deputy Chief of Staff, International Missing Persons Institute. Sarajevo, Bosnia. September 2000, July 2001.

Brkic, Marin. President, Croat Association of Families of the Missing and Forcefully Taken Croats of Brčko. Brčko, Bosnia. May 2011.

Bubalo, Goran. Project Director, Catholic Relief Services. Sarajevo, Bosnia. May 2011.

Bytyc, Avni. Executive Director, Iniciativa per progress. Pristina, Kosovo. May 2011.

Citizens Association of Srebrenica. Various members. September 2000, July 2001, June 2003.

Community Building Mitrovica. Meeting with several staff members. Mitrovica, Kosovo. May 2011.

Daidzic, Aida. Official, BISER. International Initiative of Women from Bosnia & Herzegovina. September 2000, June 2001.

Debongnie, Andre. European Commission, formerly EuroAid. Brussels, Belgium. July 2011.

Devendorf, George. Director, Public Affairs, Mercy Corps. Washington, DC. January 2006.

Dizdarevic, Ismet. University Professor, University of Sarajevo. June 2001.

Donlic, Asim. Director, Bosnia-Herzegovina Heritage Rescue Sarajevo Office of BHHR. Sarajevo, Bosnia. September 2000.

Doyle, Michael. Political Analyst, International Crisis Group. Sarajevo, Bosnia. June 2003.

Dzemailovic, Berina. CURE Foundation. Sarajevo, Bosnia. May 2011.

Dzidic, Rahela. Director, Civitas @Bosna I Hercegovina. Sarajevo, Bosnia. September 2000.

Dziedzic, Mike. Program Officer, Post-Conflict Peace and Stability Operations. United States Institute of Peace. Washington, DC. January 2006.

Dzindo, Vahidin. Catholic Relief Services. Sarajevo, Bosnia. September 2000, June 2001.

Dzino-Selajdžić, Velida. Catholic Relief Services. Sarajevo, Bosnia. September 2000, June 2001.

Ellingstad, Marc. Governance Advisor, U.S. Agency for International Development (USAID). Sarajevo, Bosnia. October 2007.

Farnsworth, Sarah W. Officer in Charge/Balkans Division. U.S. Agency for International Development. Washington, DC. June 2003, April 2006.

Finci, Jakob. President, Jewish Community of Bosnia and Herzegovina. President, Association of Citizens, Truth and Reconciliation. Sarajevo, Bosnia. June 2003, October 2007.

Furnari, John. Chief Technical Advisor Transitional Justice. United Nations Development Programme. Sarajevo, Bosnia. October 2007.

Gabelic, Aleksandr. Official, Coalition for Return. Sarajevo, Bosnia. July 2001.

Ganić, Emina. Council of Europe representative. Sarajevo, Bosnia. September 2000.

Garrett, Tom. Director, Middle East and North Africa, International Republican Institute (IRI). Washington, DC. April 2006.

Gashi, Krenar. Executive Director, Kosovo Institute for Policy Research and Development (KIPRED). Pristina, Kosovo. May 2011.

Gashi, Shukrije. Center Director, Partners—Kosova, Center for Conflict Management. Pristina, Kosovo. May 2011.

Gjoshi, Raba. Executive Director, Youth Initiative for Human Rights—Kosovo. Pristina, Kosovo. May 2011.

Goranci Brkić, Ljuljjeta. General Manager, Nansen Dialogue Centre. Sarajevo, Bosnia. May 2011.

Gowling, Elizabeth. Staff member, The Ideas Project. Pristina, Kosovo. May 2011.

Hadzic, Mujo. Advisor for Coordination of EU Assistance. Office of the Mayor. Brčko District, Bosnia. May 2011.

Hadzihalilovic, Selma. Women to Women. June 2001, June 2003.

Hajrulahovic, Katica. National Program Officer, Sida. Embassy of Sweden. Sarajevo, Bosnia. October 2007.

Harms, Danielle A. Political Officer, Second Secretary, Embassy of the United States of America. Sarajevo, Bosnia. October 2007.

Hill, Chris. President, American University of Kosovo. Pristina, Kosovo. May 2011.

Holliday, Matthew. Justice and Civil Society Initiatives, International Commission on Missing Persons. Sarajevo, Bosnia. May 2011.

Hoxha, Durata. Political Advisor to the Prime Minister. Office of the Prime Ministry. Government of Kosovo. Pristina, Kosovo. May 2011.

Hoxha, Kaltrina. Project Assistant, Balkan Investigative Reporting Network (BIRN). Pristina, Kosovo. May 2011.

Hoxha, Yll. Executive Director, Foreign Policy Club. Pristina, Kosovo. May 2011.

Idrizi, Valdete. Cofounder, Community Building Mitrovica. Pristina, Kosovo. May 2011.

Idžakovic, Fedra. Executive Director, Prava Za Sve. Sarajevo, Bosnia. June 2011.

Ilić, Saša. Center for Peace and Tolerance. Gracanica, Kosovo. May 2011.

Islamic Community Center of Mostar. Meeting with office staff. Sarajevo, Bosnia. September 2000.

Jones, Judith. Special Assistant to the Supervisor, Office of the High Representative. Brčko, Bosnia. June 2003.

Kadić, Marija. Official, Koraci Nade. Humanitarna organizacija. Mostar, Bosnia. September 2000.

Kelmendi, Migje. Owner, Rrokum TV & Java Magazine. Pristina, Kosovo. May 2011.

Klimkiewicz, Slawomir. Democratisation Team Manager, Organization for Security and Cooperation in Europe. Brčko, Bosnia. June 2003.

Ksumi, Bajram E. Director of Department for Registering and Liaison with NGOs. Government of Republic of Kosova. Ministry of Public Administration. Pristina, Kosovo. May 2011.

Kulenovic-Latal, Seila. Project Officer, Catholic Relief Services. June 2001, June 2003.

Kurti, Albin. Member of VETEVENDOSJA. Pristina, Kosovo. May 2011.

Kvitashvili, Elisabeth. Director, Office of Conflict Management and Mitigation. U.S. Agency for International Development (USAID). Washington, DC. January 2006.

Lloyd, Lindsay. Director, Europe, International Republican Institute (IRI). Washington, DC. April 2006.

Luci, Besa. Editor-in-Chief, Kosovo 2.0. Pristina, Kosovo. May 2011.

Madacki, Saša. Director, Human Rights Center, University of Sarajevo. Sarajevo, Bosnia. October 2007, May 2011.

Maksimovic, Nena. Executive Director, Center for Peace and Tolerance. Pristina, Kosovo. May 2011.

Maliqui, Sara. Youth Initiative for Human Rights. Pristina, Kosovo. May 2011.

Mamut, Lejla. Human Rights Coordinator, Advocacy Center Trial (ACT). Sarajevo, Bosnia. May 2011.

Masic, Alman. Head of Office, Youth Initiative for Human Rights. Sarajevo, Bosnia. May 2011.

Miličević, Jadranka. Officer, Fondacija CURE. Sarajevo, Bosnia. May 2011.

Miric, Milan. Coordinator, Inicijativa I civilna akcja (ICVA). Sarajevo, Bosnia. June 2003.

"Movement of Mothers of Srebrenica and Žepa Enclaves." [Association]. Meetings with several members. September 2000, July 2001, October 2007.

Murphy, Michael J. Political Counselor, Embassy of the United States of America. Sarajevo, Bosnia. October 2007.

Muscheidt, Bettina. European External Action Service. Afghanistan Desk. Brussels, Belgium. July 2011.

Nikander, Päivi. Decentralization Advisor—Local Government, International Civilian Office. Pristina, Kosovo. May 2011.

Norrgard, Lee. Programme Director, Mercy Corps (formerly Catholic Relief Services). Pristina, Kosovo. May 2011.

Parmly, Michael E. Senior Diplomatic Advisor, USAID. Local Contractor. Pristina, Kosovo. May 2011.

Pietz, Matthew. Director, AED Ideas Changing Lives. Pristina, Kosovo. May 2011.

Pliska, Alma. Methodology Development Officer. Sarajevo, Bosnia. May 2011.

Popović, Viktor. Center for Peace and Tolerance. Gracanica, Kosovo. May 2011.

Porobić Isaković, Nela. Process Specialist, Access to Justice—Facing the Past and Building Confidence for the Future. UNDP Bosnia and Herzegovina. Sarajevo, Bosnia. May 2011.

Poteat, Linda. Director, Disaster Response, InterAction. Washington, DC. January 2006.

Prins, Margariet. Senior Advisor, Office of the High Representative. Sarajevo, Bosnia. October 2007.

Pula, Vera. Program Coordinator, Kosovo Foundation for Civil Society. Pristina, Kosovo. May 2011.

Puljek-Shank, Randall. Representative for Southeastern Europe. Mennonite Central Committee. Sarajevo, Bosnia. May 2011.

Rasavac, Zineta. Civil Society Program Manager, Organization for Security and Cooperation in Europe. Sarajevo, Bosnia. September 2000.

Refaeil, Nora. Special Advisor on Dealing with the Past, International Civilian Office. Pristina, Kosovo. May 2011.

Rizvanolli, Artane. Senior Researcher, REINVEST. Pristina, Kosovo. May 2011.

Rowan, Christopher. Deputy International Civilian Representative, International Civilian Office (ICO). Pristina, Kosovo. May 2011.

Rrahmi, Bashkim. Executive Director, Foundation for Democratic Initiatives. Pristina, Kosovo. May 2011.

Rudić, Borka. Secretary General, BH Journalist Association/ REKOM. Sarajevo, Bosnia. May 2011.

Ruvic, Jadranka. Project Coordinator, HealthNet International. Sarajevo, Bosnia. September 2000.

Sahinpasic, Asim. Communications Manager, World Vision. Sarajevo, Bosnia. June 2003.

Saric, Seida. Director, Mikrokreditna Organizacja Zene za Zene International. Sarajevo, Bosnia. October 2007.

Sentic, Srdjan. Senior Advisor to Prime Minister/Director, Office for Community Affairs. Pristina, Kosovo. May 2011.

Shala, Krenar. Researcher, KIPRED. Pristina, Kosovo. May 2011.

Simić, Goran. Ministry of Justice, Federation of Bosnia and Herzegovina. Sarajevo, Bosnia. May 2011.

Simjonovic, Dijana. Center for Civil Society Development. Mitrovica, Kosovo. May 2011.

Slatina, Senad. Senior Research Coordinator, UNDP Bosnia and Herzegovina. Sarajevo, Bosnia. May 2011.

Slišković, Željka. Official, Coalition for Return. Sarajevo, Bosnia. June 2003.

Smailbegović Hadžihalilović, Aiša. President, LOTOS. Mental Health Protection. Zenica, Bosnia. September 2000.

Smidling, Tamara. Official, Center for Nonviolent Action. Sarajevo, Bosnia. May 2011.

Stanisic, Vladimir. Human Rights Officer, Human Rights/Rule of Law Department. Office of the High Representative. Sarajevo, Bosnia. September 2000.

Susnjar, Adis. Coordinator, BH Journalist Association/REKO. Sarajevo, Bosnia. May 2011.

Swerer, Daniel. Director, The Balkans Program. U.S. Institute of Peace. Washington, DC. June 24, 2003.

Sylaj, Florije. Manager, Community Building Mitrovica. Mitrovica, Kosovo. May 2011.

Sylejmani, Kreshnik. PR Manager, Consultation Process in Kosovo. Initiative for RECOM. Pristina, Kosovo. May 2011.

Tahiri, Hasim. Officer, Mundesia. Mitrovica, Kosovo. May 2011.

Tauber, Eli. High Expert Officer, University of Sarajevo. Institute for the Research of Crimes Against Humanity and International Law. Sarajevo, Bosnia. May 2011.

Tokača, Mirsad. President, Research and Documentation Center. Sarajevo, Bosnia. September 2000, June 2001, September 2007, May 2011.

Venneri, Guilio. Desk Officer for Justice, Freedom and Security. European Commission. DG Enlargement. Brussels, Belgium. June 2011.

Wilton, Robert. The Ideas Partnership. Pristina, Kosovo. May 2011.

Youth Initiative for Human Rights. Pristina, Kosovo. May 2011.

Zegiri, Adrian. Head of Office, European Centre for Minority Issues. Pristina, Kosovo. May 2011.

Zivanovic, Miroslav. Head of Documentation Department, Human Rights Centre. University of Sarajevo. Sarajevo, Bosnia. May 2011.

Zogijani, Avni, Qahu. Anti-Corruption NGO. Journalist Koha Ditore/Balkan Insight. Pristina, Kosovo. May 2011.

Zvizdic, Nuna. President, Žene Ženamy. Sarajevo, Bosnia. July 2001, May 2011.

Written Sources

Aall, Pamela. 2005. "What Do NGOs Bring to Peace Making?" In *Guide to IGOs, NGOs and the Military in Peace and Relief Operations*, edited by Daniel Miltenberger and Thomas G. Weiss, 365–83. Washington DC: USIP.

Abdelal, Rawi, Yoshiko M. Herrera, Alastair Iain Johnston, and Rose McDermott, eds. 2009. *Measuring Identity*. Cambridge: Cambridge University Press.

Abiew, Francis K., and Tom Keating. 1999. "NGOs and UN Peacekeeping Operations: Strange Bedfellows." *International Peacekeeping* 6 (2): 89–111.

Aggestam, Karin. 2003. "Conflict Prevention: Old Wine in New Bottles?" *International Peacekeeping* 10 (1): 12–23.

Ahmed, Shamima, and David M. Potter. 2006. *NGOs in International Politics*. Bloomfield: Kumarian Press.

Alger, Chadwick F. 2005. "Expanding Involvement of NGOs in Global Governance." In *Subcontracting Peace: The Challenges of the NGO Peacebuilding*, edited by Oliver P. Richmond and Henry F. Carey, 3–18. Hampshire, UK: Ashgate.

———. 2007. "There Are Peacebuilding Tasks for Everybody." *International Studies Review* 9 (3): 534–54.

Alvarez, Sonia E. 1990. *Engendering democracy in Brazil: Women's movements in transition politics*. Princeton, NJ: Princeton University Press.

Anderson, Kenneth, and David Rieff. 2005. "Global Civil Society: A Skeptical View." In *Introducing Global Civil Society 2004/05*, edited by Helmut Anheier, Marlies Glasius, and Mary Kaldor, 26–39. Thousand Oaks, CA: Sage Publications.

Anderson, Mary B. 1999. *Do No Harm. How Aid Can Support Peace—Or War*. Boulder, CO: Lynne Rienner.

Anderson, Morten. 2015. "How to Study NGOs in Practice." In *The NGO Challenge for International Relations Theory*, edited by William DeMars and Dennis Dijkzuel, 41–64. London: Routledge.

Anheier, Helmut, Marlies Glasius, and Mary Kaldor, eds. 2005. *Global Civil Society 2004/5*. London: Sage.

Archer, Sarah E. 2003. "Kosovo Present and Future." *Military Review* 83 (6): 31–40.

Autesserre, Séverine. 2014. *Peaceland: Conflict Resolution and the Everyday Politics of Intervention*. New York: Columbia University Press.

Baldwin, David A. 1989. *Paradoxes of Power*. New York: Basil Blackwell.

Barakat, Sultan, ed. 2005a. *After the Conflict: Reconstruction and Development in the Aftermath of War*. London: I. B. Tauris.

———. 2005b. "Post-War Reconstruction and Development: Coming of Age." In *After the Conflict: Reconstruction and Development in the Aftermath of War*, edited by Sultan Barakat, 7–32. London: I. B. Tauris.

Barnett, Michael. 2011. *Empire of Humanity: A History of Humanitarianism*. Ithaca, NY: Cornell University Press.

Barnett, Michael, and Jack Snyder. 2008. "The Grand Strategies of Humanitarianism." In *Humanitarianism in Question: Politics, Power, Ethics*, edited by Michael Barnett and Thomas G. Weiss, 143–71. Ithaca, NY: Cornell University Press.

Barnett, Michael, and Peter Walker. 2015. "Regime Change for Humanitarian Aid." *Foreign Affairs* 94 (4): 130–41.

Bell, Christine, and Catherine O'Rourke. 2007. "The People's Peace? Peace Agreements, Civil Society and Participatory Democracy." *International Political Science Review* 28: 293–332.

Belloni, Roberto. 2001. "Civil Society and Peacebuilding in Bosnia and Herzegovina." *Journal of Peace Research* 38 (2): 163–80.

———. 2008a. "Civil Society in War-to-Democracy Transitions." In *From War to Democracy: Dilemmas of Peacebuilding,* edited by Anna K. Jarstad and Timothy D. Sisk, 182–210. Cambridge: Cambridge University Press.

———. 2008b. *State Building and International Intervention in Bosnia.* London: Routledge.

"Better Governance for a Greater Impact." 2011. *Kosovar Civil Society Foundation.* March 11. http://civicus.org/downloads/CSI/Kosovo.pdf.

Bieber, Florian. 2002. "Governing Post-War Bosnia-Herzegovina." In *Minority Governance in Europe,* edited by Kinga Gal, 321–37. Budapest: The Open Society Institute.

Bojicic-Dzelilovic, Vesna. 2002. "World Bank, NGOs and the Private Sector in Post-War Reconstruction." In *Recovering from Civil Conflict: Reconciliation, Peace, and Development,* edited by Edward Newman and Albrecht Schnabel, 81–98. London: Frank Cass.

Briscoe, Ivan, and Megan Price. 2011. "Kosovo's new map of power: governance and crime in the wake of independence." The Hague: Netherlands Institute of International Relations.

Boutros-Ghali, Boutros. 1992. *An Agenda for Peace: Preventive Diplomacy, Peacemaking and Peace-Keeping: Report of the Secretary-General Pursuant to the Statement Adopted by the Summit Meeting of the Security Council on 31 January 1992.* New York: United Nations. http://www.un-documents.net/a47-277.htm.

———. 1995. *Supplement to* An Agenda for Peace: *Position Paper of the Secretary-General on the Occasion of the Fiftieth Anniversary of the United Nations.* http://www.un.org/documents/ga/docs/50/plenary/a50-60.htm.

———. 1996. "Foreword." In *NGOs, the UN and Global Governance,* edited by Thomas G. Weiss and Leon Gordenker. Boulder, CO: Lynne Rienner.

Bowen, John R. 1996. "The Myth of Global Ethnic Conflict." *Journal of Democracy* 7 (4): 3–14.

Brouwer, Imco. 2000. "Weak Society and Civil Society Promotion: The Cases of Egypt and Palestine." In *Funding Virtue: Civil Society Aid and Democracy Promotion,* edited by Marina Ottaway and Thomas Carothers, 21–48. Washington, DC: The Carnegie Endowment for International Peace, 2000.

Brown, Keith. 2009. "How (Not) to Export Civil Society. Do We Know How Yet? Insider Perspectives on International Democracy Promotion in the Western Balkans." *Southeastern Europe* 33 (1): 1–25.

Brown, Michael Edward. ed., 1993. *Ethnic Conflict and International Security.* Princeton, NJ: Princeton University Press.

———. 1996. The international dimensions of internal conflict. CSIA Studies in International Security, no. 10. Cambridge, MA: MIT Press.

"Building the new Libya." Bulletin of the United Nations Department of Political Affairs, Winter-Spring 2012. http://www.un.org/wcm/webdav/site/undpa/shared/undpa/pdf /Politically%20Speaking%20Winter%20Spring%202012.pdf.

Burg, Steven L., and Paul S. Shoup. 1999. *The War in Bosnia-Herzegovina: Ethnic Conflict and International Intervention*. New York: M. E. Sharpe.

CAD, DAC. 1997. "Guidelines on Conflict, Peace and Development Co-operation."

Call, Charles T. 2008. "Building States to Build Peace?" In *Building States to Build Peace*, 1–25. Boulder, CO: Lynne Rienner.

Call, Charles T., and Elizabeth M. Cousens. 2008. "Ending Wars and Building Peace: International Responses to War-Torn Societies." *International Studies Perspectives* 9: 1–21.

Campbell, Susanna, David Chandler, and Meera Sabaratnam. 2011. *A Liberal Peace? The Problems and Practices of Peacebuilding*. London: Zed Books.

Carothers, Thomas. 1999. *Aiding Democracy Abroad: The Learning Curve*. Washington, DC: The Carnegie Endowment for International Peace.

———. 2006. "Backlash against Democracy Promotion." *Foreign Affairs* 85 (2).

Center for Global Prosperity. 2008. *Index of Global Philanthropy 2008*. Washington, DC: Hudson Institute. https://www.hudson.org/files/documents/2008%20Index%20-%20 Low%20Res.pdf.

"The Challenges of Change." 1992. Conference on Security and Co-operation in Europe Summit, July 9–10.

Chandler, David. 2000. *Bosnia: Faking Democracy after Dayton*. London: Pluto Press.

———. 1998. "Democratization in Bosnia: The limits of civil society building strategies." *Democratization* 5 (4): 78–102.

———. 2001. "The Road to Military Humanitarianism: How the Human Rights NGOs Shaped a New Humanitarianism Agenda." *Human Rights Quarterly* 23 (3): 687–700.

Chaundhary Wimpelmann, Torunn, Orzala Ashraf Nernat, and Astri Suhrke. 2011. "Promoting Women's Rights in Afghanistan: The Ambiguous Footprint of the West." In *The Liberal Peace? The Problems and Practices of Peacebuilding*, edited by Susanna Campbell, David Chandler, and Meera Sabaratnam, 106–20. London: Zed.

Chayes, Sarah. 2006. *The Punishment of Virtue: Inside Afghanistan after the Taliban*. Queensland: University of Queensland Press.

Christopher, Warren. 1993. "New Steps toward Conflict Resolution in the Former Yugoslavia." U.S. Department of State. New Conference on Former Yugoslavia, Office of theSpokesman.http://dosfan.lib.uic.edu/ERC/briefing/dossec/1993/9302/930210dossec. html.

Civil Society in Bosnia and Herzegovina: Seeking the Way Forward. 2011. UN Volunteers Report.

Clinton, William J. 1994. "Address before a Joint Session of the Congress on the State of the Union." [speech]. January 25. Online by Gerhard Peters and John T. Woolley, The American Presidency Project. http://www.presidency.ucsb.edu/ws/index.php?pid=504 09#ixzz1qRc3GZNk.

———. 1993. "Inaugural Address." [speech] January. Online by Gerhard Peters and John T. Woolley, The American Presidency Project. http://www.presidency.ucsb.edu/ws/?pid=46366.

Cohen, Michael A., Maria Figueroa Kupcu, and Parag Khanna. 2008. "The New Colonialists." *Foreign Policy* 167: 74–79.

Cooley, Alexander, and James Ron. 2002. "NGO Scramble: Organizational Insecurity and the Political Economy of Transnational Action." *International Security* 27 (1): 5–39.

"Congressional Presentation Fiscal Year 1998 Europe and the Newly Independent States." 1999. Washington, DC: USAID.

Country Assistance Strategy for Bosnia and Herzegovina 2009–2013. May 20, 2009, http://pdf.usaid.gov/pdf_docs/PDACP613.pdf.

Cousens, Elizabeth M., and Charles K. Cater. 2001. *Toward peace in Bosnia: implementing the Dayton accords.* Boulder, CO: Lynne Rienner.

Coyne, Christopher K. 2013. *Doing Bad by Doing Good.* Stanford, CA: Stanford University Press.

Crawford, Beverly, and Ronnie D. Lipschutz, eds. 1998. *The Myth of "Ethnic Conflict": Politics, Economics, and "Cultural" Violence.* Berkeley: University of California Press.

CSO Sustainability Index for Central and Eastern Europe and Eurasia. 2013, June. Washington, DC: USAID.

Currion, Paul. 2010. "Strength in Numbers: A Review of NGO Coordination in the Field. Case Study: Kosovo 1999–2002." Report by the Geneva International Council of Voluntary Agencies.

Daalder. 1999. Getting to Dayton: The Making of America's Bosnia Policy. Washington DC: The Brookings Institution.

Daalder, Ivo H., and James G. Stavridis. 2012. "NATO's Victory in Libya: The Right Way to Run an Intervention." *Foreign Affairs* 91 (2): 2–7.

Dabelko, Geofrrey D. 1999. "The Environmental Factor." *Washington Quarterly* 23 (4): 14–19.

David, Stephen. 2008. *Catastrophic Consequences.* Baltimore: Johns Hopkins Press.

Deak, Istvan. 1993. "A World Gone Raving Mad." *New York Times.* March 28. https://www.nytimes.com/books/98/12/06/specials/kaplan-balkan.html.

Deaton, Angus. 2013. *The Great Escape: Health, Wealth and the Origins of Inequality.* Princeton, NJ: Princeton University Press.

de Jonge Oudraat, Chantal, and Virginia Haufler. 2008. *Global Governance and the Role of NGOs in International Peace and Security.* AICGS.

DeMars, William E. 2005. *NGOs and Transnational Networks: Wild Cards in World Politics.* London: Pluto Press.

DeMars, William E., and Dennis Dijkzeul. 2015. *The NGO Challenge to IR Theory.* London: Routledge.

Devine, Vera. 2011. *NGOs and Corruption in Post-War Reconstruction: The Case of Bosnia's Refugee Return.* U4 Practice Insight Report 3. Bergen, Norway: CMI.

Diehl, Paul F. 2008. *Peace Operations.* Cambridge: Polity.

Diehl, Paul F., and Daniel Druckman. 2010. *Evaluating Peace Operations.* Boulder, CO: Lynne Rienner.

Dizdarević, Drdan et al. 2006. "Democracy Assistance in Bosnia and Herzegovina." Open Society Fund Bosnia & Herzegovina. Sarajevo, Bosnia. http://pdc.ceu.hu/archive/00003187/01/democracy_assessment_in_BiH.pdf.

Dobbins, James. 2003. *America's Role in Nation-Building*. RAND Corporation.

———. 2012. "Organizing for Nation Building." In *The International Community and Statebuilding: Getting its Act Together?* edited by Patrice McMahon and Jon Western, 41–56. New York: Routledge.

Dobbins, James, Seth G. Jones, Keith Crane, Andrew Rathmell, and Brett Steele. 2001. *The UN's Role in Nation-Building: From the Congo to Iraq*. Washington, DC: The Rand Corporation.

Dobbins, James, John G. McGinn, Keith Crane, Seth G. Jones, Rollie Lal, Andrew Rathmell, Rachel M. Swanger et al. 2003. *America's Role in Nation-Building: From Germany to Iraq*. Washington DC: The Rand Corporation.

Dobbins, James, Seth G. Jones, Keith Crane, Christopher S. Chivvis, Andrew Radin, F. Stephen Larrabee, Nora Bensahel et al. 2008. *Europe's Role in Nation-Building: From the Balkans to the Congo*. Washington DC: The Rand Corporation.

Donini, Antonio. 2007. "Local Perceptions of Assistance." *International Peacebuilding* 14 (1): 158–72.

Doyle, Michael W., and Nicholas Sambanis. 2006. *Making War and Building Peace: United Nations Peace Operations*. Princeton, NJ: Princeton University Press.

Duffield, Mark. 1994. "Bosnia and the Future of Military Humanitarianism." *Middle East Report* No. 187/188: 16–17.

Durch, William J. 2004. "Strengthening UN Secretariat Capacity for Civilian Post-Conflict Response," Paper presented at the Strengthening the UN's Capacity on Civilian Crisis Management Conference.

Easterly, William. 2006. *The White Man's Burden: Why the West's Efforts to Aid the Rest Have Done So Much Ill and So Little Good*. New York: Penguin.

Edstrom, Hakam, Janne Haaland Matlary, and Magnus Petersson, eds. 2011. *NATO: The Power of Partnerships*. New York: Palgrave Macmillan.

Edwards, Michael, and David Hulme, eds. 1996. *Beyond the Magic Bullet: NGO Performance and Accountability in the Post-Cold War World*. West Hartford, CT: Kumarian Press.

Edwards, Michael, David Hulme, and Tina Wallace. 1999. "NGOs in a Global Future: Marrying Local Delivery to Worldwide Leverage." *Public Administration and Development* 19 (2): 117–36.

EU assistance to BiH. 2007. "Bosnia and Herzegovina 2007 Progress Report." November 6, 2007. http://ec.europa.eu/enlargement/pdf/mipd_bosnia_herzegovina_2007_2009_en.pdf.

Fagan, Adam. 2005. "Civil society in Bosnia ten years after Dayton." *International Peacekeeping* 12 (3): 406–19.

———. 2012. *Europe's Balkan Dilemma: Paths to Civil Society or State-Building*. London: I. B. Tauris.

———. 2006. "Transnational aid for civil society development in post-socialist Europe: Democratic consolidation or a new imperialism?" *Journal of Communist Studies and Transition Politics* 22 (1): 115–34.

Fearon, James, and David Latin. 2003. "Ethnic Insurgency and Civil War," *American Political Science Review* 97 (1): 75–90.

Ferati-Sachsenmaier, Flora. 2015. *Postwar Kosovo: The Challenge of Pursuing Interethnic Reconciliation in a Politically Contested Territory (1999–2008).* PhD diss., University of Bremen.

Fisher, Joanna. 2005. "The Role of NGOs in Institution-Building in Rwanda." In *Subcontracting Peace: The Challenges of NGO Peacebuilding,* edited by Oliver P. Richmond and Henry F. Carey, 183–89. Hampshire, UK: Ashgate.

Fisher, Julie. 1998. *Non-Governments: NGOs and the Political Development of the Third World.* West Hartford, CT: Kumarian Press.

Fischer, Martina. 2006. "Civil Society in Conflict Transformation." Berlin: Berghof Research Center for Constructive Conflict Management. http://www.berghof-foundation. org/fileadmin/redaktion/Publications/Handbook/Articles/fischer_cso_handbookII .pdf. Accessed September 20, 2011.

Fitzduff, Mari, and Cheyanne Church. 2004. "Stepping Up to the Table." In *NGOs at the Table: Strategies for Influencing Policies in Areas of Conflict,* edited by Mari Fitzduff and Cheyanne Church, 1–22. Lanham, MD: Rowman & Littlefield.

Flores, Thomas Edward, and Irfam Nooruddin. 2009. "Financing the Peace: Evaluating World Bank Post-Conflict Assistance Programs." *The Review of International Organizations* 4 (1): 1–27.

Forsythe, David. 2007. *Human Rights in International Relations,* 2nd ed. Cambridge: Cambridge University Press.

Forsythe, David and Patrice C. McMahon. 2016. *American Exceptionalism Revisited U.S. Foreign Policy, Human Rights, and World Order.* London: Routledge.

FSG. 2013. *Ahead of the Curve. Insights for the International NGO of the Future.* Report funded by The William and Flora Hewlett Foundation.

Fukuyama, Francis. 2004. *State-Building: Governance and World Order in the 21st Century.* Ithaca, NY: Cornell University Press.

Gagnon, Chip. 2006. "Catholic Relief Services, USAID, and Authentic Partnership in Serbia." *Transacting Transition: The Micropolitics of Democracy Assistance in the Former Yugoslavia* (2006): 167–68.

Gagnon, Chip, Stefan Senders, and Keith Brown. 2014. "Introduction." In *Post Conflict Studies: An Interdisciplinary Approach,* edited by Chip Gagnon and Keith Brown, 1–16. London: Routledge.

Galtung, Johan. 1975. *Essays in Peace Research.* Copenhagen: Christian Ejlers.

George, Alexander, and Andrew Bennett. 2005. *Case Studies and Theory Development in Social Sciences.* Cambridge, MA: MIT Press.

Gheciu, Alexandra. 2011. "Divided Partners: The Challenges of NATO-NGO Cooperation in Peacebuilding Operations." *Global Governance* 17: 95–113.

Gidley, Ruth. 2005. "NGOs Respond to Crackdown from Afghan Government." *ReliefWeb,* April 8. http://reliefweb.int/report/afghanistan/ngos-respond-crackdown-afghan -government.

Gingrich, Tara, and Marc Cohen. 2015. "Turning the Humanitarian System on its Head," Oxfam Research Reports, July. Oxford: Oxfam.

Goodhand, Jonathan. 2006. *Aiding Peace? The Role of NGOs in Armed Conflict*. Boulder, CO: Lynne Rienner.

Goodhand, Jonathan, Nick Lewer, and David Hulme. 1999. "NGOs and Peace Building: Sri Lanka Study." Bradford & Manchester: Department of Peace Studies, University of Bradford, Institute for Development Policy and Management, University of Manchester.

Goodhand, Jonathan and Oliver Walton. 2009. "The limits of liberal peacebuilding? International engagement in the Sri Lankan peace process. *Journal of Intervention and Statebuilding*, 3 (3): 303–23.

Goonatilake, Susantha. 2006. *Recolonisation: Foreign Funded NGOs in Sri Lanka*. New York: Sage.

Gordenker, Leon, and Thomas G. Weiss. 1996. "Pluralizing Global Governance." In *NGOs, the UN, and Global Governance*, edited by Thomas Weiss and Leon Gordenker, 17–47. Boulder, CO: Lynne Rienner.

Grodeland, Ase Berit. 2006. "Public Perceptions of Non-Governmental Organizations in Serbia, Bosnia & Herzegovina, and Macedonia." *Communist and Post-Communist Studies* 39: 221–46.

Gurr, Ted Robert. 2002. "Containing Internal War in the Twenty-First Century." In *From Reaction to Conflict Prevention*, edited by Fen Oslder Hampson and David M. Malone, 41–62. Boulder, CO: Lynne Rienner.

Hall, Peter, and Rosemary Taylor. 1996. "Political Science and the Three New Institutionalisms," *Political Studies* 44 (5): 936–57.

Halliday, Fred. 2001. "The romance of non-state actors." In *Non-state actors in world politics*, 21–37. London, UK: Palgrave Macmillan.

Hampson, Fen Olser. 2002. "Preventive Diplomacy at the United Nations and Beyond." In *From Reaction to Conflict Prevention*, edited by Osler Hampson and David Malone, 139–58. Boulder, CO: Lynne Rienner.

Harpviken, Kristian Berg, Arne Strand, and Karin Ask. 2002. *Afghanistan and Civil Society*. Paper Commissioned by the Norwegian Ministry of Foreign Affairs, Peshawar/Bergen December 8. CMI Commissioned Report: CMI.

Hassan, Fareed M. A. 2004. "Lessons Learned from World Bank Experience in Post-Conflict Reconstruction," OED Conference Note, September 21. Washington, DC: World Bank. http://www-wds.worldbank.org/external/default/WDSContentServer/WDSP/IB/2013/1 2/13/000442464_20131213143256/Rendered/PDF/820830WP0OED0c00Box379853B00P UBLIC0.pdf.

Helman, Gerald B., and Steven R. Ratner. 1992. "Saving Failed States." *Foreign Policy* 89: 3–20.

Henderson, Sarah L. 2003. *Building Democracy in Contemporary Russia: Western Support for Grassroots Organizations*. Ithaca, NY: Cornell University Press.

Henriksen, Dag. 2007. *NATO's Gamble Combining Diplomacy and Airpower in the Kosovo Crisis, 1998–1999*. Annapolis, MD: Naval Institute Press.

Hertel, Shareen. 2006. *Unexpected Power: Conflict and Change among Transnational Activists*. Ithaca, NY: Cornell University Press.

Hertic, Zlatko, Amela Sapcanin, and Susan L. Woodward. 2000. "Bosnia and Herzegovina." In *Good intentions: Pledges of Aid for Post-conflict Recovery*, edited by Shepard Forman and Stewart Patrick, 315–66. Boulder, CO: Lynne Rienner.

Hilhorst, Dorothea. 2003. *Discourses, Diversity and Development: The Real World of NGOs*. London: Zed.

Hill, Felicity. 2002. "NGO Perspectives: NGOs and the Security Council" *Disarmament Forum* 1: 27–30.

"History of the NATO-led Stabilisation Force (SFOR) in Bosnia and Herzegovinia." NATO website, http://www.nato.int/sfor/docu/d981116a.htm.

Hitchens, Christopher. 2011. "From Abbottabad to Worse." *Vanity Fair*.

Holbrooke, Richard, 1998. *To End a War: Sarajevo to Dayton The Inside Story*. New York: Random House.

Howell, Jude et al. 2008. "The Backlash Against Civil Society in the Wake of the Long War on Terror," *Development in Practice* 18 (1): 82–93.

Human Rights Security Report Project. 2007. http://www.hsrgroup.org/docs/Publica tions/HSB2007/Figures/2007HSBrief_fig3_1-StateBasedArmedConflictsByType .jpg.

Human Security Research Project. 2009. http://www.hsrgroup.org/docs/Publications /HSR20092010/Figures/20092010Report_Fig10_2_NumberOfWars.pdf.

Human Security Research Project. 2010. http://www.hsrgroup.org/docs/Publications/HSR 20092010/Figures/20092010Report_Fig6_6_BattleDeathsYearMillionPopulation.pdf

Human Security Report Project. 2012. Human Security Report 2012: *Sexual Violence, Education, and War: Beyond the Mainstream Narrative.* Vancouver: Human Security Press. http://hsrgroup.org/docs/Publications/HSR2012/2012HumanSecurityReport-FullText-LowRes.pdf.

Huntington, Samuel. 1996. *The Clash of Civilizations and the Remaking of World Order.* New York: Simon & Schuster.

———. 1973. "Transnational Organizations in World Politics," *World Politics* 25 (3): 333–68.

ICVA. 2000. *ICVA Directory of Humanitarian and Development Agencies in Bosnia and Herzegovina.* Sarajevo: International Council of Voluntary Agencies.

Ignatieff, Michael. 2003. *Empire Lite.* New York: Random House.

"In the Wake of War: Improving U.S. Post-Conflict Capabilities." 2005. Report of an Independent Task Force. New York: Council on Foreign Relations.

Irvine, Jill. A. 2013. "Electoral Breakthroughs in Croatia and Serbia: Women's Organizing and International Assistance," *Communist and Post-Communist Studies* 46.

Irvine, Jill A., and Patrice McMahon. 2013. "From International Courts to Grassroots Organizing: The Obstacles to Transitional Justice in the Balkans." In *Transitional Justice and Civil Society in the Balkans,* edited by Olivera Simic and Zala Volcic, 217–38. London: Springer.

Jalali, Rita. 2013. "Financing Empowerment? How Foreign Aid to Southern NGOs and Social Movements Undermines Grass-Roots Mobilization." *Sociology Compass* 7 (1): 55–73.

Jarstad, Anna K. 2008. "Dilemmas of war-to-democracy transitions: Theories and concepts." In *From War to Democracy: Dilemmas of peacebuilding*: 17–36.

Jarstad, Anna K., and Timothy D. Sisk, eds. 2008. *From War to Democracy: Dilemmas of Peacebuilding.* Cambridge: Cambridge University Press.

Johnson, Chris, and Jolyon Leslie. 2004. *Afghanistan: The Mirage of Peace.* London: Zed Books.

Kaldor, Mary. 2007. *Human Security*. Cambridge: Polity Press.

———. 1999. *New and Old Wars: Organized Violence in a Global Era*. Stanford, CA: Stanford University Press.

Kalyvas, Stathias. 2001. "'New' and 'Old' Civil Wars: A Valid Distinction?" *World Politics* 54 (1): 99–118.

Kaplan, Robert D. 1993. Balkan ghosts: A journey through history. New York: St. Martin's Press.

———. 1994. "The Coming Anarchy: How scarcity, crime, overpopulation, tribalism, and disease are rapidly destroying the social fabric of our planet." *The Atlantic* (Feb): 44–76.

Keating, Thomas F., and W. Andy Knight, eds. 2004. *Building Sustainable Peace*. New York: United Nations University Press.

Keck, Margaret, and Kathryn Sikkink. 1998. *Activists Beyond Borders: Advocacy Networks in International Politics*. Ithaca, NY: Cornell University Press.

Kelly, Kevin. 1999. "Development for Social Change: The Challenge of Building Civil Society in Rwanda." *Trocaire Development Review*: 57–80.

Keohane, Robert O. (1984) 2005. *After Hegemony: Cooperation and Discord in the World Political Economy*, revised edition. Reprint, Princeton, NJ: Princeton University Press.

Kerlin, Janelle A., and Supaport Thanasombat. 2006. "The International Charitable Nonprofit Subsector: Scope, Size, and Revenue," *Non-Profits in Focus*, Urban Institute Policy Brief, No. 2, September. Washington, DC: Urban Institute.

King, Iain, and Whit Mason. 2006. *Peace at any price: how the world failed Kosovo*. Ithaca: Cornell University Press.

Klarreich, Kathie, and Linda Polma. 2012. "The NGO Republic of Haiti," *The Nation*, November 19.

Klein, Naomi. 2007. *The Shock Doctrine: The Rise of Disaster Capitalism*. New York: Macmillan.

Korten, David. 1987. "Third Generation NGO Strategies: A Key to People-Centered Development," *World Development* 15: 145–59.

Kostovicova, Denisa. 2008. "Legitimacy and International Administration: The Ahtisaari Settlement for Kosovo from a Human Security Perspective." *International Peacekeeping* 15 (5): 631–47.

Krakauer, Jon. 2013. "Is It Time to Forgive Greg Mortenson?" *Daily Beast*. April 8. http://www.thedailybeast.com/articles/2013/04/08/is-it-time-to-forgive-greg-mortenson.html.

———. 2011. *Three Cups of Deceit: How Greg Mortenson, Humanitarian Hero, Lost His Way*. Expanded and updated. Byliner Inc.

Kristoff, Madeline, and Liz Panarelli. 2010. "Haiti: A Republic of NGOs?" *Peacebuilding Brief* 23, April 26. Washington, DC: USIP.

Kristof, Nicholas. 2011. "Three Cups of Tea Spilled." *New York Times*. April 20.

Leo, Benjamin. 2013. "Is Anyone Listening? Does US Foreign Assistance Target People's Top Priorities?" Center for Global Development Report No. 348, December.

Lindenberg, Marc, and Coralie Bryant. 2001. *Going Global: Transforming Relief and Development NGOs*. Hampshire, UK: Ashgate.

Llamazares, Monica, and Laina Reynolds Levy. 2003. "NGOs and Peacebuilding in Kosovo" Working Paper No 13. Bradford, UK: University of Bradford. http://www.brad.ac.uk/acad/confres/papers/pdfs/CCR13.pdf.

Lorezo-Capussela, Andrea. 2015. *State-Building in Kosovo: Democracy, Corruption and the EU in the Balkans*. I.B. Tauris.

Lowrey, Annie. 2011. "Don't Build Schools in Afghanistan: The real lesson of the Three Cups of Tea scandal." *Slate*. http://www.slate.com/articles/business/moneybox/2011/05/dont_build_schools_in_afganistan.html.

Maas, Peter. 1997. *Love Thy Neighbor*. New York: Vintage.

Mac Ginty, Roger. 2011. *International Peacebuilding and Local Resistance: Hybrid Forms of Peace*. London: Palgrave Macmillan.

Maglajilic, Reima Ana, and Edin Kodzic. 2008. "Political Space in Participation: Is There Full Citizen Participation in Public Life?" in *Democracy Assistance in Bosnia & Herzegovina,* edited by Dobrila Govedarica, 313–51. Sarajevo: Open Society Fund Report.

Manheim, Jarod B., and Richard C. Rich. 1995. *Empirical Political Analysis*. White Plains, NY: Longman.

Mapping and Analysis of Kosovo Civil Society. 2005. Kosovar Civil Society Foundation Prishtina: Kosovo. http://www.kcsfoundation.org/repository/docs/03_03_2014_4035052_KCSF_2005_Mapping_and_analysis_of_Kosovo_civil_society.pdf.

Mapping Study of Non-State Actors (NSA) in Bosnia-Herzegovina. 2005. The European Commission http://europa.ba/wp-content/uploads/2015/05/delegacijaEU_2013052914554860eng.pdf.

Marten, Kimberly Zisk. 2005. *Enforcing the Peace. Learning from the Imperial Past*. New York: Columbia University Press.

Martens, Kerstin. 2005. NGO's and the United Nations: Institutionalization, Professionalization and Adaptation. New York: Springer Press.

Mathews, Jessica Tuchman. 1997. "Power Shift," *Foreign Affairs* 76 (1). https://www.foreignaffairs.com/articles/1997-01-01/power-shift.

———. 1989. "Redefining Security." *Foreign Affairs* 68 (2): 162–77.

McCleary, Rachel M. 2009. *Global Compassion: Private Voluntary Organizations and US Foreign Policy since 1939*. Oxford: Oxford University Press.

McMahon, Patrice C. 2002. "What Have We Wrought?: Assessing International Involvement in Bosnia." *Problems of Post-Communism* 49 (1): 18–29.

McMahon, Patrice C. 2004. "Rebuilding Bosnia: A Model to Emulate or to Avoid?" *Political Science Quarterly* 119 (4): 569–93.

McMahon, Patrice C., and Jon Western. 2009. "The Death of Dayton." *Foreign Affairs* 88 (5): 69–83.

———, eds. 2012. *The International Community and Statebuilding: Getting Its Act Together?* New York: Routledge.

Mearsheimer, John. 1994. "The False Promise of International Institutions," *International Security* 19 (3): 5–49.

Mertus, Julie. 1999. *Kosovo: How Myths and Truths Started a War*. Berkeley: University of California Press.

———. 2004. "Improving International Peacebuilding Efforts: The Example of Human Rights Culture in Kosovo." *Global Governance* 10 (3): 333–51.

———. 2000. *War's Offensive on Women: The Humanitarian Challenge in Bosnia, Kosovo and Afghanistan.* West Hartford, CT: Kumarian Press.

Mikail, Barah. 2013, *Civil Society and Foreign Donors in Libya.* (AFA, Fride and Hivos). July 23. http://www.medea.be/2013/07/civil-society-and-foreign-donors-in-libya-part -1/, accessed February 20, 2014.

Molaeb, Amjad. 2014. "The Changing Face of Islam in Kosovo," *The New Context*, July 18. http://thenewcontext.milanoschool.org/the-changing-face-of-islam-in-kosovo /, accessed August 1, 2015.

Moore, Adam. 2013. *Peacebuilding in Practice: Local Experiences in Two Bosnian Towns.* Ithaca, NY: Cornell University Press.

Mortenson, Greg. 2006. *Three Cups of Tea: One Man's Mission to Promote Peace . . . One School at a Time.* New York; Penguin Books.

Mueller, John. 2000. "The Banality of Ethnic War," *International Security* 25 (1): 42–70.

Mulalic, Muhidin. 2011. "Women's NGOs in Bosnia," *Epiphany* 4 (1): 40–55. http://english.nahla.ba/tekstovi10.aspx?tid=232.

Murdie, Amanda. 2014. *Help or Harm. The Human Security Effects of International NGOs.* Stanford, CA: Stanford University Press.

Murithi, Tim. 2009. *The Ethics of Peacebuilding.* Edinburg: Edinburg University Press.

Musahara, Herman, and Chris Huggins. 2005. "Land Reform, Land Scarcity and Post-Conflict Reconstruction: A Case Study of Rwanda," In *From the Ground Up: Land Rights, Conflict and Peace in Sub-Saharan Africa*, edited by Chris Huggins and Jenny Clover, 269–346. ISS Africa. https://www.issafrica.org/uploads/6LAND.PDF

NATO. 2005. "Bringing Peace and Stability to the Balkans." NATO in the Balkans Briefing Report, February. Brussels: NATO Public Diplomacy Division.

Nilsson, Annika, Joakim Anger, and Jim Newkirk. 2010. "Evaluation of Support to the Civil Society in the Western Balkans." Sida Review 20.

Nordland, Rod. 2013, "Foreign Projects Give Afghans Fashion, Skate Park and Now 10,000 Ballons" *The New York Times.* May 25.

Nye, Joseph S. 2004. "The Rising Power of NGOs." *Project Syndicate.* http://www .project-syndicate.org/commentary/nye10/English.

Nye, Joseph J., and Robert Keohane. 1971. "Transnational Relations and World Politics: An Introduction," *International Organization* 25 (3): 329–49.

O'Brien, Paul. 2004. "Old Woods, New Paths, and Diverging Choices for NGOs." In *Nation-Building Unraveled? Aid, Peace and Justice in Afghanistan*, edited by Antonio Donini, Norah Niland, and Karin Wermester, 187–203. Hartford, CT: Kumarian Press.

O'Neill, William. G. 2002. *Kosovo: An Unfinished Peace.* Lynne Rienner.

OECD. 2013. Aid for CSOs. OECD. DOE: http://www.oecd.org/dac/peer-reviews /Aid%20for%20CSOs%20Final%20for%20WEB.pdf.

———. 2014. Development Co-operation Report 2014: Mobilising Resources for Sustainable Development. Paris: OECD. DOI: http://dx.doi.org/10.1787/dcr-2014-en.

———. 2008. "Financing Development 2008: Whose Ownership?" http://www.oecd.org /dataoecd/52/6/40729854.pdf. Accessed August 1, 2012.

———. 1998. *Reports for the DAC High Level and OECD Ministerial Council Meetings on Progress Made on Conflict, Peace and Development Cooperation and Addressing Excessive Military Expenditures in Developing Countries.* OECD Document, DCD/DAC (98) 8/REV1, 16 February. Paris: OECD.

Ohanyan, Anna. 2009. "Policy Wars for Peace: Network Model of NGO Behavior," *International Studies Review* 11 (3): 475–501.

O'Neill, William. 2002. *Kosovo: An Unfinished Peace.* Boulder, CO: Lynne Rienner.

Orjuela, Camilla. 2004. *Civil Society in Civil War.* Gothenburg, Sweden: Gothenburg University.

———. 2010. "Sri Lanka: Peace Activists and Nationalists." In *Civil Society & Peacebuilding: A Critical Assessment*, edited by Thannia Paffenholz, 297–320. Boulder, CO: Lynne Rienner.

Ottaway, Marina and Thomas Carothers, eds. 2000. *Funding virtue: Civil Society Aid and Democracy Promotion.* Washington DC: Carnegie Endowment for International Peace.

Paffenholz, Thania, and Christoph Spurk. 2006. "Civil Society, Civic Engagement, and Peacebuilding." *Social Development Papers*, No. 361, October. The World Bank.

Papić, Žarko. 2001. "Policies of international support to South-East European countries: Lessons (not) learnt from Bosnia-Herzegovina."

Papić, Žarko, Ranka Ninković, and Omer Čar. 2007. "Integrity in Reconstruction: Corruption, Effectiveness and Sustainability in Post-War Countries." Sarajevo: IBHI.

Paris, Roland. 2004. *At War's End: Building Peace after Civil Conflict.* Cambridge: Cambridge University Press.

———. 2011. "Critiques of Liberal Peace." In *A Liberal Peace? The Problems and Practices of Peacebuilding*, edited by Susanna Campbell, David Chandler, and Meera Sabaratnam, 31–54. London: Zed.

Paris, Roland, and Timothy D. Sisk, eds. 2009. *The Dilemmas of Statebuilding: Confronting the Contradictions of Postwar Peace Operations.* New York: Routledge.

Paul, James A. 2010. *A Short History of the NGO Working Group.* New York: NGO Working Group on the Security Council. http://www.ngowgsc.org/content/short-hisotyr-ngo-working-group.

"Peace and Conflict-Sensitive Approaches to Development." 2000. A Briefing for the OECD DAC Task Force on Conflict, Peace and Development Cooperation and the Conflict Prevention and Reconstruction Network (CPRN), December.

Pickering, Paula May. 2012. "Explaining the varying impact of international aid for local democratic governance in Bosnia-Herzegovina." *Problems of Post-Communism* 59 (1): 31–43.

———. 2007. *Peacebuilding in the Balkans: The View from the Ground Floor.* Ithaca, NY: Cornell University Press.

Poole, Lydia. 2013, "Funding at the Sharp End: Investing in National NGO Response Capacity." Catholic Agency for International Development. London: UK.

Posen, Barry, R. 1993. "The security dilemma and ethnic conflict." *Survival* 35 (1): 27–47.

Pouligny, Béatrice. 2005. "Civil Society and Post-Conflict Peacebuilding: Ambiguities of International Programmes Aimed at Building 'New' Societies." *Security Dialogue* 36 (4): 495–510.

Ramalingam, Ben, Bill Gray, and Giorgia Cerruti. 2013. "Missed Opportunities: The Case for Strengthening National and Local Partnership-based Humanitarian Responses." Christian Aid Report, 3 November.

Rashid, Ahmed. 2008. *Descent into Chaos: The U.S. and the Disaster in Pakistan, Afghanistan, and Central Asia.* New York: Penguin Press.

"Redefining Security" A Report to the Secretary of Defense and the Director of the Central Intelligence. February 28, 1994.

Reid, Elizabeth J., and Janelle A. Kerlin. 2006. *The International Charitable Nonprofit Subsector in the United States.* Washington, DC: Urban Institute.

Reimann, Kim D. 2006. "A View from the Top: International Politics, Norms and the Worldwide Growth of NGOs." *International Studies Quarterly* 50 (1): 45–67.

Reshaping International Priorities in Bosnia and Herzegovina, 2001. Part III The End of the Nationalist Regimes and the Future of The Bosnian State. European Stability Initiative Report. March 22.

Richmond, Oliver P. 2005. "Introduction: NGOs, Peace and Human Security." In *Mitigating Conflict: The Role of NGOs*, edited by Oliver Richmond and Henry F. Carey, 2–11. London: Routledge.

——. 2011. A Post-Liberal Peace. New York: Routledge.

——. 2011. "Resistance and the Post-Liberal Peace." In *A Liberal Peace? The Problems and Practices of Peacebuilding,* edited by Susanna Campbell, David Chandler, and Meera Sabaratnam, 226–44. London: Zed.

Richmond, Oliver P., and Henry F. Carey, eds. 2005. *Subcontracting Peace: The Challenge of NGOs in Peacebuilding.* Hampshire, UK: Ashgate.

Richmond, Oliver P., and Jason Franks. 2009. *Liberal Peace Transitions. Between Statebuilding and Peacebuilding.* Edinburgh: Edinburgh University Press.

Rieff, David. 2003. A Bed for the Night: Humanitarianism in crisis. New York: Simon and Schuster.

——. 2000. "Kosovo's Humanitarian Circus." *World Policy Journal* 17(3): 25–32.

——. 1995. *Slaughterhouse: Bosnia and the Failure of the West.* New York: Simon and Schuster.

Risse, Thomas, Stephen C. Ropp, and Kathryn Sikkink, eds. 1999. "The Power of Human Rights." International Norms and Domestic Change. Cambridge University Press.

Roberts, Adam. 2003. *A Bed for the Night. Humanitarianism in Crisis.* New York: Simon and Schuster.

——. 2000. "Kosovo's Humanitarian Circus," *World Policy Journal*, 17 (3): 25–32.

——. 2010. "Lives and statistics: Are 90% of war victims civilians?" *Survival* 52 (3): 115–36.

Salamon, Lester M., Wojciech S. Sokolowski, and Regina List. 2003. *Global Civil Society: An Overview.* Washington DC: Johns Hopkins University Institute for Policy Studies.

Sampson, Steven. 2002. "Weak States, Uncivil Societies and Thousands of NGOs: Benevolent Colonialism in the Balkans." In *The Balkans in Focus: Cultural Boundaries of the Balkans,* edited by Sanimir Resic and Barbara Tornquist-Plewa, 27–44. Lund, Sweden: Lund University Press.

Schimmelfennig, Frank, and Ulrich Sedelmeier. 2005. *The Europeanization of Central and Eastern Europe.* Ithaca, NY: Cornell University Press.

Schmitz, Hans Peter, Paloma Raggo, and Tosca Bruno-van Vijfeijken. 2012. "Accountability of Transnational NGOs: Aspirations vs. Practice," *Nonprofit and Voluntary Sector Quarterly* 41 (6): 1175–94.

Schuller, Mark. 2012. *Killing with Kindness: Haiti, International Aid and NGOs*. Rutgers, NJ: Rutgers University Press.

Sejfija, Ismet. 2006, "From the "Civil Sector" to Civil Society?" In *Peacebuilding and Civil Society in Bosnia-Herzegovina: Ten years after Dayton*, edited by Martina Fischer, 125–40. Münster: Lit-Verlag.

Serwer, Daniel. 2012. "Statebuilding In Iraq: An American Failure, Lately Redeemed." In *The International Community and Statebuilding: Getting its Act Together?* edited by Patrice C. McMahon and Jon Western, 169–83. London: Routledge Press.

Silverstein, Ken. 2011. "Silence of the Lambs: For do-gooder NGOs in Cambodia, accommodation with the regime is very profitable." *Slate*. June 20. http://slate.com/articles/news_and_politics/foreigners/2011/06/silence_of_the_lambs.html.

Sita-Sucic, Daria. 2013. "Politicking Paralyzes Divided Bosnian Town of Mostar." *Reuters*. http://www.reuters.com/article/2013/02/05/us-bosnia-mostar-idUSBRE9140O620130205.

Smillie, Ian. 1995. *The Alms Bazaar: Altruism Under Fire: Non-Profit Organizations and International Development*. Ottawa: International Development Research Centre.

———. 2001. *Patronage or partnership: Local capacity building in humanitarian crises*. IDRC.

Smillie, Ian, and Goran Todorovic. 2001. "Reconstructing Bosnia, constructing civil society: disjuncture and convergence." Patronage or partnership: Local capacity building in humanitarian crises (2001): 25–50.

Smith, Brian H. 2014. *More Than Altruism: The Politics of Private Foreign Aid*. Princeton, NJ: Princeton University Press.

Snyder, Jack. 1993. "Nationalism and the crisis of the post-Soviet state." *Survival* 35 (1): 5–26.

Sogge, K. Bickart, and J. Saxby, eds. 1996. *Compassion and Calculation: The Business of Private Foreign Aid*. London: Pluto Press.

Stephenson, Max O., and Laura Zanotti. 2012. *Peacebuilding through community-based NGOs: paradoxes and possibilities*. Sterling, VA: Kumarian Press.

Sterland, Bill. 2006. *Civil society capacity building in post-conflict societies: The experience of Bosnia and Herzegovina and Kosovo*. Oxford, UK: INTRAC.

Stiglmayer, Alexandra. 1993. *Mass Rape: The War against Women in Bosnia*. Lincoln: University of Nebraska Press.

Stoddard, Abby. 2006. *Humanitarian alert: NGO information and its impact on US foreign policy*. Bloomfield, CT: Kumarian Press.

Storey, Andy. 1997. "Non-Neutral Humanitarianism: NGOs and the Rwanda Crisis," *Development in Practice* 7 (4): 384–94.

Strand, Arne. 2005. "Aid Coordination: Easy to Agree On, Difficult to Organize." In *After Conflict Reconstruction and Development in the Aftermath of War*, edited by Sultan Barakat, 87–100. London: I. B. Tauris.

Strategy for Western Balkans 2012–2015. 2011. Olof Palme International Centre Report, 15 April. http://www.palmecenter.se/Documents/ENGLISH%20DOCUMENTS/Western%20Balkan/OPC%20Strategy%20Western%20Balkans%202012-2015.pdf.

"Supporting Democracy in Kosovo." 2002. Organization for Security and Cooperation in Europe http://www.osce.org/kosovo/37661?download=true.

Suri, Jeremi. 2011. *Liberty's Surest Guardian: American Nation-Building from the Founders to Obama*. New York: The Free Press.

Tarrow, Sidney. 2005. The New Transnational Activism. Cambridge University Press.

Telford, John. 2001. *Evaluation of UNHCR's Role in Strengthening National NGOs*. Evaluation and Policy Unit, UNHCR paper, EPAU/2001/01. Geneva, Switzerland: UNHCR. http://www.stranieriinitalia.it/briguglio/immigrazione-e-asilo/2002/luglio/unhcr-valutaz-rafforz-ong.pdf.

Terry, Fiona. 2002. *Condemned to Repeat? The Paradox of Humanitarian Action*. Ithaca, NY: Cornell University Press.

Thelen, Kathleen. 1999. "Historical Institutionalism in Comparative Perspective." *Annual Review of Political Science* 2: 369–404.

Toal, Gerard, and Carl T. Dahlman. 2011. *Bosnia Remade: Ethnic Cleansing and Its Reversal*. Oxford: Oxford University Press.

Tschirgi, Necia. 2004. *Post-Conflict Peacebuilding Revisited: Achievements, Limitations, Challenges*. Unpublished paper prepared for the WSP International Peace Academy Peacebuilding Forum Conference, New York, 7 October.

Ullman, Richard H. 1983. "Redefining Security." *International Security* 8 (1): 129–53.

Un, Kheang. 2006. "State, Society and Democratic Consolidation: The Case of Cambodia," *Pacific Affairs* 79 (2): 139–63.

UNDP. 2008. *Civil Society and Development*. Kosovo Human Development Report. Pristina, Kosovo: UNDP. http://hdr.undp.org/sites/default/files/nhdr_2008_kosovo_en.pdf.

———. 2003. *Human Development Report 2003: Millennium Development Goals: A Compact among Nations to End Human Poverty*. New York: Oxford University Press.

UN Office of the Resident Coordinator for Development Operations, 2001.

UN Security Council Resolution 1325. 2000. S/RES/1323(2000).

UN Security Council. 1999. *Report of the Secretary-General on the United Nations Interim Administration Mission in Kosovo*. S/1999/779, 12 July. New York: UN Security Council.

Urquhart, Brian. 2004. "The Good General." *The NY Times Review of Books*. September 23.

USAID. 2006. *2006 NGO Sustainability Index for Central and Eastern Europe and Eurasia*. Washington, DC: USAID.

———. 2008. *2008 NGO Sustainability Index for Central and Eastern Europe and Eurasia*. Washington, DC: USAID.

U.S. Overseas Loans and Grants. Obligations and Loan Authorizations. 2007. USAID. Washington, DC.

Uvin, Peter. 2001. "Difficult Choices in the New Post-Conflict Agenda: the International Community in Rwanda after the Genocide." *The Third World Quarterly* 22 (2): 177–89.

———. 1995. "Scaling Up the Grassroots and Scaling Down the Summit: The Relations between Third World NGOs and the UN." *Third World Quarterly* 16 (3): 495–512.

Walsh, Martha. 2000. *Aftermath: The Role of Women's Organization in Post-conflict Bosnia and Herzegovina*. Center for Development Information and Evaluation Working Paper No. 308. July. Washington, DC: USAID.

Waltz, Kenneth. 1979. *Theory of international relations. Reading: Addison-Wesley.* Weiss, Thomas G., and Leon Gordenker, eds. 1996. *NGOs, the UN and Global Governance.* Boulder, CO: Lynne Rienner.

Wedel, Janine R. 2011. "Will Foreign Aid Dollars Help or Hurt Democracy in the Middle East?" *World Post.* http://www.huffingtonpost.com/janine-r-wedel/will-foreign-aid-dollars_b_870131.html.

Wells II, Linton, and Charles Hauss. 2008. "Odd Couples: The DoD and NGOs." *Inside Defense.* Palgrave Macmillan US, 237–48.

West, Katrina. 2001. *Agents of Altruism: The Expansion of Humanitarian NGOs in Rwanda and Afghanistan.* Hampshire, UK: Ashgate.

Western, Jon, and Joshua Goldstein. 2011. "Humanitarian Intervention Comes of Age" *Foreign Affairs* 90 (6): 48–59.

Willets, Peter. 2000. "From Consultative Arrangements to Partnership: The Changing Status of NGOs in Diplomacy at the UN." *Global Governance* 6: 191–212.

———. 2010. *Non-Governmental Organizations in World Politics: The Construction of Global Governance.* London: Routledge.

Woehrel, Steven. 2013. "Bosnia and Herzegovina: Current Issues and U.S. Policy" *Congressional Research Report,* January 24.

Wong, Wendy H. 2012. *Internal Affairs. How the Structure of NGOs Transforms Human Rights.* Ithaca, NY: Cornell University Press.

World Bank. 2007. *Civil Society and Peacebuilding: Potential, Limitations and Critical Factors.* Report no. 36445-GLB. December 20. Washington, DC: World Bank. http://siteresources.worldbank.org/EXTSOCIALDEVELOPMENT/Resources/244362-1164107274725/3182370-1164110717447/Civil_Society_and_Peacebuilding.pdf.

———. 1998. *Post-Conflict Reconstruction: The Role of the World Bank.* Washington, DC: World Bank. http://documents.worldbank.org/curated/en/175771468198561613/Post-conflict-reconstruction-the-role-of-the-World-Bank.

Yearbook of International Organizations. 2001. Munich: K. G. Saur Verlag.

———. 2007. Munich: K. G. Saur Verlag.

Zherka, Elizabeth. 2013. "Building Gendered Human Security Inside and Out: A Case Study in Post-Conflict Kosovo." PhD diss., University of Washington.

Živanović, Miroslav. 2006. "Civil Society in Bosnia and Herzegovina: Lost in Transition." In *Civil Society and Good Governance in Societies in Transition,* edited by Wolfgang Benedek, 23–53. Wien: Neuer Wissenschaftlicher Verlag.

Index

Note: Italic page numbers refer to figures.